TEACHER MENTORING and INDUCTION

The State of the Art and Beyond

Hal Portner
EDITOR

Afterword by Dennis Sparks

CORWIN PRESS
A SAGE Publications Company
Thousand Oaks, California

For information:

Corwin Press
A Sage Publications Company
2455 Teller Road
Thousand Oaks, California 91320
www.corwinpress.com

Sage Publications Ltd.
1 Oliver's Yard
55 City Road
London EC1Y 1SP
United Kingdom

Sage Publications India Pvt. Ltd.
B-42, Panchsheel Enclave
Post Box 4109
New Delhi 110 017 India

Printed in the United States of America

Library of Congress Cataloging-in-Publication Data

Teacher mentoring and induction: The state of the art and beyond/edited by Hal Portner.
    p. cm.
Includes bibliographical references and index.
ISBN 1-4129-0979-1 (cloth)—ISBN 1-4129-0980-5 (pbk.)
    1. Mentoring in education. 2. Teachers—Training of. I. Portner, Hal.
LB1731.4.T453 2005
370.' 71' 55—dc22   2004028754

This book was printed on acid-free paper.

05   06   07   08   09   10   9   8   7   6   5   4   3   2   1

Acquisitions Editor:	Rachel Livsey
Editorial Assistant:	Phyllis Cappello
Production Editor:	Beth Bernstein
Copy Editor:	Ruth Saavedra
Typesetter:	C&M Digitals (P) Ltd.
Proofreader:	Scott Oney
Indexer:	Rick Hurd
Cover Designer:	Rose Storey

Contents

Preface

The phrase *state of the art* is ambiguous. Understood in terms of a president's state-of-the-nation address, for example, the expression implies an overview of current conditions, perhaps reviews how conditions got to be the way they are, and most likely proposes strategies for improving those conditions. On the other hand, when used to describe the latest product introduced by a high-tech manufacturer, for instance, the term *state of the art* carries with it the notion of "cutting-edge" or "top-of-the-line." This book applies both of these concepts of *state of the art* to the rapidly expanding field of teacher induction and mentoring.

THE BOOK'S PERSPECTIVE

A comprehensive examination into the state of the art of contemporary teacher induction and mentoring calls for viewing through a variety of sharply focused lenses. This book provides such a varied perspective. The insights and vision of over a dozen authors are represented here. These contributing authors are a select group of distinguished educators, researchers, and practitioners who are not only recognized leaders in the development of the field's knowledge base, but also are sought after as consultants by induction and mentoring program developers and policymakers. They have been deeply and passionately involved for many years in the important issues underlying the induction, mentoring, and nurturing of new teachers. Through a synthesis of research and experience, the authors describe and discuss a variety of issues and practices that not only define contemporary induction and mentoring but do so in ways that may well channel its future. As a group, they write from the same conviction. Individually, however, they write in their own voice. I trust that the reader will find their stylistic diversity to be both enlightening and refreshing.

THE BOOK'S FORMAT

The twelve chapters of the book are grouped into three sections. Part I, Developing and Designing Mentoring and Induction Programs, describes the developmental processes, organizational structures, and philosophical underpinnings that make up exemplary teacher induction programs. Part II, Mentoring Constructs and Best Practices, focuses on significant and emerging aspects within the larger context of induction and mentoring. Part III, Connecting Mentoring and Induction to Broader Issues, looks beyond individual programs and practices and examines their extended relationships and interactions.

DEVELOPING AND DESIGNING INDUCTION AND MENTORING PROGRAMS

Perhaps the most pronounced change over the past decade or two in the way teacher induction and mentoring takes place in a school or district has been its planning and structure. Although there were notable exceptions, earlier induction activities were often limited to an orientation day— usually the day before students arrived—in which new teachers signed a bevy of forms, met each other and their resident colleagues, were introduced to an array of handbooks and policy manuals, and were sent off to ready their classrooms and themselves for their first class—sink or swim!

Mentoring, also with notable exceptions, was either an informal process whereby a veteran teacher would take a novice under wing, or it was formalized to the extent that an experienced teacher might receive some sort of training, was teamed up with a new teacher, and then was expected to show the novice "the ropes." The five chapters in Part I illustrate the extent to which the development and structure of induction and mentoring programs have evolved.

In Chapter 1, Tom Ganser draws on his years of extensive research to remind us that mentoring programs already have a history that can, in some cases, offset the need to reinvent the wheel when creating new programs or enhancing existing ones. Another advantage of this history, Ganser finds, is that more and more school leaders readily support mentoring programs because they themselves have experienced firsthand the benefits of mentoring. Although Ganser discusses the potential of existing mentoring programs to offer examples of good practice, he emphasizes the exciting opportunities current research and experience present for developing even more effective induction and mentoring programs in the future.

In Chapter 2, Mark Bower describes how he and a team of dedicated staff members, representing a variety of interests and positions in a suburban school district, spent two years developing the specifics of a program designed to achieve their vision: new teachers excelling in situations where they are empowered to enable their students to succeed.

In Chapter 3, Harry Wong documents a variety of programs that eschew teacher retention as their primary goal. The developers of these programs have designed them to focus on teacher effectiveness and student learning. They consist of an organization or structure having many activities and emphasizing the involvement of many people. They feature clearly articulated goals, administrative supervision, long-term objectives, networks that allow for structural and nurturing collaboration, demonstration classes where teachers can observe and be observed, and portfolio assessments to assess pedagogical knowledge and skills. Wong describes how the induction process is rigorously monitored and evaluated in such programs and how the process flows seamlessly into sustained lifelong professional development.

In Chapter 4, Ellen Moir relates how, when in the mid-1980s California found itself facing a crisis caused primarily by exceptionally low rates of teacher retention, she was called upon to oversee the creation of a new program for teacher induction that resulted in a comprehensive new teacher support program with mentoring at its core. The program, The Santa Cruz New Teacher Project (SCNTP), was led by the University of California, Santa Cruz, in partnership with the Santa Cruz County Office of Education and all school districts in the area. Ellen describes what developing, implementing, and replicating SCNTP in several districts throughout the United States has taught us about the essential components of an effective induction program and the role of mentors.

In Chapter 5, Hal Portner contends that a major task for developers of an induction and mentoring program is to plan for its survival so that it can sustain and expand its vitality and positive impact on teaching and learning. Portner argues that an effective way to ensure induction and mentoring's longevity is to embed the program firmly into the culture of a school. He presents a set of three principles—Systems-Thinking, Collaborative-Doing, and Committed-Leading—that provide a framework upon which developers can create the conditions needed to do just that. He describes in detail how those principles were applied to the enhancement of a school system's existing induction and mentoring program.

MENTORING CONSTRUCTS AND BEST PRACTICES

Effective induction and mentoring programs incorporate a well-planned set of practices. Part II examines several of these approaches that are proving to be powerful mechanisms for achieving valued goals.

In Chapter 6, Jean Casey and Ann Claunch trace the stages of mentor development from novice to expert. The five stages include *predisposition, disequilibrium, transition, confidence,* and *efficacy.* Although individuals experience professional learning in a variety of ways, each stage of learning to mentor has identifiable attributes or characteristics. Casey and Claunch have found that mentors often reveal their developmental stage through the language they use to describe their work.

In Chapter 7, James Rowley articulates the qualities of the good mentor by means of a framework that clearly defines the diverse roles a mentor teacher plays. Rowley defines high performing mentor teachers as having six essential qualities, each conceptualized as a personal or professional belief realized in the form of a set of congruent behaviors. Over the past few years, Rowley has found that of the six essential qualities, preparing mentor teachers to coach for classroom success has proved to be the most challenging for practitioners. Rowley discusses institutional resistance to mentor-as-coach, stresses the value of the process, asks policymakers to reflect on where their state or school district program is at the present time in terms of their readiness to embrace the practice, and predicts its future development.

In Chapter 8, Barry Sweeny argues that people who lead and participate in induction and mentoring programs must purposefully redefine the way they and their institutions use professional time—even if doing so changes the culture of their school. They must, Sweeny insists, design their programs' activities to make the time available and not leave it to teachers to steal time from kids. Sweeny offers a variety of strategies for finding, making, and funding time for induction and mentoring and provides examples illustrating the application of some of those strategies.

In Chapter 9, Laura Lipton and Bruce Wellman emphasize the power of mentoring relationships to foster improved student learning. Lipton and Wellman define the three functions of learning-focused relationships— offering support, creating challenge, and facilitating a professional vision—that distinguish them from other types of possible interaction. They go on to present a continuum of learning-focused interactions that includes methods for navigating across three stances—consulting, collaborating, and coaching—to increase the effectiveness and productivity of the mentor-protégé relationship. The chapter concludes with an exploration of mentoring practices to support transitions from novice to more expert forms of teaching and provides indicators of those transitions.

CONNECTING MENTORING AND INDUCTION TO BROADER ISSUES

Induction and mentoring models have come to exert some powerful influences on people and programs outside of their immediate venue and in turn have been strongly influenced by other paradigms and systems.

In Chapter 10, Susan Villani maintains that school communities need to nurture leadership in many different ways if schools are to offer the opportunities for students and adults to learn and achieve at new heights. The concept of *parallel leadership* whereby teachers and their principals engage in collective action to build school capacity is especially effective, she postulates, and she suggests that induction and mentoring programs have the potential, perhaps more than any other initiative, to both culti-vate and provide opportunity for such leadership.

In Chapter 11, Janice Hall contends that state support of local induction and mentoring is essential. In order to ascertain the extent and influence of such support, Janice compares the involvement of states between 1998 and 2004, draws conclusions based on that comparison, and suggests ways such support can be strengthened.

In Chapter 12, Ted Britton and Lynn Paine describe the salient features of comprehensive teacher induction programs they have studied exten-sively in five countries around the world: China (limited to the city of Shanghai), France, Japan, New Zealand, and Switzerland. Britton and Paine suggest that U.S. induction and mentoring programs in general can benefit greatly by taking a critical look at the components that make up those successful programs.

Each chapter ends with an exercise designed to guide readers through reflecting on the possibilities of applying the chapter's material to their own programs.

Finally, Dennis Sparks reminds us that strong induction programs are the starting point of a continuum of professional learning that can extend across a teacher's career. When embedded in school cultures that value collaboration, view professional learning as part of teachers' daily work rather than as something separate from it, and promote continuous improvement in teaching and student achievement, induction programs are the starting point for a career-long commitment to professional growth and innovation.

ACKNOWLEDGMENTS

Several months ago I set out to examine the extent of diversity among teacher induction and mentoring programs in the United States in order to determine how and why various programs developed as they did, to iden-tify areas where programs are effective, to consider where and how they might become even more successful, and to publish the results. It soon became apparent, however, that this would be a Herculean task not to be tackled by one individual. A project such as this would require the direct involvement of more than a few knowledgeable and committed people capable of bringing a variety of experiences and informed viewpoints to bear. In addition, these would need to be individuals who were willing to contribute their time and advice along with their expertise.

I contacted the educators, authors, practitioners, and consultants whom I most respected for their insights in and contributions to the field of induc-tion and mentoring and invited them to be contributing authors to a pro-posed book I would edit. These are busy people, and I fully expected polite "thank you, but . . . " responses. Not so! Everyone I asked immediately and graciously accepted. These individuals not only agreed to share their expertise; they also agreed to share themselves. They made this book a truly collaborative effort by reviewing and critiquing each other's chapters and by offering me and each other suggestions and support along the way. I am profoundly grateful to each contributing author and am delighted to acknowledge their time, energy, and cooperation.

Carol Mullen is another colleague to whom I am very grateful. Dr. Mullen is an associate professor at the College of Education, University of Southern Florida, and coeditor of *Mentoring and Tutoring,* an international peer-review journal. Carol's advice and encouragement, especially in regard to the intricacies and niceties of editing a publication such as this, are very much appreciated.

I also want to acknowledge and thank Robb Clouse, editorial director for Corwin Press, for recognizing the significance of this book. Robb immediately set the wheels in motion needed to bring about its publication. Corwin's Rachel Livsey, acquisitions editor, and Phyllis Cappello, senior editorial assistant, were always helpful and understanding partners. I truly value their insightful comments and suggestions.

Finally, I am most grateful to my wife, Mary, for her liberal and unequivocal encouragement and support and her practical suggestions (she is, after all, an English teacher).

—*Hal Portner*

The contributions of the following reviewers are gratefully acknowledged:

D. Leonard
Staff Development Resource Teacher
BTSA: Beginning Teacher Support and Assessment
Torrance, CA

Audrey F. Lakin
Teacher Induction and Mentoring Coordinator
Community Unit School District #300
Carpentersville, IL

Carole Cooper
Director of Academic Accountability
St. Charles Community Unit District #303
St. Charles, IL

Theresa Rouse
Assessment and Program Evaluation Coordinator
Administrator, Monterey County Office of Education
Salinas, CA

Gail A. Rachor, Ed.D.
Consultant and Adjunct Instructor
Eastern Michigan University
Ypsilanti, MI

About the Editor

Hal Portner is the author of *Mentoring New Teachers* (1998 and 2003), *Training Mentors Is Not Enough: Everything Else Schools and Districts Need to Do* (2001), and *Being Mentored: A Guide for Protégés* (2002), all published by Corwin Press. He is a former public school teacher and administrator and was a staff consultant for the Connecticut State Department of Education where, among other responsibilities, he served as coordinator of the Connecticut Institute for Teaching and Learning and worked closely with school districts to develop and carry out professional development and teacher evaluation plans and programs. He also served as professional development consultant for the faculty of Holyoke (Massachusetts) Community College. He writes, develops materials, trains mentors, facilitates the development of new-teacher induction programs, and presents to and consults with school districts and other educational organizations and institutions. He is a member the editorial board of *Mentoring & Tutoring*, an international peer-reviewed journal.hportner@comcast.net. http://www.portner.us/Hal

About the Contributors

Mark Bower is the director of staff development and continuing education for the Hilton Central School District in New York State. In addition to his role in staff development and overseeing the teacher mentoring program, he has been a primary school principal for the district. He has just finished serving a three-year, elected term as a board of trustees member for the National Staff Development Council (NSDC). He is an adjunct professor for the State University of New York, College at Brockport, where he teaches in the graduate program for teacher education. He also works as an educational consultant to several districts and BOCES (Board of Cooperative Educational Services) in New York State.

mbower@hilton.k12.ny.us

Ted Britton, associate director of WestEd's National Center for Improving Science Education, is an editor or contributor to almost thirty books and reports. Much of his recent research and writing focuses on the subject-specific aspects of secondary teacher induction. This work includes an emphasis on comparing teacher induction systems among countries and builds upon his prior international studies, including the Third International Mathematics and Science Study (TIMSS) and a study of innovations for science and mathematics education conducted for the Organisation for Economic Co-operation and Development (OECD).

tbritto@wested.org

Jean Casey is coordinator of the Secondary Teacher Induction and Resident Teacher Program at the University of New Mexico. In that role, she is responsible for providing structured support and mentoring for over 200 beginning teachers in both rural and urban school districts. She has been in public school education for over thirty years, and her expertise includes curriculum development in graduate level teacher education, mentoring, and the design and evaluation of educational programs. She is currently a consultant to the New Mexico Public Education Department on issues of teacher evaluation and licensure.

nintynine@aol.com

Ann Claunch is the elementary coordinator of the Resident Teacher Program and the Teacher Induction Program at the University of New Mexico in Albuquerque, New Mexico. As the induction coordinator, her responsibilities include the systematic induction of all first-year teachers in four different school districts and the professional development of mentor teachers. Her research interests include mentoring and induction as well as curriculum development for elementary students. She is currently a consultant for National History Day.

aclaunch@unm.edu

Tom Ganser is the director of the Office of Field Experiences at University of Wisconsin-Whitewater and an associate professor in the Department of Curriculum and Instruction. He has served as a trainer, workshop facilitator, and consultant for organizations throughout the United States, including the National Education Association and state affiliates, and in Bermuda, Finland, Jamaica, and Sweden. He is a frequent presenter and keynote speaker at state, national, and international meetings and has published in a variety of research- and practitioner-oriented journals, including *American School Board Journal, Educational Forum, Journal of Staff Development*, and *Phi Delta Kappan*.

gansert@uww.edu

Janice L. Hall is the director of field experiences in the Secondary Education Department, College of Education and Human Services at Utah State University. She has placed and supervised student teachers for seventeen years for three universities. At Indiana State University she worked as the coordinator of the Beginning Teacher Internship program and is currently working collaboratively with the Cache County School District in Logan, Utah, to set up a teacher mentor training program. She also serves on the Quality Teaching Committee with the State of Utah, working with them to establish state guidelines for the role of the trained mentor.

hall@cc.usu.edu

Laura Lipton is Codirector of MiraVia, LLC. She is an international consultant whose writing, research, and seminars focus on effective and innovative instructional practices and on building professional and organizational capacities for enhanced learning. She engages with schools and school districts, designing and conducting workshops on learning-focused instruction, literacy development, and strategies to support beginning teachers. She applies her extensive experience with adult learners to workshops and seminars conducted throughout the United States, Canada, Europe, Australia, and New Zealand on such topics as learner-centered instruction, data-driven dialogue, teacher leadership, action research, and learning-focused mentoring.

lelipton@miravia.com

Ellen Moir is executive director of the New Teacher Center (NTC) at the University of California, Santa Cruz, a national resource for high quality new teacher and new administrator induction programs. Ellen has also served for fifteen years as director of the Santa Cruz New Teacher Project, and from 1985 to 2000, she was UCSC director of teacher education. In 2003, she received the California Council on Teacher Education Distinguished Teacher Educator Award. She has authored several book chapters related to induction and produced video documentaries on teacher induction and bilingual education. Her induction work has been supported by fifteen private foundations and by the National Science Foundation.

moir@catsucsc.edu

Lynn Paine is a faculty member at Michigan State University in the Department of Teacher Education, where she works with preservice, beginning, and experienced teachers. Her research focuses on understanding teaching and teacher learning. She has conducted extensive fieldwork in China, the United Kingdom, and the United States. Her publications include work on mentoring, teacher collaboration, and teacher education. She is currently engaged in exploring how policies and programs can support the learning of beginning mathematics and science teachers.

painel@msu.edu

James Rowley is professor of teacher education at the University of Dayton and president of Teacher-development.com. He is the codeveloper of *High Performance Mentoring*, a multimedia training program for school districts, published by Corwin Press. Over the past fifteen years he has helped school districts throughout the United States and Canada develop mentor-based entry-year programs. He is also the cocreator of other multimedia training programs including *Recruiting and Training Successful Substitute Teachers*, *Becoming a Star Urban Teacher*, and *Mentoring the New Teacher*. All of the above programs use video case studies supported by print media to engage teachers in personal reflection and group problem solving.

james.rowley@notes.udayton.edu

Dennis Sparks is executive director of the 10,000-member National Staff Development Council. He is author of *Leading for Results: Transforming Teaching, Learning, and Relationships in Schools* (Corwin, 2005); *Designing Powerful Professional Development for Teachers and Principals* (NSDC, 2002); *Conversations That Matter* (NSDC, 2001), a collection of his *Journal of Staff Development* interviews since 1991; coauthor with Stephanie Hirsh of *Learning to Lead, Leading to Learn* (NSDC, 2000); coauthor with Joan Richardson of *What Is Staff Development Anyway?* (NSDC, 1998); and coauthor with Stephanie Hirsh of *A New Vision for Staff Development* (ASCD/NSDC, 1997). All of his interviews and articles are accessible on the NSDC Web site at www.nsdc.org/library/authors/sparks.cfm.

sparksnsdc@aol.com

Barry Sweeny was a teacher for twenty-two years, during which time he supervised and mentored numerous student and novice teachers and chaired the committee that developed his district's mentor program, and during the following four years, he was the program's coordinator. Since 1998, he has been a full-time mentoring and coaching consultant, trainer, and program evaluator. He is author of over 120 articles, books, chapters, videos, and training manuals and has developed and manages four mentoring Web sites.

sweenyb@earthlink.net
http://www.teachermentors.com

Susan Villani is an educator who cares deeply about the growth of adults and children. As a teacher, principal, and college professor she has collaborated with students, staff, and families to create safe school cultures that honored each member and promoted their achievement and self-actualization. She works with school systems, departments of education, and educational organizations to design and implement mentoring programs for new teachers, support the wisdom and learning of experienced faculty, and empower administrators to work with teacher leaders and other staff. She is the author of *Are You Sure You're the Principal?*, *Mentoring Programs for New Teachers,* and *Mentoring Programs for New Principals* (Corwin Press, forthcoming).

susanvillani@yahoo.com

Bruce Wellman is codirector of MiraVia, LLC, a publishing, training and consulting firm. He consults with school systems, professional groups, and organizations throughout the United States and Canada, presenting workshops and courses for teachers and administrators on learning-focused patterns and practices, learning-focused supervision and mentoring, presentation skills, and facilitating collaborative groups. He is an award-winning author and coauthor of numerous publications related to organizational and professional development, mentoring, quality teaching, and improving professional cultures.

bwellman@miravia.com

Harry K. Wong is a former high school teacher and, presently, a new teacher advocate. He and his wife, Rosemary, are the authors of *The First Days of School* (Harry K. Wong Publications), which has sold over two million copies. They also write a monthly column for www.teachers.net, where their articles on induction can be found. He is coauthor of *New Teacher Induction: How to Train, Support, and Retain New Teachers* (Harry K. Wong Publications). He has also authored more than twelve articles on induction; these can be seen at www.NewTeacher.com. He is one of the most sought after speakers in education today.

harrykrose@aol.com

Introduction

When President Clinton's *Call to Action for American Education in the 21st Century* (1997) informed us that nationally, two million teachers will be needed during the ensuing ten years to replace retirements and accommodate rapidly growing student enrollment, the education establishment geared up its teacher education and recruitment efforts. Yes, more teachers were being trained and recruited, but the supply did not seem to catch up to the demand. The assumption was that there was a shortage of available teacher candidates. However, an analysis of national data by Ingersoll (2001) showed that widely publicized school staffing problems were not solely—or even primarily—the result of too few teachers being trained and recruited. Rather, the data indicated that school staffing problems were to a significant extent a result of a revolving door, where large numbers of teachers were departing teaching long before retirement. Research by Susan Moore Johnson (2001) supported a wealth of previous research and experience by suggesting that the key to addressing shortages lies not in attractive recruitment policies but in mentoring, which she describes as "support and training for new teachers at the school site."

Schools and districts throughout the United States rushed to add the word *mentoring* to their vocabularies and hastily instituted mentoring programs. A number of states followed the lead of California and Connecticut and established mentoring regulations. Although mentoring activities flourished—some of them comprehensive, others merely perfunctory—educational leaders began to realize that new teachers needed more. Recruiting New Teachers, Inc. (2000), a national nonprofit organization based in Belmont, Massachusetts, asserted that beginning teachers also needed to go through "induction," the process RNT describes as "socialization to the teaching profession, adjustment to the procedures and mores of a school site and school system, and development of effective instructional and classroom management skills."

On June 23, 2004, the Alliance for Excellent Education released a report which revealed that American schools spend more than $2.6 billion annually replacing teachers who have dropped out of the teaching profession.

The report cites comprehensive induction, which includes mentoring, especially in a teacher's first two years on the job, as the single effective strategy to stem the rapidly increasing teacher attrition rate. According to the report, one out of every two new teachers will quit within five years. About 207,000 teachers, nearly 6 percent of the teaching workforce, will not return to teaching next fall. The Alliance for Excellent Education research goes on to show that comprehensive induction cuts attrition rates in half and develops new teachers more rapidly into highly skilled, experienced professionals. Although the report indicates that induction has been shown to create a payoff of $1.37 for every one dollar invested, only 1 percent of beginning teachers currently receive the ongoing training and support that constitutes comprehensive induction when they enter the teaching profession.

As induction and mentoring were introduced into more and more schools and districts, researchers reinforced what had already become evident to practitioners: When these programs were well designed and implemented, novice teachers were not only staying longer; they were also developing into better teachers—and doing so at a faster rate—than had many before them.

INDUCTION AND MENTORING TODAY

The proliferation of teacher induction and mentoring has accelerated at such a rapid pace that the time has come to take a deep breath and step back from the headlong rush into the induction and mentoring frenzy into which most states and many school districts have catapulted themselves. What do we mean by induction and mentoring? Where are we in our induction and mentoring efforts? How and why did we get where we are, and where might we be headed?

The time has come to put induction and mentoring into perspective *vis-á-vis* itself and its relationship with educational reform in general, and with contemporary professional development practices in particular. What is the state of the art of teacher induction and mentoring? That is what this book is about.

AN INVITATION

The development of induction and mentoring programs is not over; it is an ongoing process that requires the reflection and work of many. Therefore we, the editor, collaborating authors, and publisher, invite you, the reader, to contribute to that process. To that end, we have appended an exercise to each chapter designed to encourage you (1) to assess the extent that your induction and mentoring program addresses some issues discussed in that chapter and (2) to envision ways your program can embrace and possibly expand on the application and further development of those issues. We then encourage and invite you to share with us any actions or epiphanies elicited by the exercises. The authors' e-mail addresses are included along with their biographies for this purpose.

—*Hal Portner*

REFERENCES

Alliance for Excellent Education. (2004, June 23). *Tapping the potential: Retaining and developing high quality new teachers.* Washington, DC: Author.

Clinton, W. J. (1997). *Call to Action for American Education in the 21st Century.* From the president's State of the Union address, February 4, 1997.

Ingersoll, R. M. (2001). Teacher turnover and teacher shortages: An organizational analysis. *American Educational Research Journal, 38*(3), 499–534.

Johnson, S. M. (2001, July/August). Retaining the next generation of teachers: The importance of school-based support. *Harvard Education Letter.*

Recruiting New Teachers, Inc. (2000). *A guide to developing teacher induction programs.* Belmont, MA: Author.

PART I

Developing and Designing Mentoring and Induction Programs

1

Learning From the Past—Building for the Future

Tom Ganser

Establishing a mentoring program for beginning teachers is not a new idea; it is an idea that has gained considerable momentum in recent years. The results of a survey of 5,253 teachers in the fifty states and the District of Columbia published by the National Center for Educational Statistics (2001) reveal that 26 percent of the respondents had served as a mentor and 23 percent of the respondents had been mentored by another teacher. Most states now recommend or require induction programs for beginning teachers. A recent report of the National Commission on Teaching and America's Future (2003) indicates that the number of state induction programs has increased from seven states in 1996–1997 to thirty–three states in 2002; however, not all of these programs call for on-site mentors.

Formally organized mentoring programs for beginning teachers in the United States have existed for more than a generation of teachers (Darling-Hammond & Sclan, 1996). Accordingly, mentoring programs already have a history that can be assumed to offset the need to "reinvent the wheel" in creating new programs or enhancing existing programs. Another advantage of this history is that more and more school leaders readily support mentoring programs because they themselves have experienced the benefits of mentoring as beginning teachers or as mentors. For example, as a new teacher in 1993, Tracy Hein participated in the University of Wisconsin–Whitewater Beginning Teacher Assistance Program, a mentoring program organized for local school districts. Today, Tracy is principal of Prairie View Elementary School in Mukwonago, Wisconsin, and she reflects,

> My experience as a beginning teacher cements in my mind the importance of mentoring. I would have been lost if I didn't have a mentor. My mentor was a safe person for me. I didn't worry about being judged and had open communication with her. I think sometimes beginning teachers don't ask the questions they should because they are afraid of looking unqualified. The mentor opens up the venue for these conversations. I believe that because I experienced such a solid network of support and guidance, I make a conscious effort to offer that to our beginning teachers at Prairie View Elementary School.

As a result of her experience as a teacher, Tracy is now a strong advocate for the school district's own mentoring program for beginning teachers (and, as Tracy reminds me, even those teachers that aren't so "beginningish").

CURRENT AND EMERGING TRENDS

The history of mentoring programs sets traps for limiting the design, implementation, and evaluation of a mentoring program to what worked in the past. Leading mentoring programs today calls for the ability to understand basic principles of good mentoring that continue to form the bedrock of strong mentoring programs. But leadership also requires expertise at expanding the vision of effective programs beyond enduring principles by taking into account current trends, some evident and others just starting to emerge, that must influence the look and feel of today's mentoring programs to maximize their effectiveness. The purpose of this chapter is to explore these trends in answer to seven critical questions about mentoring programs for beginning teachers:

- Who provides the leadership for the program?
- On what principles or standards is the program based?
- What are the characteristics of the beginning teachers that the program serves?
- Who serves as the mentors in the program?
- How long does the program last?
- How is the program evaluated?
- Where does the program fit into teaching as a profession?

Who Provides the Leadership for the Program?

Early on in the history of organized mentoring programs for beginning teachers, typically the director of instruction, curriculum supervisor, manager of staff development, or someone serving in a similar capacity was solely responsible for designing and overseeing the program. Moreover, a working knowledge of the program, including its intended goals and activities, may have been shared by relatively few members of the school community beyond the program's director and participants. School administrators (e.g., superintendents, principals), teacher leaders (e.g., grade level team leaders, department chairpersons), other teachers, student support professionals (e.g., counselors, social workers, psychologists), and clerical and building maintenance staff may have had scant knowledge about the mentoring program and its relationship to them as members of the school community.

Today, it is still probable that a director of instruction, curriculum supervisor, or manager of staff development is administratively responsible for the operation of a mentoring program. However, it has become increasingly common for these individuals to assemble a steering committee for support in designing the program and in carrying out critical functions such as

- Selecting, training, and supporting mentors
- Pairing mentors and mentees
- Specifying mentoring activities (e.g., conferences, classroom visits, development)
- Professional development plans
- Organizing the various types of meetings typically associated with mentoring programs (e.g., orientation/welcoming meetings, periodic topical meetings, end-of-year celebrations)
- Addressing interpersonal conflicts
- Designing strategies for program evaluation, interpreting results, and using results for program improvement

The members of the steering committee, appropriately described by Portner (2001) as "*partners* in building and maintaining an exemplary mentoring program" (p. 18, emphasis added), can represent a wide variety of interested parties from within the school (e.g., nonmentoring veteran teachers), within the school district (e.g., members of the board of education), and outside the school and school district (e.g., service organizations such as the Rotary Club).

An important aspect of this trend is to include as members of the steering committee representatives of the local teachers' union and faculty from nearby colleges and universities. The two largest teachers' unions in the United States, the National Education Association and the American Federation of Teachers, have become very active in supporting mentoring programs for their members (American Federation of Teachers, 2001; National Education Association [NEA] Foundation for the Improvement of Education, 1999). Since 2001, the NEA-Saturn-UAW Partnership Award has recognized 'best practices' mentoring programs that are created and sustained through the joint efforts of both the school district and the union, and have resulted in substantially assisting new teachers in their education careers (National Education Association, 2004). At the local level, memoranda of understanding and labor agreements articulate important features of mentoring programs, including qualifications and selection of mentors and clarifying the nonevaluative role of mentors.

Efforts to include representatives of higher education on steering committees are fitting since changes in state licensing requirements for teachers can include a mentoring component, as well as the participation of representatives of higher education in meeting continuing licensing requirements, such as the development of a professional development plan. More important, linking K–12 schools with colleges and universities responsible for preparing teachers with mentoring programs during their early years of teaching acknowledges the permeability of institutional boundaries and the "seamless" connection between preservice education and the professional development of teachers.

Expanding the leadership of a mentoring program beyond an individual to a variety of program stakeholders shares program ownership among many people who might otherwise feel like outsiders. It also multiplies the number of perspectives and ideas that can address the challenges of program implementation that are sure to arise. However, involving different groups in this way also calls for skill at building consensus.

On What Principles or Standards Is the Program Based?

Although formally organized mentoring programs for beginning teachers are relatively new, as long as there have been schools and teachers working in them, at least some portion of beginning teachers have benefited by being mentored by their veteran colleagues. With the opportunity and backing to overcome the isolation among teachers that the structure of schools all too often promotes, many experienced teachers are predisposed to offer emotional support and encouragement to their new colleagues as they make the transition from "student of teaching" to "teacher of students" at the start of their careers. Clarifying policies and procedures for teachers new to a school, and offering insights into the subtleties of the local school culture, also come naturally to teachers who find themselves serving as mentors with or without the formal title.

As formally organized mentoring programs began to emerge in the 1960s and 1970s, they reflected such intuitive dimensions of mentoring as (1) support and encouragement, especially for young beginning teachers experiencing the day-to-day survival phase of teaching, and (2) assistance in negotiating the uncertain terrain of school policies and procedures. However, without program goals laying out expectations for mentoring directly related to effective instruction, mentors tended to construct a definition of mentoring that was largely personal in nature and limited in scope.

In recent years, the approach to designing mentoring programs has been significantly influenced by the emergence of professional standards for teaching. Examples include the Interstate New Teacher Assessment and Support Consortium [INTASC] core standards (Council of Chief State School Officers, 1992), the National Board for Professional Teaching Standards (1989), Educational Testing Service's Praxis III PATHWISE assessment system (Pathwise Formative Observation Form, 1995), and Danielson's (1996) framework for teaching. In some instances, these principles have been modified in the creation of state standards, as is the case with the Wisconsin Teacher Standards (Wisconsin Department of Public Instruction, 2004) that are variations of the INTASC core standards.

The relationship of mentoring programs to teaching standards is evident in many ways. For example, the roles, responsibilities, and training of mentors; the topics presented at program meetings; and the logging of discussions or planning sessions between mentors and their mentees can be linked to specific standards. Since teaching standards are generally comprehensive, there is little danger that any important aspect of teaching cannot be related to an appropriate standard. Used appropriately, teaching standards provide a foundation for mentoring programs that extends mentoring beyond emotional support, encouragement, and help with routines to address the knowledge, skills, and dispositions associated with effective teaching and improved student learning. Using teaching standards as a template for mentoring takes much of the guesswork out of where mentors and mentees should focus their efforts.

What Are the Characteristics of the Beginning Teachers That the Program Serves?

The image of beginning teachers as young adults, typically female, white, and middle class, trained in a four-year baccalaureate degree program, and at the start of a lifetime career in teaching, has always predominated, and justifiably so, even today. However, since the emergence of formal mentoring programs a generation of teachers ago, the percentage of beginning teachers who do not share these characteristics has grown tremendously. Increasing numbers of beginning teachers are older adults who are changing careers, sometimes in dramatic fashion. There is also evidence that some young beginning teachers do not intend to make teaching their career for life. Perhaps even more important, a growing proportion of new teachers have been prepared in alternative route certification programs rather than in traditional undergraduate four-year programs.

In 1984, only 3 percent of teachers began their career after finishing a post-baccalaureate preparation program. By 1999, that number had increased ninefold to 27 percent. As a group, these teachers were about eight years older than undergraduate-program completers. They were also nearly five times more likely to be transitioning into teaching from an occupation outside the field of education. Finally, over a third of them had taught in some capacity previously, compared with about 14 percent of other beginning teachers (Feistritzer, 1999). All in all, their characteristics are quite different when compared with their younger counterparts, and they are increasing in number. These older beginning teachers tend to be more proactive than younger beginning teachers in taking advantage of induction assistance available to them, including mentoring, but they often can feel more scrutinized by family and friends as they make a middle-age move from one line of work to another. And the intensity of their experiences as older beginning teachers can be very powerful indeed.

> I've waited thirteen years to teach school, and it's finally time to begin the school year. It scares me to death! Will I be able to discipline students who need it? Can I gain respect in and out of the classroom from my peers? These are just a few of the questions I keep asking myself. After thirteen years of working outside as a carpenter, I wonder if I will get the "itch" to go back outside and swing a hammer.

Another emerging trend suggests that greater numbers of beginning teachers may not enter teaching for the long haul. In *The Project on the Next Generation of Teachers* (http://www.gse.Harvard.edu/~ngt/), Susan Moore Johnson (2004) and a team of six Harvard researchers have found that some young, beginning teachers consciously plan on testing the waters of teaching for two or three years before making a commitment. Others approach teaching from the start as a limited-term public service, similar to serving in the Peace Corps, and never plan on teaching for more than a few years before moving on to another occupation.

Alternative Route Preparation Programs

Regardless of age, career stage, and career objectives, more and more beginning teachers come to teaching via alternative route preparation programs rather than through traditional four- or five-year programs, a growing phenomenon highlighted by keynote speakers at the First Annual Conference (February 1–3, 2004, San Antonio, Texas) on Alternative Certification sponsored by the National Center for Alternative Certification. The structure and quality of alternative certification programs varies considerably from programs that essentially are traditional programs redesigned to meet the needs of working, nontraditional students to programs that are based almost exclusively on on-the-job training. Alternative certification programs often aim at supplying teachers to urban school districts where staffing demands outstrip the pool of traditionally prepared teachers and at preparing teachers in hard-to-staff areas like mathematics, science, and special education.

The No Child Left Behind Act of 2001 (2004) supports alternative route programs by funding two programs offering "Innovative and Alternative Routes to Licensure": (1) Troops to Teaching and (2) Transition to Teaching. The Transition to Teaching program also includes "teacher mentoring" among funded "pre- and post-placement induction or support activities that have proven effective in recruiting and retaining teachers" (Sec. 2313 (g)(2)(B)(i)).

Finally, in order to assist states in meeting the "highly qualified" teacher requirement of No Child Left Behind, the U.S. Department of Education permits teachers in some rural districts who are highly qualified in at least one subject to have three years to become highly qualified in the additional subjects that they teach if they are provided with relevant professional development, intense supervision, or structured mentoring.

Variety of Characteristics Requires Flexibility in Mentoring Programs

The primary target of teacher mentoring programs today continues to be the young adult, trained in a traditional fashion and embarking on a career intended for a lifetime, as was the case thirty years ago. However, the continuing and increasing influx of beginning teachers with significantly different characteristics—older, changing careers, not intending to teach for more than a few years, and prepared in nontraditional ways— suggests that one-size-fits-all teacher mentoring programs cannot be viable in the long run. The need for flexibility in mentoring programs is even more critical if they are also intended to serve the large number of experienced teachers who migrate from one school district to another and who are yet another kind of beginning teacher.

Who Serves as the Mentors in the Program?

In the early years of formally organized teacher mentoring programs, the teachers sought out to serve as mentors were hoped to have about eight to fifteen years of teaching experience, to be in a teaching assignment identical in grade level or content area to their mentees, and to teach in a nearby classroom. Having a shared lunch or preparation period was an added bonus. Each mentor was assigned to a single mentee, and mentoring was conceptualized as a one-on-one, face-to-face relationship.

Although these conditions remain desirable today, changes in the pool of prospective mentors and improvements in communications technology have resulted in a more expansive notion of what works in teacher mentoring programs when it comes to mentors and the nature of the mentor-mentee relationship. For example, one of the trends that has resulted in the need for new teachers—the retirement wave of teachers hired in the 1960s and 1970s—also means that there are fewer veteran teachers available to serve as mentors. Moreover, the same teachers likely to be courted to become mentors are also in high demand to serve in other leadership roles in their schools, school districts, local teachers' associations, and professional organizations and as cooperating teachers for preservice teachers participating in early field experiences, student teaching, and internships. Not surprisingly and as a result, increasing numbers of mentors have either relatively few years of teaching experience or many years of experience compared with their counterparts twenty or thirty years ago. It is also more and more common today that mentors may have different teaching assignments than their mentees, work in different schools—or even be recently retired from teaching.

Mentoring Configurations

It is ironic that just as the expectations for mentoring links are rising, the number of desirable prospective mentors who can both articulate how they conduct their work and guide beginning teachers in mastering rigorous teaching standards and qualifying for more strenuous licensing requirements is getting smaller. In response to this situation, teacher mentoring programs are often organized around a "mentoring team" or "mentoring mosaic" rather than exclusively on a one-on-one relationship between one mentor and one beginning teacher. When a team approach is used, typically one teacher serves as a primary mentor while one or more other teachers step in as secondary mentors. In those cases where the primary mentor's teaching assignment (and possibly teaching experience in general) differs greatly from that of the mentee, another teacher may serve as the grade level or content area mentor. Similarly, if the primary mentor works in a different school, another teacher working in the mentee's school may function as a local mentor. Another variation is that one teacher serves as a mentor for two or more beginning teachers. Naturally, these variations on one-on-one mentoring require clearly described and understood differences in roles and responsibilities.

Impact of Communications Technology

Advances in communications technology have reduced the dependency of mentoring on a face-to-face relationship. Futurist Michael Zey (2001) predicts the emergence of "virtual" mentoring. In Allen, Texas, the Collin County Community College offers the Teacher Certification Program Mentoring Program to support new teachers. "Telementoring" is included to "enhance face-to-face mentor support though electronic means." This is typically done through computer-mediated communications such as e-mail, videoconferencing, or Internet discussion or chat. Via Internet discussion, mentors provide intern teachers with tested models of support, guidance, and encouragement (Collin County Community College, 2002).

It is possible to combine multiple mentors and communications technology. For instance, a teacher with expertise in some area of teaching, assessment for example, might be asked to host an electronic chat room for beginning teachers for a week or two, focusing on issues related to student assessment. Over the course of the year, other teachers who are not official mentors might interact with new teachers in the school or the entire school district in this way on a variety of topics, for a limited period of time and at a relevant point in the school year.

As necessary and useful as these variations on one-on-one, face-to-face mentoring may be in the context of today's schools, a close professional relationship between mentees and their (primary) mentors continues to be the sign of an effective and successful teacher mentoring program.

How Long Does the Program Last?

In the early days, mentoring programs for beginning teachers were almost always a year in length, starting in August or September and lasting until the end of the academic year. This schedule continues to be the most common format today. Viewing this as the appropriate length of a mentoring program fits with the notion that after a year of experience, a novice teacher is no longer a beginner. Practically speaking, the financial cost associated with mentoring programs can also be an obvious reason for limiting them to a year.

When it comes to program length, the trend in recent years is to extend teacher mentoring programs beyond one year to the second or even third year of a new teacher's employment. Less frequently, the period of time is extended backward by initiating formalized mentoring during preservice preparation in a traditional or alternative certification program. The wisdom of viewing beginning teachers' need for mentoring beyond their first year of work is obvious when experienced teachers are asked, "When did you stop feeling like a beginning teacher?" They usually answer, "After about three or four years."

Multiyear Mentoring

That beginning teachers can derive tremendous benefit from working with a mentor beyond their first year is supported with evidence that new teachers, along with beginners in virtually all other professions, go through predictable stages of professional development over their career (Fessler, 1995; Piland & Anglin, 1993). Most novice teachers move from an early survival and discovery phase as they adjust their preconceptions of teaching based on biography and limited preservice classroom experiences, through a period of experimentation and consolidation of skills, and into a phase of mastery and stabilization characterizing midcareer.

After an initial period of time developing a working knowledge of day-to-day policies, procedures, and routines; becoming somewhat familiar with the characteristics of the students; and learning more about the curriculum, beginning teachers are ready to focus their energies on developing their capacity to be good teachers. While they may start to reach this stage during their first year of teaching, it is more likely to emerge during the next year. It also can be disappointing to mentors who are eager to guide their mentees in becoming more effective teachers to find that they may not be fully ready for this during their first year on the job.

Extending a teacher mentoring program into a second year or beyond requires modifications of goals, appropriate mentoring activities, and the relationship between mentors and their mentees to maximize effectiveness. In short, more of the same may result in little net gain. For example, the required contact between mentors and mentees may be reduced during the second year and occur at a more subtle level; mentees are likely to be more proactive in determining the direction that mentoring takes. Certainly, the quality of what can be expected during a second or third year is directly related to the quality of the program's foundation as built during the first year.

How Is the Program Evaluated?

The expectations for monitoring formal mentoring programs have changed over time. From the beginning, most mentoring programs included strategies for capturing the perspectives of program participants regarding various dimensions of the program. At a minimum, surveys were conducted near the end of the year to determine participants' satisfaction regarding a host of program elements, ranging from appropriateness of mentor-mentee pairings to the value of guest speakers at program meetings, and even to the quality of the snacks provided at meetings. Less frequently, surveys with similar or identical items were administered at the beginning and midpoint of the year in order to capture changes in participants' perceptions over time. The objective of these efforts was program improvement, but seldom to document the impact of the program on program participants. In some cases, program evaluation was little more than an afterthought.

Since the 1990s, more sophisticated—and useful—evaluation techniques have become a critical part of teacher mentoring programs (and staff development in general, as articulated by Sparks & Hirsh, 1997). Those responsible for developing mentoring programs now aim at systematic program evaluation that extends beyond the reactions of mentors and mentees to what they learn as a result of participating in the program, to how they are applying what they learn to their work, and to the impact of the program on mentors, mentees, their students, and even the broader school community.

Planning for Evaluation

Planning for program evaluation occurs early on as an integral part of program design and in response to several critical questions:

- What is the purpose of each element of the evaluation plan?
    To improve the program?
    To increase program effectiveness?
    To judge the value of the program?
    To communicate the value of the program?
    To show how the program and its activities are related to school priorities and professional teaching standards?

- What sources of information are most important for each purpose?
    Surveys?
    Individual or group interviews?
    Journals or anecdotal records?
    Self-assessments linked to rubrics?
    Audiotapes or videotapes (e.g., meetings between mentors and their mentees)?
    Employment data (related to teacher retention)?
    Electronic data (e.g., frequency and duration of e-mail communications or visits to a chat room)?
    Student data (e.g., attendance, achievement)?

- When will the information be collected?
    At the beginning of the year? Midpoint? End of year?
    Across the years (for comparison)?

- Who is responsible for collecting and analyzing the information?
    The program coordinator?
    An outsider (e.g., a retired teacher or administrator, or a faculty person from a local college or university)?

- Who will assure that the results of program evaluation are actually used?
- How will the program evaluation plan be evaluated?

Today's greater emphasis on the careful evaluation of teacher mentoring programs is understandable, although, ironically, in other parts of the world the value of a mentoring program for beginning teachers is believed to be so self-evident as to preclude the need for very much in the way of program evaluation (Britton, Paine, Pimm, & Raizen, 2003). Limited resources for mentoring as one of many worthwhile staff development activities force hard decisions as to which activities to support; typically the decision to support a program is based on evidence of its probable or actual effectiveness. It is reasonable to expect sound evidence that a staff development program like mentoring works, even though it is probably impossible to produce the incontrovertible proof that some look for (Guskey, 2000). However, the lack of absolute proof that mentoring works should never dampen the spirit of educators who know the value of mentoring and who are committed to developing mentoring programs as an essential component of high-quality teacher induction.

Where Does the Program Fit Into Teaching as a Profession?

For most of their history, organized teacher mentoring programs have been a nicety for beginning teachers. School districts have supported mentoring programs voluntarily, assuming the availability of at least minimum resources and knowing that it is difficult to make a case against the value of connecting novice teachers with their experienced colleagues. Mentoring programs were viewed as a part of staff development but certainly not a top priority. However, during the past fifteen years, the significance of mentoring programs as part of the profession of teaching has grown exponentially.

As a Requirement for Teacher Licensure

Perhaps the most important change regarding formalized beginning teacher mentoring is that mentoring is increasingly linked to the administrative codes and state statutes as a requirement for teaching licenses. The state of Ohio provides an example. Since July 1, 2002, new teachers and principals in Ohio have been issued a provisional license and have been required to "successfully complete an entry year program with guidelines provided by the Ohio Department of Education" (3301-24-04(A)(2)) (Ohio Department of Education, 2004). In addition, "school districts, chartered community schools, and chartered nonpublic schools, are required to provide a formal structured program of support, including mentoring, to all entry year teachers and principals" (3301-24-04(B)(2)).

A significant change of teacher licensure in Wisconsin, effective August 31, 2004, also requires school districts to provide a mentor for at least one year for teachers, administrators, and other student services personnel (e.g., guidance counselors) who are issued a nonrenewable "initial educator" license (Wisconsin Department of Public Instruction, 2005). Qualifying for the next step, the "professional educator" license, requires the successful design, implementation, and completion of a "professional development plan." This plan must be approved by a three-person team (teacher, administrator, representative of higher education), submitted to the Wisconsin Department of Public Instruction at the start of the initial educator's second year of employment, and successfully completed within two to four years. In some instances, mentors are likely to serve as the teacher on the three-person team. However, even if mentors are not on the team, they will certainly be called upon to support their mentees during their first year as they formulate their professional development plan.

When mentoring of beginning teachers is tied to licensure, as it is in Ohio, Wisconsin, and thirty other states today (Hall, Chapter 11, this volume), it is no longer just one element of beginning teacher induction support, available if possible and entered into voluntarily, but a high-stakes venture upon which continuing licensure (and, in turn, employability) depends. This context provides a compelling argument for taking great care in the design and implementation of organized teacher mentoring programs with respect to such elements as mentor selection, mentor training, and mentoring activities.

Mentoring Programs as Incentive

Today's mentoring programs differ from programs thirty years ago in yet another very different way. Competition among school districts for hiring teachers, particularly in difficult-to-staff areas, has resulted in the emergence of incentives unimagined in the past, including signing bonuses, forgivable loans, and subsidized housing. Not surprisingly, the availability and quality of a mentoring program also can be an important factor for candidates as they consider applying for or accepting a teaching position, especially if licensure in the state is tied to mentoring. Given comparable opportunities, candidates are even willing to accept a somewhat lower salary if they believe that the available mentoring program will be superior. In effect, the program becomes a recruitment device.

FINAL THOUGHTS

Mentoring programs for beginning teachers have matured since their emergence a generation of teachers ago. They have reached an important stage in their growing status and acceptance as a critical professional development activity that can positively impact the career trajectory of new teachers for a lifetime. Accordingly, it is not surprising that mentoring and mentoring programs are common topics at the annual conferences of influential educational organizations such as the American Association of Colleges of Teacher Education, American Educational Research Association, Association of Supervision and Curriculum Development, Association of

Teacher Educators, International Mentoring Association, and National Staff Development Council.

High-quality mentoring is readily identified today as the heart of effective teacher induction, complemented by a variety of other strategies (Smith & Ingersoll, 2004). For example, *Tapping the Potential: Retaining and Developing High-Quality New Teachers,* a recent report by the Alliance for Excellent Education (2004), recommends providing beginning teachers with common planning time and opportunities for collaboration, ongoing professional development, participation in external networks of teachers, and standards-based evaluation, in addition to mentoring. Indeed, when it comes to preventing an inhumane "sink or swim" introduction to teaching that serves neither beginning teachers nor the children they teach, Harry Wong (2001) is accurate in cautioning that "mentoring can't do it all."

There is something remarkable about mentoring that underscores its lasting value for the profession of teaching. Beginning teachers who have benefited from mentoring readily seek opportunities to give back to their profession, often by becoming mentors themselves. And as they enter into leadership roles at the local, state, or national level, they carry an experience-based vision of the powerful bond among teachers that inevitably results whenever mentoring is a supported priority. In this regard, there is no better form of professional development for teachers than a thoughtfully designed and carefully implemented mentoring program.

REFLECTIONS AND APPLICATIONS

This chapter advocates expanding the vision of effective mentoring programs for beginning teachers beyond established principles by taking into account current trends in seven critical areas. Exercise 1.1 asks you to assess how your program currently addresses each of these critical issues and how each might be enhanced based on material in the chapter.

Exercise 1.1   Seven Critical Issues

Directions: In the first column following each critical issue, describe the current status of that issue in your mentoring program and reflect on its effectiveness. In the next column, speculate how applying material from Chapter 1 might enhance the effectiveness of that issue in your program.

Critical Issue	Current Status	Potential Enhancement
Who provides the leadership for the program?		
On what principles or standards is the program based?		
What kinds of beginning teachers does the mentoring program serve?		
Who serves as the mentors in the program?		
How long does the program last?		
How is the program evaluated?		
Where does the program fit into teaching as a profession?		

REFERENCES

Alliance for Excellent Education. (2004). *Tapping the potential: Retaining and developing high-quality new teachers.* Retrieved July 4, 2004, from www.a114ed.org/publications/TappingThePotential/index.html

American Federation of Teachers. (2001). *Beginning teacher induction: The essential bridge* (AFT Educational Issues Policy Brief No. 13). Washington, DC: AFT Educational Issues Department. Retrieved May 30, 2004, from http://www.aft.org/pubs-reports/downloads/teachers/policy13.pdf

Britton, E., Paine, L., Pimm, D., & Raizen, S. (2003). *Comprehensive teacher induction: Systems for early career learning.* Dordrecht, The Netherlands: Kluwer Academic Publishers.

Collin County Community College. (2002). *Teacher Certification Program Mentoring Program.* Retrieved May 31, 2004, from http://iws.ccccd.edu/telementoring/resources.asp

Council of Chief State School Officers. (1992). *Model for beginning teacher licensing and development: A model for state dialogue.* Retrieved on May 30, 2004, from http://iws.ccsso.org.content/pdfs/corestrd.pdf

Danielson, C. (1996). *Enhancing professional practice: A framework for teaching.* Alexandria, VA: Association for Supervision and Curriculum Development.

Darling-Hammond, L., & Sclan, E. M. (1996). Who teaches and why: Dilemmas of building a profession for the twenty-first century. In J. Sikula, T. J. Buttery, & E. Guyton (Eds.), *Handbook of research on teacher education* (2nd ed., pp. 67–101). New York: Macmillan.

Feistritzer, C. E. (1999). *The making of a teacher: A report on teacher preparation in the U.S.* Washington, DC: Center for Education Information. Retrieved May 31, 2004, from http://www.ncei.com/MakingTeacher-rpt.htm

Fessler, R. (1995). Dynamics of teacher career stages. In T. R. Guskey & M. Huberman (Eds.), *Professional development in education: New paradigms & practices* (pp. 171–192). New York: Teachers College.

Guskey, T. R. (2000). *Evaluating Professional Development.* Thousand Oaks, CA: Corwin.

Johnson, S. M. (Ed.). (2004). *Finders and keepers: Helping new teachers survive and thrive in our schools.* Hoboken, NJ: Wiley & Sons.

National Board for Professional Teaching Standards. (1989). *What teachers should know and be able to do: The five core propositions of the National Board.* Retrieved July 5, 2004, from http://www.nbpts.org/about/coreprops.cfm

National Center for Educational Statistics. (2001). *Teacher preparation and professional development: 2000* (NCES 2001-088). Washington, DC: U.S. Department of Education, Office of Educational Research and Improvement. Retrieved June 1, 2004, from http://nces.ed.gov/pubs2001/2001088.pdf

National Commission on Teaching and America's Future. (2003). *No dream denied: A pledge to America's children.* Retrieved May 30, 2004, from http://documents.nctaf.achieve3000.com/report.pdf

National Education Association. (2004). *NEA-Saturn/UAW Partnership Award.* Retrieved July 30, 2004, from www.nea.org/members/mentoraward.html

National Education Association Foundation for the Improvement of Education. (1999). *Creating a teacher mentoring program.* Retrieved May 30, 2004, from http://www.nfie.org/publications/mentoring.htm

No Child Left Behind Act of 2001. (2004). Retrieved May 2, 2004, from http://www.ed.gov/policy/elsec/leg/esea02/

Ohio Department of Education. (2004). *Entry Year.* Retrieved June 3, 2004, from http://www.ode.state.oh.us/teaching-profession/teacher/certification_licensure/standards/pdf/TE_LS_Entry_Year.pdf

PATHWISE Formative Observation Form. (1995). Princeton, NJ: Educational Testing Service.

Piland, D. E., & Anglin, J. M. (1993). It is only a stage they are going through: The development of student teachers. *Action in Teacher Education, 15*(3), 19–26.

Portner, H. (2001). *Training mentors is not enough: Everything else schools and districts need to do.* Thousand Oaks, CA: Corwin.

Smith, T. M., & Ingersoll, R. M. (2004). What are the effects of teacher induction and mentoring on beginning teacher turnover? *American Educational Research Journal, 41,* 681–714.

Sparks, D., & Hirsh, S. (1997). *A new vision for staff development.* Oxford, OH: Association for Supervision and Curriculum Development, National Staff Development Council.

Wisconsin Department of Public Instruction. (2005). *Teacher education and licensing, PI 34 Rules.* Retrieved May 30, 2004, from http://www.dpi.state.wi.us/dpi/dlsis/tel/pi34.html

Wong, H. (2001). Mentoring can't do it all. *Education Week, 22*(43), 46, 50.

Zey, M. (2001). Cybermentoring, telementoring, and beyond: The emerging role of computer and electronic mediated relationships in business formal mentor programs. Proceedings of the Annual Meeting of the Institute of Behavioral and Applied Management, Charleston, SC.

2

Developing a District's Mentoring Plan

From Vision to Reality

Mark Bower

The State of New York Board of Regents at their November 2003 meeting approved an amendment to Section 100.2 of the Commissioner's Regulations requiring school districts and BOCES to develop a mentoring program. Beginning September 2004, candidates for professional certification must participate in a one year mentored experience.

(Joseph B. Porter, Nov. 2003)

The development of a district-based mentoring program starts with a vision. In the case of the Hilton Central School District, a public school district in upstate New York, the vision was of new teachers excelling in situations where they are empowered to enable their students to succeed.

In pursuit of its vision, the developers of the Hilton program designed it to assist new teachers in the critical areas of classroom management, curriculum implementation, instructional practices, and assessment of student learning. With over 375 teachers and five school buildings, Hilton's desired outcomes for its program were developed to increase the likelihood that beginning teachers receive the highest quality mentoring possible given the current problems of teacher shortage, attrition, and the fact that novice teachers leave the profession in disproportionate numbers. The program also looked to increase the mentor teacher's knowledge, skill, and abilities in providing ongoing formal assistance as well as day-to-day support to the new teacher.

PUTTING TOGETHER THE GUIDING TEAM

In this district, it was critical, as it would be in most districts, to assemble a team of influential staff members who represent a variety of interests and positions. In the initial development of Hilton's mentoring program, the local teachers' association, teachers from each building at different stages in their careers, as well as administrators, met regularly over a period of two years to study the research on mentoring, review the New York State Education Department's guidelines for mentoring programs, and draft a plan that would meet the unique needs of the district. Over the course of the two years that the team of three administrators, two association representatives, and three classroom teachers worked together, information was distributed to the local board of education, administrative and teacher groups, and other districtwide committees who would, over time, have involvement in the mentoring program.

BEING CLEAR ABOUT MENTORS AND INTERNS: DEFINITIONS AND ROLES

In Hilton, the mentoring process is defined as

> a process that facilitates instructional improvement wherein an experienced educator (mentor) works with a novice or less experienced teacher (intern) collaboratively and nonjudgmentally to study and deliberate on ways instruction in the classroom may be improved.

While it may seem overly simplistic, in a district-based mentoring program, it is important from the onset to clearly define *mentor* and *intern*. In Hilton's program, the mentor is defined as a permanently certified, tenured teacher who has demonstrated outstanding knowledge and skill in the classroom in an effort to promote student learning and achievement. The mentor exhibits a personal interest in mentoring new teachers and a willingness to coach, assist, and provide specific feedback to new teachers.

Mentors should demonstrate the ability to analyze, communicate, and collaborate. They should possess the ability to influence others and at the same time command respect and be trustworthy and collegial.

Additionally, the mentor is involved in professional development, teaches in the same building as the intern, and is as close to the same grade and subject as the intern, wherever and whenever possible.

Mentors are seen as facilitators of instructional improvement, providers of an alternative form of supervision, and supporters of teachers' professional growth and development. It is important for the district to be clear that mentors are not critics or judges, formal evaluators, or administrative informants.

Considerable time is also spent with the mentors on looking at their own professional expertise and their ability to work with interns in the development of those areas, which include

- Knowledge and expertise in the content areas
- Management of the physical and affective environment
- Management of student behavior
- Knowledge and use of appropriate resources to advance learning
- Ability to demonstrate positive human relation skills
- Ability to demonstrate skill in lesson, unit, and yearly planning
- Understanding of child growth and development
- Use of a wide range of effective instructional practices

Hilton frames the mentor's role with the following scenario. The mentor meets with the intern to discuss plans. The mentor explains that mentors have no evaluative authority and they will keep their conversations confidential. Although the intern will have at least three formal observations by the principal over the course of the semester, the mentor will not in any way participate in the evaluation process. "My job," explains the mentor, "is to work with you as much as possible on areas we both feel need improvement."

Over the next several months the mentor and the intern develop a close professional relationship. The intern realizes that the mentor in fact does not have any evaluative input, and confidence grows daily. "You know," says the intern, "I feel I can really open up to you. You have given me realistic suggestions for improving my teaching. I know you are not sitting in judgment of my work in the classroom."

The intern's skills improve dramatically over the next several months. The mentor shares with the intern the evidence of the students' trust in the intern as a teacher and the quality of the work that the students are doing in the classroom. The intern credits much of this success to the friendly, expert assistance received from the mentor.

In looking at a scenario such as this one, the role of the mentor becomes much clearer and the mentor sees that the real power in the work with the intern lies in establishing a strong working relationship.

Simultaneously, it is important to define *intern*. In Hilton, for our mentoring program, an intern is a teacher or staff member new to the teaching profession and in his or her first full year of employment with the district. Given that a district program will potentially need to serve a large number of new teachers over the next several years, the determining factor for assigning mentors to teachers who are not new to teaching but new to the district, and to those teachers working in part-time or long-term substitute positions, will be the availability of qualified mentors who closely match grade and subject areas, as well as the degree to which these teachers are in need of a mentor. When necessary and possible, qualified mentors may also need to work with teachers on an as-needed basis during their probationary period.

Roles and Responsibilities

A mentoring program needs to have established guidelines for the roles and responsibilities of both mentors and interns.

The Mentor

In any district, no matter what the program, the responsibilities of a mentor are great.

> During the first few months of the beginning teacher's induction year, the mentor may become fully responsible for various instructional and socialization activities. Mentoring has an evolutionary quality (Gray & Gray, 1985); the experienced teacher assists the beginning teacher gradually to gain competency, confidence, realistic values, experience, self-evaluative skills, and curricular knowledge. Interaction between the mentor and beginning teacher may involve modeling, supervision, coaching, and discussion and curriculum collaboration. Eventually as beginning teachers gain more confidence and competence, the mentors minimize their instructional leadership. The beginning teacher demonstrates acquired skills and knowledge by becoming self-directing, self-evaluating, and eventually responsible for the development of his own professional development program. During this period as the beginning teacher learns and grows, so does the mentor. (Andrews & Wideen, 1987, p. 150)

The major responsibilities of a mentor in Hilton are modeling different instructional methodologies, providing regular observation and feedback, working jointly on the introduction of new curriculum materials, assisting in classroom action research, and serving in a resource and consultant role to the intern. These responsibilities are connected to the more explicit parts of a mentor's role, which include

- Recognizing the confidentiality of their work with interns
- Providing ongoing information, support, feedback, and assistance to the intern

- Helping the intern refine present skills and develop new ones, particularly in the areas of management, curriculum, instruction, and assessment
- Enhancing the intern's ability to reflect, problem solve, and make decisions that are certain to promote student learning
- Scheduling any helpful visits to classrooms in the district and providing the intern with a framework for observing another teacher's specific use of a management, curriculum, instruction, or assessment practice
- Keeping a journal or log of all work involved with the intern
- Scheduling time to take the online learning course on mentoring offered through the district and/or attend a regional mentoring initiative entitled Mentoring that Matters
- Being willing to put in the time needed to help the intern learn, grow, and develop as an educator
- Attending a maximum of four meetings per year—one during the New Teacher Summer Orientation, one fall, one winter, and one spring end-of-year meeting with district personnel
- Completing an end-of-year survey

The Intern

It is important to ensure that interns are extremely clear about their role, particularly since their probationary years in a district can be quite unnerving. We more completely spelled out some of the additional components of the intern's role as indicated below:

- Recognize the confidentiality of your work with mentors.
- Be open to feedback given to you by the mentor.
- Be prepared to be visited by the mentor during classroom instruction time so that the mentor has an opportunity to observe your work with students.
- For any follow-up conference or conversation with your mentor, be on time and be prepared.
- Work on your own ability to reflect, problem solve, and make decisions that are in the best interest of the students.
- Keep a journal or log of all work involved with the mentor.
- Attend the end-of-year spring meeting with your mentor.
- Complete an end-of-year survey.
- Know what your professional goals are.
- Recognize and appreciate that difference is healthy.
- Learn to work cooperatively with your mentor.
- Encourage yourself to learn in your preferred ways.
- Be accepting of new ideas, practices, and strategies.
- Be a good listener.
- Ask good questions.
- Be open to feedback.

COMING TO TERMS WITH
THE FORMAL STRUCTURE

Vision without action is a daydream; action without vision is a nightmare. Hilton's induction and mentoring plan provides the structure by which its vision can be put into action.

Procuring Mentors

The program annually advertises for mentors. Prospective mentors submit a brief written application indicating their interest in mentoring (see Figure 2.1). This application speaks to the criteria for mentors stated in both the definition and roles and responsibilities.

Once applications are submitted, building administrators, a teachers' association representative, and the district's staff development director will review applications, and a mentoring pool will be created so that, as hiring takes place each summer, new teachers (interns) can be matched appropriately with same-building mentors. In rare cases, some mentor-intern matches may need to be made outside a building for positions such as counselor, psychologist, and speech and language. For these positions, a district pool may be created.

Once in a building or district pool, a mentor will remain there unless the mentor or the building administrator, teachers' association representative, and director of staff development indicate otherwise. Each spring, the district will advertise for new mentors, recognizing that the pool of available mentors needs to grow each year. The local board of education will also approve the list of mentors on an annual basis.

Matching Mentors With Interns

A major piece of the structure of this district's mentoring program is to pair all new teachers with qualified mentors. Whenever and wherever possible, the program looks to place one intern with each mentor. There is the flexibility in the structure, however, to place a maximum of two interns with each mentor. In the first three pilot years of this formalized program, the structure will involve creating a mentoring pool in each of the district's five buildings. From this mentoring pool, the building administration, one teachers' association representative, and the district's staff development director will match mentors with interns.

Once matching is completed, mentors and interns will meet each other either during the rolling orientation schedule or the New Teacher Summer Orientation. The rolling orientation is a series of dates during the summer months when new hires schedule appointments to meet with the human resource, staff development, and curriculum and instruction office staffs in order to learn about, in a more intimate setting, the goals and objectives of the district, the staff development for new teachers, and the mentoring

(Text continues on page 29)

Figure 2.1   Mentoring Application

Name _____

School building _____

Grade(s), subject(s) taught _____

Number of years in the district _____

Number of years in your assignment for 2004–2005 school year _____

In one paragraph, summarize the reasons why you would want to be a mentor to a new teacher.

Speak to the following issues which would comprise your roles and responsibilities if you were to work with an intern in the future:

- How important would confidentiality be to you in a mentoring role you would have with a new teacher?

- In what ways, in the past, have you already provided ongoing information, support, feedback, and assistance to another teacher(s)?

- What strengths do you possess in the areas of management, curriculum, instruction, and assessment, as these are the primary areas for which you would be providing mentoring?

(Continued)

Figure 2.1 (Continued)

Name _____ p. 2

- What skills/strategies/practices have you/would you employ to enhance an intern's ability to reflect, problem solve, and make decisions that are certain to promote student learning?

- If you were to suggest your intern visit another classroom/classroom teacher, what framework would you offer that would assist your intern in observing the teacher?

- Do you currently keep your own learning journal/log? What suggestions would you have for your intern in maintaining one on his/her own?

For your information:

- Attend the two half-day staff development on August 30–31.
- Carve out time on your own (when the online courses are ready) to learn more about mentoring (you will receive inservice credit for this).
- Be willing to put in the time to help your intern learn, grow, and develop as an educator.
- Attend a maximum of four meetings per year (one is a part of the summer orientation and the other three are fall, winter, and/or spring) and one end-of-year meeting.
- Complete an end-of-year survey.

program and to receive curriculum documents that they are responsible for enacting in the classroom. The New Teacher Summer Orientation is the time (three full days at the end of the summer) when all new hires come together for the district's formal orientation which includes, among other things, meeting with their mentors. This summer orientation leads into a yearlong, monthly support group which is in place to continue the orientation into the year and is Hilton's means of inducting new teachers to the district and to the profession. Mentors will be given some release time at the administration's discretion to visit and observe their interns' classrooms. In turn, interns will be given some release time at the building administrator's discretion to visit the mentors' classrooms or other teachers' classrooms (at the recommendation of the mentor). Time to conference and meet will take place beyond the workday and work year.

If a mentor feels that there need to be any changes made in matching, he or she can field these concerns to the district's director of staff development, who will work with the building administration and the teachers' association representative to do so. In the special case where an intern feels that the relationship is not productive, the intern can involve any individual in the building's selection team that he or she feels comfortable with (building principal, vice principal, association representative, or director of staff development). These situations will be dealt with as confidentially as is humanly possible and with a high degree of respect and tact.

Time: A Critical Issue

When will induction and mentoring take place? The Hilton program developers realized that as much time as possible must be made available in order for induction and mentoring to have the impact they envision. Therefore, the plan requires mentors and interns to meet during the summer rolling orientation or the more formal New Teacher Summer Orientation. Additionally, the mentors, as a group, are responsible for meeting three times per year (once each during the fall, winter, and spring) for one and a half to two hours each with the director of staff development and any other guests as deemed necessary by the mentors or because of issues that need to be discussed. The interns are responsible for attending the end-of-year spring meeting with their mentor. There are no set rules for the amount of time during the year that mentors and interns must meet. The amount of time they will spend together is dependent on the intern's needs. A suggested guideline is to schedule time to meet monthly, recognizing that the first several months of school may require more time than subsequent months. As much as possible, it would be advantageous to make use of any time during the course of the normal school day to schedule time to meet. As mentioned previously, the administration has discretion to use release time as necessary to allow mentors and interns time to visit and observe classrooms.

EVALUATING THE MENTORING PROGRAM

A formative evaluation of the mentoring program will take place annually. All mentors and interns will be surveyed (see Figure 2.2), as will the building administrators and teachers' association representatives. This data will be reported anonymously to the overseeing committee in the district (the staff development advisory council), who will conduct an annual review of the program, suggesting any necessary changes to the district's director of staff development who, in turn, will work with the teachers' association executive committee, two administrative representatives, and other district personnel, as needed, to enact the changes.

A formal evaluation will take place every two years and will be broadened to include additional evaluation instruments such as focus groups conducted by an outside evaluator.

ORIENTATION AND STAFF DEVELOPMENT TO SUPPORT MENTORS AND INTERNS

The district expects mentors to participate in orientation and staff development. The following topics make up this staff development experience for mentors:

- Skills and strategies for effective mentoring
- Meaningful feedback and conferencing skills
- Special challenges that face the mentor
- Dealing with a teacher in crisis
- The components of a mentoring plan
- Developing your plan for mentoring

A yearlong staff development plan is in place focusing on each of these topics in depth. The plan also provides for mentors to convene as a group at least four times during the school year to support each other, collaborate, share effective practices, and troubleshoot. The support of mentors is as important in the Hilton district as is the mentoring process itself. Some of the basic skills and strategies to be explored during staff development sessions for mentors include

- Determining goals
- Listening
- Building rapport
- Sharing information and sources
- Focusing on human and emotional needs
- Choosing your words carefully
- Challenging for high achievement

(Text continues on page 33)

Figure 2.2   End-of-Year Survey

For the Intern:

1. To what degree did the mentor provide quality support, assistance, feedback, and suggestions? (circle one)

1	2	3	4	5
Low				High

Please explain.

2. To what degree did you believe your classroom work/practice was enhanced due to the work you did with the mentor? (circle one)

1	2	3	4	5
Low				High

Please explain.

3. More than anything else, what about your work as a teacher this year was strengthened due to your work with the mentor?

4. What advice or suggestions might you have for future mentors as they carry out their responsibilities with their interns?

5. What suggestions do you have for the district in terms of how they organized and managed the mentoring program?

(Continued)

Figure 2.2 (Continued)

For the Mentor:

1. To what degree did you believe you were able to provide quality support, assistance, feedback, and suggestions to the intern? (circle one)

       1   2   3   4   5

   Low   High

   Please explain.

2. To what degree did you believe your work with the intern improved his/her classroom work/practice? (circle one)

       1   2   3   4   5

   Low   High

   Please explain.

3. More than anything else, what is it that you believe you learned as a result of mentoring a new teacher?

4. What advice would you give interns in the future as to how they may engage the mentors in work related to major classroom responsibilities?

5. What suggestions do you have for the district in terms of how they managed and carried out the mentoring program?

- Identifying strengths and areas in need of improvement
- Coaching for development
- Providing appropriate support
- Recognizing accomplishments

Feedback and Conferencing Skills

Advanced strategies for supporting the beginning teacher through mentoring include, for example, meaningful feedback. What does meaningful feedback look like, and conversely, what doesn't it sound and look like? Here are the key elements of meaningful feedback:

- Keep feedback specific to two areas:
  - Behavior to reinforce.
  - Behavior to "grow" with.

- It's a "remembered" teaching situation.
- It focuses on what the receiver, not you, the sender, needs.
- New teachers are capable of doing something with the feedback they receive.
- Ideas are expressed as more-less, rather than either-or.

THE BEGINNING TEACHER IN CRISIS: THE MENTOR'S CHALLENGE

I know it has been rough because it is the first year. And it is always going to be rough in your first year. But I never expected it to be like this. I never thought I'd feel so down and incompetent. . . . There have been times where I felt so small I couldn't even scrape myself off the floor.

Rebecca, a third-grade teacher

As part of its mentor training, the Hilton district decided to use case studies to help the mentor more clearly examine the needs of interns, particularly those interns they would be working with who may be in crisis. Following are a few of these case studies.

Case Study 1

A kindergarten teacher in a small rural district is in his first year of teaching. He has 20 kindergarten students for a full day program. He prides himself as a beginning teacher in being organized and prepared. While he is working on developing positive relationships with his students, he is dealing with five chronically misbehaving students. On a recent visit to his classroom, you, the mentor, observed these five students consistently shouting out, and on numerous occasions running around the room; in more than one instance they were annoying both verbally and physically to other students in the classroom. The kindergarten teacher tried the following:

"Students, please take your seats and sit down."

"Boys and girls, this is not the way we act in kindergarten."

"Mr. Richardson expects you to behave in this class."

"I'm giving you till the count of five to stop shouting out and get in your seats."

Case Study 2

A fourth-grade teacher in an urban district is beginning her second year of teaching. While she is new to the district, she has spent one year teaching in a suburban district. She has twenty-four students in a blended program. She is assisted for part of the day by a special education teacher and teacher assistant who are primarily serving the seven identified students in her class. This teacher has established routines and procedures and has spent considerable time ensuring that students follow her behavioral expectations.

As her mentor, you're observing a large-group math lesson dealing with fractions. She has introduced the concept of fourths. She asks the students if they have any questions about this concept. She immediately puts the students to work on a worksheet comprised of thirty computational problems dealing with fractions. At least ten students' hands are raised, and many of them are indicating they do not know how to do the first problem. Other students are getting to work, but within minutes are experiencing similar problems. The teacher responds by saying, "I don't know what's the matter with you students. You indicated that you didn't have any questions about this a few minutes ago. I'll try to come around and help each one of you."

Case Study 3

In a suburban district a fifth-grade art teacher new to a middle school building and new to teaching has a classroom of thirty eighth graders. Her personal portfolio demonstrates her high degree of skill as an artist. Many of the students she is working with are not motivated in the area of art. A small number of the students do not have the prerequisite skills needed in this art class, and the remainder of the students are extremely talented as artists and extremely motivated as students. You, as mentor, are observing her introductory lesson to a unit on watercolors. She shows the students her display of four watercolor paintings that are part of her personal portfolio. She has set up a still life of four pieces of fruit in a bowl, a decanter, and a vase of simple flowers. The materials are ready at each of the large art tables in the room. She tells the students that they can begin sketching the still life and she will be available for help. Many students begin moaning and are verbally negative. Other students are near tears as they make their first attempts (albeit floundering) at the sketch. A small group of students get started with a high degree of success. The teacher, trying to provide one-on-one help to the verbally negative and the floundering groups of students, is completely frustrated and disappointed.

Case Study 4

In a large suburban high school with a high percentage of academically talented students, a first-year technology teacher who came with the highest recommendations is working with one section of twenty-two students in a high school technology course. While he is a content expert, he has limited experience in teaching high school students, particularly students who are from affluent, academically oriented homes. You, the mentor, are observing a lesson on simple machines. The first twenty minutes of the lesson have gone by and the teacher is the only person in the room who has done any talking. At this point you notice many students whose heads are on desks. Other students have not taken one note; some students in the corner of the room are having a private conversation. It is apparent to you that they have tuned out the teacher and little, if any, learning is taking place. The teacher now notices your level of concern as the mentor observing this situation. He stops the lesson and asks students what the problem is. He gets the following responses:

"I already know everything about simple machines."

"When am I ever going to need to know any of this? I am taking advanced placement courses and am going to an Ivy League college."

"I hate to tell you this, Mr. Lucas, but technology is not supposed to be a lecture-based course and all you have done is lecture."

"I don't even know what I should be taking notes on. You haven't told us what the purpose or objective of this lesson is."

In each of the four case studies, the mentor needs to recognize that there is a pattern to the problems each of the four teachers is experiencing. When these cases are used during mentor training, some critical questions for a mentor would be the following:

- What are the core problems inherent in each scenario?
- How would you prioritize from high to low all of the issues that need to be addressed with the intern?

- What action plan would assist the intern in immediately putting into action steps to overcome the high-need areas?
- How would you assist the intern in working on the remaining problems over time?

TEN ESSENTIALS FOR DESIGNING AN INDUCTION/MENTORING PLAN

1. Determine and honor the principal, building, and district expectations for the mentor and intern.

2. Determine and honor any unique expectations that the teachers' union may have for this program.

3. Clarify your personal beliefs related to mentoring.

4. Determine how you will introduce yourself to an intern and in turn have the intern introduce him- or herself to you.

5. Clarify the personal goals you have for the mentor-intern relationship.

6. Work out a realistic schedule for observations and conferences.

7. Design an evaluation component for collecting data showing whether students benefit from the mentor-intern relationship.

8. Continue to learn and study the research that supports mentoring.

9. Identify and consider all components that will affect the program.

10. Above all, remain true to your vision.

CLOSING THOUGHTS

Districts across the country have been and will continue to be dealing with significant turnover of teachers. Veteran teachers will be retiring, and a high proportion of novice teachers will be leaving the profession. It is crucial to have a comprehensive plan that addresses this issue and looks at the manner in which novice teachers are supported during their first years of employment.

What, more than anything, is important in the development of a district-based mentoring plan and program is the collective ownership of the plan by multiple stakeholders in the district. Second, the plan needs to be guided by a group of individuals who are invested in the growth and development of novice teachers. Last, staff development to assist both mentors and interns, over time, must address key issues in the mentor-intern relationship that a district wants to promote.

Without question, it is the ongoing support that a district provides in terms of resources, time, and staff development that will further strengthen the mentoring program and turn the vision of an effective induction and mentoring program into reality.

REFLECTIONS AND APPLICATIONS

This chapter advocates turning the vision of effective induction and mentoring programs for beginning teachers into reality by designing a methodical and pragmatic structure. One of the essential elements of that structure is the comprehensive training of mentors. Exercise 2.1 asks you to assess to what extent your program currently provides some of these critical training issues, and how, based on the chapter's discussions and examples, the effectiveness of such training might be enhanced.

Exercise 2.1   Basic Skills and Strategies

Directions: Below are some of the basic skills and strategies explored by the Hilton Central School District's mentors during their staff development sessions. In the box to the right of each skill or strategy, describe how it takes place in your mentor training program and reflect on its effectiveness. In the next box, speculate how, by applying material from this chapter, you might enhance the training's effectiveness.

Skills & Strategies	How Applied	Potential Enhancement
Determining goals		
Building rapport		
Challenging for high achievement		
Sharing information and sources		
Providing appropriate support		
Identifying strengths and areas in need of improvement		
Coaching for development		

REFERENCES

Andrews, I., & Wideen, M. (1987). *Staff development for school improvement: A focus on the teacher.* London: Falmer Press.

Gray, W. A., & Gray, M. M. (1985). Synthesis of research on mentoring beginning teachers. *Educational Leadership, 43,* 37–43.

3

New Teacher Induction

The Foundation for Comprehensive, Coherent, and Sustained Professional Development

Harry K. Wong

Induction is a comprehensive process of sustained training and support for new teachers. The process of induction has been growing successfully for the past twenty years, and this chapter provides an opportunity to talk about where we are and where are we going with the training and retaining of new teachers. Let's begin with some startling facts on why new teachers fail.

- Thirty-three percent of new teachers are hired after the school year has already started, and 62 percent are hired within thirty days of when they start teaching (Kardos & Liu, 2003).
- Fifty-six percent of new teachers report that no extra assistance is available to them as new teachers (Kardos & Liu, 2003).
- While 87 percent of the new teachers in a particular state said they had a mentor, only 17 percent said their mentors ever observed them teach (Kardos & Liu, 2003).
- Few teachers began teaching with a clear, operational curriculum in hand and even fewer received curricula that aligned with state standards (Kauffman, Johnson, Kardos, Liu, & Peske, 2002).

- Only 1% of beginning teachers currently receive the ongoing support that constitutes comprehensive induction when they enter the profession (Alliance for Excellent Education, 2004a).

Now for the good news. There are some exciting state-of-the-art induction programs that are providing the proper training and support for the professional development of effective teachers and that lead to lifelong learning.

- Switzerland, Japan, New Zealand, Shanghai (China), and France have cultures of lifelong learning that begin with induction processes that are comprehensive, coherent, and sustained.
- The Flowing Wells School District of Tucson, Arizona, has a structured eight-year process that develops their new teachers from novices to expert teachers.
- Ninety-nine percent of the teachers in the Lafourche Parish Schools of Louisiana in 2002 successfully completed the performance-based Louisiana Teacher Assistance and Assessment Program required for state teacher certification.
- In the Forsyth County Schools of Georgia, their Induction Academy is focused on the quality of student work, where they "Work on the Work" (WOW).
- In the Carlsbad School District in New Mexico, the induction program is focused on teaching teachers how to teach the required benchmarks and standards.
- The Homewood-Flossmoor High School District in Flossmoor, Illinois, has a lifelong professional development program called Homewood-Flossmoor University.
- The Dallas Public Schools in Texas have a comprehensive new teacher initiative that is composed of learning opportunities for future teachers in high school, student teachers, and beginning teachers and advanced studies for veteran teachers.
- Connecticut, California, and South Carolina have structured, multi-year induction programs with specific protocols for teacher effectiveness and student learning.
- These comprehensive and organized induction programs train and support teachers to focus on student learning.

INDUCTION AND MENTORING ARE NOT SYNONYMOUS

The term *mentoring* is often misused for *induction*. It must be clarified that induction and mentoring are not the same. The fact that the two terms are used interchangeably and synonymously does not make it correct.

- Induction is a noun. It is the name given to a comprehensive, coherent, and sustained professional development process that is organized by a school district to train, support, and retain new teachers, which then seamlessly guides them into a lifelong learning program.

- Mentoring is most commonly used as a verb or adjective, because it describes what mentors do. A mentor is a single person, whose basic function is to help a new teacher. Mentoring is not induction; it is a component of the induction process.

The terms *mentoring* and *induction* cannot be used interchangeably. Mentors are important, but they are only one component of the induction process. Mentors cannot replace or be the only form of induction assistance. To do so would be to use a "one-size-fits-all" mentality that says a mentor is all a new teacher needs to become an effective teacher.

In many school districts, mentoring is carried out one-on-one, in isolation, with no coherence to any district or school curriculum, plan, goals, or standards, whereas good induction programs are comprehensive, last several years, have clearly articulated goals, and provide a structured and nurturing system of professional development and support. Or, as Johnson and Birkeland (2003b) quote a new teacher in an induction program, "It was the perfect blend: caring, very structured, and a lot of supervision!"

Mentoring: Some Critical Reviews

Bennetts (2001), Hawk (1986–1987), and Little (1990) report that there is little empirical evidence to support specific mentoring practices.

Sharon Feiman-Nemser writes in her 1996 *ERIC Digest* article, "Teacher Mentoring: A Critical Review," that mentoring burst onto the educational scene in the early 1980s, yet a review of twenty years of claims about mentoring reveals that few studies exist that show the context, content, and consequences of mentoring. Thus more direct studies are needed about mentoring and its effects on teaching and teacher retention.

Four significant reports expand on Feiman-Nemser's contention.

1. A research review written by Richard Ingersoll and Jeffrey Kralik (2004) states, "While current research does not yet provide definitive evidence of the value of mentoring programs in keeping new teachers from leaving the profession, it does reveal that there is enough promise to warrant significant further investigation (p. 15)."

2. Susan Moore Johnson and The Project on the Next Generation of Teachers (2004) state, "Although a few new teachers in our study said they would have been lost without their mentors, most provided little evidence that one-on-one mentoring offered much support (pp. 196–197)."

3. A report from the Public Education Network (2004), *The Voice of the New Teacher* says, "Although the value of mentoring is indisputable, the evidence of stand-alone 'mentoring as induction' programs has been called into question."

4. *Tapping the Potential: Retaining and Developing High-Quality New Teachers,* a report from the Alliance for Excellent Education (2004b), says, "While mentoring is the most widely practiced component of induction, mentoring by itself is not enough to retain and develop teachers. Mentoring programs vary widely and may do little more than ask mentors to check in with new teachers a few times per semester to chat (p. 12)."

The use of mentoring alone, without the other components of induction, is not supported by research as being a proven strategy.

Mentoring: The Focus Is on Survival

The issue is not mentoring. The issue is when mentoring is used as an isolated event. Studies have shown that mentoring does not teach teacher effectiveness; rather, it is designed to answer questions of survival. Susan Moore Johnson (2003), director of the Harvard Graduate School of Education's Project on the Next Generation of Teachers, said at an Association for Supervision and Curriculum Development (ASCD) presentation, "Mentoring is all the rage. There is some sort of deep hope on the part of everyone that if you get the right mentor, your life will be saved and you will be the teacher you remember. But the truth is that mentoring pairs seldom are anything but haphazard. They are driven by the schedule. They are often not pairs of people who really know the subjects that the individual is teaching."

It is the belief of some people that all a new teacher needs to succeed is a mentor. In a paper for WestEd, Britton, Raizen, Paine, and Huntley (2000; summarized in Wong, Britton, & Ganser, 2005) report that currently in more than thirty states, the universal practice seems remarkably narrow. Mentoring predominates, and often there is little more. In many schools, one-on-one mentoring is the dominant or sole strategy for supporting new teachers, often lacking real structure and relying on the willingness of the veteran and new teacher to seek each other out. Many mentors are assigned to respond to a new teacher's day-to-day survival teaching tips, functioning primarily as a safety net for new teachers.

Britton further reports that mentoring, in and of itself, has no purpose, goal, or agenda for student learning. Thus, mentoring fails to provide evidence of the connection between well-executed professional development and student learning.

Schmoker (quoted in Breaux & Wong, 2003, p. 23) writes, "So called 'mentors' are everywhere these days, but they aren't often given release time or a clear, compelling charge." Mentors may show up after school begins and may not have been trained, compensated, or given direction or goals to attain. Many mentors do not consult with other mentors and may never even visit the mentee's classroom.

Head, Reiman, and Thies-Sprinthall (1992) confirm that negative outcomes have been reported and that unstructured buddy mentoring can have harmful results and can actually be worse than no mentoring at all. Hargreaves and Fullan (2000), in describing mentoring in the new millennium, claim that beginning teachers may know more about some current strategies than the mentor.

Induction: Structured, Comprehensive, and Focused on Professional Learning

Mentors are very important, but they must be part of an induction process aligned to the district's vision, mission, and structure. For a mentor to be effective, the mentor must be trained and then used in combination with the other components of the induction process.

Every company, every nonprofit organization, every locally run store or restaurant has a continuous training program. Teachers are no different. They want training, they want to fit in, and they want their students to learn and achieve. For the most part, education has failed to recognize what industries have always recognized—training matters. Formalized, sustained training matters.

Even the best educated of new employees need on-the-job training. Despite completing college and medical school, doctors spend years working as hospital residents before entering private practice. Newly elected judges, armed with law degrees and years of experience, attend judicial college before assuming the bench. It stands to reason, then, that teachers, who have earned college degrees and teaching credentials, have much to gain from on-the-job training.

Demonstration Classrooms and Networking: Other Induction Components

As important and as appreciated as mentors may be, Wong has discovered in communicating with hundreds of new teachers via the Web site www.teachers.net that they want two other components that induction programs provide: (1) demonstration classes where they can see other teachers model good teaching, a component that is central to the five foreign induction processes reported by Britton, Paine, Raizen, and Pimm (2003) and (2) collaboration. It has been found that teachers remain with a district when they feel strong bonds of connection to a professional learning community that has, at its heart, high-quality interpersonal relationships founded on trust and respect (Wong & Asquith, 2002).

In the United States, Breaux and Wong (2003) report that teachers are typically viewed as independent operators, encouraged to be creative, and expected to do a good job behind closed doors. Collaboration is rare. Worse yet, new teachers seldom see another classroom. "I never sat in anyone else's classroom even once," laments first-year teacher Gail A. Saborio of Wakefield, Rhode Island. "Mine is the only teaching style I know. I felt that sometimes I was reinventing the wheel." Loneliness and lack of support further exacerbate the problems of beginning teachers.

Kardos and Liu (2003), at Harvard's Project on the Next Generation of Teachers, found that of 110 new teachers in New Jersey, 87 percent said they had a mentor, but only 17 percent of the new teachers said that their mentors ever actually watched them teach in the classroom.

Wong (2003b) writes that what keeps good teachers are structured, sustained, intensive professional development programs that allow new teachers to observe others, to be observed by others, and to be part of networks or study groups where all teachers share together, grow together, and learn to respect each other's work.

Shields et al. (2003) report that only 6 percent of new teachers received in-class mentoring or coaching at least monthly. In addition, new teachers were more likely to receive superficial support (e.g., their mentors prepared or sent materials) than support that might help improve their skills and knowledge of instructional techniques and classroom management, such as observing their mentors or having their mentors demonstrate a lesson.

Johnson and Birkeland (2003a), reporting on their study of fifty teachers in Massachusetts, conclude, "Our work suggests that schools would do better to rely less on one-on-one mentoring and, instead, develop schoolwide structures that promote the frequent exchange of information and ideas among novice and veteran teachers." Induction builds a community of teachers, bringing together beginning teachers, experienced teachers, and school leaders in a collaborative setting where they can observe each other teach and engage in a culture of cooperation and continuous learning (Wong, 2004a).

On Sustained Professional Development

Induction programs can run for two or more years and then seamlessly flow into a comprehensive and sustained professional development process. Christopher Cross (Cross & Rigden, 2002) writes that a study of seven urban districts reported that the only reform effort that clearly resulted in student achievement gains had clear instructional expectations, supported by extensive (sustained) professional development, over a period of several years.

Caroline Hendrie (2002) writes that after several urban school districts spent half a billion dollars of Annenberg Challenge funds, the money that delivered the best return was the money invested in giving teachers sustained opportunities to improve their classroom skills.

Hiebert, Gallimore, and Stigler (2002) state that professional development yields the best results when it is long-term, school-based, collaborative, focused on students' learning, and linked to curricula. Thus, the induction process must be systematic and sustained.

In a paper presented to the American Educational Research Association, Garet, Porter, Desmoine, Birman, and Kwang (2001) report that after working with 1,027 teachers, they found that teachers learned more in teacher networks and study groups than with mentoring and that longer, sustained, and intensive professional development programs make a greater impact than shorter ones.

Components of Successful Induction Programs

Induction is a comprehensive, multiyear process designed to train and acculturate new teachers in the academic standards and vision of the district. It is worth repeating that all effective induction programs have three basic characteristics (Wong, 2002b). They are

1. Comprehensive. There is an organization or structure to the program consisting of many activities and many people who are involved. There is a group that oversees the program and rigorously monitors it to be sure that it stays the course toward student learning.

2. Coherent. The various activities and people are logically connected to each other.

3. Sustained. The comprehensive and coherent program continues for many years.

According to the Public Education Network (2004), researchers have identified the following components of effective induction program practices:

- Long-term planning for improving teaching and learning, aligned with the instructional philosophy of the school
- Practices aligned with professional standards as well as state and local student learning standards
- A strong sense of institutional commitment incorporating with strong administrator support and involvement
- Participation by all new teachers, whether entering the profession from traditional or alternative pathways
- Input from beginning and veteran teachers on program design and structure
- A time frame that begins prior to, extends throughout, and continues beyond the new teacher's first year of teaching
- Opportunities for inductees to visit demonstration classrooms
- Study groups in which new teachers can network and build support, commitment, and leadership in a learning community

- Adequate time and resources for implementation
- Reduced workloads, release time, and placement in classes with less, rather than more, demanding students
- Quality mentoring, with careful selection, training, and ongoing support for mentors
- Ongoing assessment to determine whether the program is having its desired impact

STRATEGIES USED BY EXEMPLARY INDUCTION PROGRAMS

Effective induction programs have all or many of the following strategies incorporated into a comprehensive, formalized process to train, support, and retain new teachers.

Administrative Support

In each of the induction programs of the five countries reported by Britton, Paine, Raizen, & Pimm (2003) there is an administrative group that oversees, coordinates, sets policy, provides goals, and rigorously monitors the induction program to ensure effective teacher performance.

Welcome Center

The Dallas Independent School District in Texas and the Clark County Schools in Nevada have a "welcome center" for their new teachers. The centers help new teachers find housing and set up utilities, provide maps, recommend banking facilities, and assist with all the other practical needs of teachers who are new in town.

Script

In Oklahoma, the El Reno School District's two-year induction program teaches new teachers how to script their first day of school so teachers can begin with a plan of action. A sample of one of these scripts can be found at www.teachers.net/wong, June 2000 and March 2003.

Preschool Workshop

Four staff developers in the Lafourche Parish Schools of Thibodaux, Louisiana, conduct four days of instruction, immersing new teachers in the district's culture and uniting them with everyone in the district to form a cohesive, supportive instructional team.

Bus Tour

The superintendent acts as a tour guide on a chartered bus trip through-out the Flowing Wells School District of Tucson, Arizona, providing a rite of passage into the culture of the community.

Demonstration Classrooms

In the Mesa, Arizona, schools, there are monthly scheduled demonstration classes across a variety of grade levels and subjects.

Networking

The induction program of the Islip Public Schools of New York features collaborative study group activities, led by the director of human resources, who facilitates the program, and enhanced by veteran teachers and curriculum leaders. Study groups focus on skill-building strategies such as conducting parent conferences, managing classrooms, crafting lesson plans, and implementing cooperative discipline. The groups constantly work on team-building and problem-solving techniques. They use model lessons and hold sharing sessions in which teachers learn from each other and build respect for one another (Wong, 2004c).

Cooperative Education

Workshops and college classes are held in the Blue Valley School District 229 of Overland Park, Kansas, as a cooperative effort between the school district, the local teachers' union, and the University of Kansas. This approach won them the NEA-AFT Saturn/UAW Partnership Award in 2001.

Mentor Training

Effective mentors are not only trained, but have a district vision toward which they mentor. In the Forsyth County Schools of Georgia, mentors receive 100 hours of training. The mentors in Prince George's County, Maryland, receive forty hours of training in peer coaching skills when they initially join the mentor teacher cohort. In addition, they receive monthly training on topics such as presenting effective professional development, coaching on instructional strategies, and analyzing assessment data. They are also encouraged to attend districtwide professional development, especially regarding changes in curriculum and instruction or data management.

Long-Term Learning

In Community Consolidated School District 15 of Palatine, Illinois, the new teacher induction program is a mandatory four-year professional development program that helps prepare new teachers for national board certification. In the Medford, Oregon, school district's professional development program, there is a catalog showing an array of activities that are offered every year on a regularly scheduled basis, beginning with induction components.

Multiple Support

Each new teacher in the Hopewell, Virginia, school district gets three support providers: a mentor, a coach, and a lead teacher. In the Lafourche Parish Schools of Louisiana, the new teacher gets a mentor and a curriculum facilitator. In the Dallas Independent School District, new teachers have access to a mentor and an instructional coach.

Campus Coordinator

On each campus of the Flowing Wells schools, the new teachers meet every week or biweekly for informal meetings, chaired typically by the assistant principal.

Formative Assessment

In the two-year induction process of the California Beginning Teachers Support and Assessment (BTSA) program, new teachers are given more than ten hours of orientation and classroom management training before the school year, followed by workshops throughout the first two years. They are guided by an ongoing formative assessment process which includes (1) developing an individual learning plan (ILP); (2) being monitored as they progress through the California Formative Assessment and Support System for Teachers (CFASST), which is a series of twelve "events" aligned with the California Standards for the Teaching Profession; (3) being assessed in relation to a Developmental Continuum of Teacher Ability rubrics; (4) keeping a collaborative assessment log; (5) participating in formal and information observations; (6) analyzing student work according to content standards; and (7) presenting their portfolios to colleagues at a colloquium.

Graduation

Many districts, like the Lafourche Parish Schools of Louisiana, have formalized graduation ceremonies for new teachers at the end of induction. These ceremonies include multimedia presentations, stirring speeches, and the awarding of diplomas that signify entry into a family of collaborative learners.

Albion (New York) Central School District's Comprehensive Induction Program

- Seven-day new teacher induction prior to the beginning of school
- Comprehensive three-year professional and staff development plan with follow up into year 5 using Danielson's Framework for Enhancing Professional Practice
- Mentoring component
- Release time for classroom peer visitations, group work, mini-workshops, out-of-district conferences and workshops, peer coaching, and study teams
- Extensive training over three years (for all stakeholders) on best practices, effective instructional strategies, cooperative learning, multiple intelligences, design, and assessment
- Off-campus opportunities for socialization and connecting
- Administrative involvement in and support of program components at all levels
- Full-time program coordinator who works with all stakeholders to provide ongoing support (during the summer as well)

THE FOCUS IS ON STUDENT LEARNING

The Dallas Independent School District's New Teacher Initiative is an induction program that provides support and development for new teachers and leads them into lifelong advanced studies that focus on student learning (Wong, 2004b). They have activities for future teachers in high school, student teachers, and beginning teachers. There is help provided by a district Web site, mentors, coaches, workshops, institutes, and advanced studies, all monitored by a support team that focuses on teacher effectiveness and student learning.

The Flowing Wells School District of Tucson, Arizona, has had an induction program for eighteen years. So many people write to or visit the school system that they hold an annual workshop to share their induction model with others. A staff developer, after attending one of their workshops, said, "I have never visited a school district where there is a culture of everyone sharing the same attitude of 'What is it we need to do to enhance student learning?'"

Student learning is the focus in both the Forsyth County Schools of Georgia and the Carlsbad Municipal Schools in New Mexico. In the Forsyth County Schools they have an Induction Academy with a goal of "Quality learning and superior performance for all." To achieve this they work on the work (WOW). Throughout the school district, there is a clear focus on students and the quality of the work provided to students—work that students find interesting, challenging, and satisfying and that results in their learning what is expected by schools, parents, and the community.

In the Carlsbad Municipal Schools, Charlotte Neill, superintendent, says, "We teach our teachers how to teach the required benchmarks and standards, manage the classroom environment, set appropriate procedures, and maximize instructional time. We are a very cohesive district and we want new staff to feel wanted, valued, and respected by the way we support them through the induction process. We want them to be comfortable in taking risks of trying new things and in learning from their peers and their coaches."

In the Homewood-Flossmoor High School District, they use the North Central Regional Educational Laboratory (NCREL) model (Hassel, 2002) to structure their induction and professional development program. The model answers the question, "What do we need to do to improve student learning?" To formulate a clear plan of what kind of instructional practice they want to promote, they design an induction and professional development structure with the following plan for improving student learning:

| What are our student educational goals? | − What are our actual student performances? | = What are our student learning gaps? |
| What staff skills are needed to close student gaps? | − What are our actual staff skills? | = What are our professional development needs? |

When schools and school districts have an organized, coherent, and sustained induction and professional development process, they will most likely demonstrate improved teaching and student learning.

With an organized, coherent, and sustained induction and professional development process, the Islip Schools on Long Island in New York, for example, saw a concomitant improvement in student learning, which they view as resulting from improved teacher performance (see Figure 3.1).

The issue today is not new teacher retention. The issue is student learning, and the research on student learning is unequivocal. Over 200 studies have shown that the only way to improve student learning is with a knowledgeable and skillful teacher (Breaux & Wong, 2003; Wong, 2003a). Student learning is directly linked to teacher effectiveness; the better the teacher is able to manage the classroom and deliver the instruction, the more students will learn. Just as it is an indisputable fact that students learn best from teachers who are effective, it is also an indisputable fact that effective teachers are produced from comprehensive, coherent, and sustained professional development programs (Wong, 2002a). It is noteworthy that as a teacher improves in effectiveness through training, the first groups of students to profit from improved learning are the lower ability students (Breaux & Wong, 2003). Principals and teacher leaders have the largest roles to play in fostering such experiences.

Figure 3.1   Islip, New York, Public Schools

1998–1999	2001–2002
Before Induction Program	After Induction Program
40% Regents diploma rate 80 students enrolled in advanced placement classes, with 50% achieving 3 or higher	70% Regents diploma rate 120 students enrolled in advanced placement classes, with 73% achieving 3 or higher

Include the Principal and the Entire Community of Learners in the Process

To go beyond current state-of-the-art programs, effective induction programs are now moving to the inclusion of principals in the induction process. Breaux and Wong (2003) report on the existence of induction programs for administrators, mainly for principals and staff developers, the two most important people in the leadership role of preparing effective teachers. These induction programs help administrators develop the skills of organizing a sustained professional development program and a learning community.

State-of-the-art research on the value of principals was released in the spring of 2004 by the Mid-Continent Research on Education and Learning (MCREL). Reporting on 30 years of research, Waters, Marzano, and McNulty (2004) tell us that effective principals can increase a school's test scores between 10 and 19 percent if their leadership (1) directs, provides for, and monitors a professional development program that creates effective teachers and (2) provides for a learning community where there is a culture of collegiality. Good teachers do not choose to remain at schools where administrators perform poorly. Effective leadership means involving teachers in key instructional decisions and providing opportunities for teachers to learn from each other within a coherent overall improvement plan for the staff. Good teachers know that they must have colleagues who have similar standards and expectations. Accomplished teachers are more likely to choose to work in schools when there will be a "critical mass" of like-minded colleagues who share their commitment to student achievement and where the principal is the key to establishing this commitment to teacher improvement and student achievement.

There is no research to show that teachers become more effective by working in isolation. Johnson and The Project on the Next Generation of Teachers (2004) have found that, paradoxically, the presence of a mentoring program may actually reduce the scope of assistance and support that new teachers receive, because when everyone assumes that a new teacher's needs will be met by an assigned mentor, other experienced teachers are less likely to interfere when they see a novice in need. However, a novice teacher is far less likely to be left confused when there is shared responsibility by all experienced teachers in the school for the induction of all new teachers. A novice need not depend on a single relationship to learn when the school has a web of professional support, as in a school with an integrated professional culture.

Induction, because it is a group activity, immediately fosters and continues an integrated professional culture. New teachers want to learn; they are eager to contribute; they are anxious to help make a difference. Most important, they want to belong to a community of learners.

What motivates and creates leadership is a structured, sustained, intensive professional development program that allows new teachers to observe others, to be observed by others, and to be part of networks or study groups where all teachers share together, grow together, learn to respect each other's work, and collaboratively become leaders together (Wong, 2004a).

INDUCTION: FOUNDATION FOR SUCCESS

The teachers we hire today will become the teachers for the next generation. Their success will determine the success of an entire generation of students. We can no longer condone the shortsighted practice of giving a new teacher a mentor and instructing them to reflect, one-on-one in isolation, with no coherence to or collaboration with any state, district, or school curriculum, plan, goals, or standards.

We know that student learning is directly linked to teacher effectiveness, which begins with an organized and structured process called induction. Induction programs have clearly articulated goals, administrative supervision, long-term objectives, networks that allow for structural and nurturing collaboration, demonstration classes where teachers can observe and be observed, portfolio assessments to assess pedagogical knowledge and skills, and effective mentoring. The entire process is rigorously monitored and evaluated, and it flows seamlessly into a sustained lifelong professional development process. That is why comprehensive induction is the foundation of a coherent and sustained professional development process on which we can build.

REFLECTIONS AND APPLICATIONS

This chapter lists and discusses strategies used by exemplary induction programs. Exercise 3.1 asks you to assess how your program currently addresses some of these critical issues and, based on material in the chapter, to project how your program's provision of each strategy might be improved.

Exercise 3.1 Seven Induction Strategies

Directions: Below are some of the strategies used by exemplary induction programs. In the box to the right of each strategy, describe how it takes place in your teacher induction program and reflect on its effectiveness. In the next box, speculate how, by applying material from this chapter, you might enhance the strategy's effectiveness.

Strategy	How Applied	Potential Enhancement
Administrative support		
Welcome center		
Preschool workshop		
Demonstration classrooms		
Mentor training		
Long-term learning		
Multiple support		

REFERENCES

Alliance for Excellent Education. (2004a). *Tapping the potential: Retaining and developing high-quality new teachers.* Washington, DC: Author. Retrieved September 10, 2004, from www.NewTeacher.com [Reporting on the work of Thomas Smith and Richard Ingersoll, "What Are the Effects of Induction and Mentoring on Beginning Teacher Turnover?" *American Educational Research Journal, 41,* 2, Summer 2004.]

Alliance for Excellent Education. (2004b). *Tapping the potential: Retaining and developing high-quality new teachers.* Washington, DC: Author. Available at www.NewTeacher.com

Bennetts, C. (2001). Lifelong learners: In their own words. *International Journal of Lifelong Education, 20*(4), 272–288.

Breaux, A., & Wong, H. (2003). *New teacher induction: How to train, support, and retain new teachers.* Mountain View, CA: Harry K. Wong.

Britton, E., Paine, L., Raizen, S., & Pimm, D. (2003). *Comprehensive teacher induction: Systems for early career learning.* Dordrecht, The Netherlands: Kluwer Academic Publishers. Available from www.WestEd.org

Britton, E., Raizen, S., Paine, L., & Huntley, M. (2000). *More swimming, less sinking: Perspectives from abroad on U.S. teacher induction.* Paper presented at the National Commission on Mathematics and Science Teaching in the 21st Century, San Francisco.

Cross, C., & Rigden, D. (2002, April). Improving teacher quality. *American School Board Journal, 1989*(4), 24–27.

Danielson, C. (2002). *Enhancing student achievement: A framework for school improvement.* Alexandria, VA: Association for Supervision and Curriculum Development.

Feiman-Nemser, S. (1996). Teacher mentoring: A critical review. *ERIC Digest* (ED 397 060).

Garet, M., Porter, M., Desmoine, L., Birman, B., & Kwang, S. (2001, Winter). What makes professional development effective? *American Educational Research Journal,* pp. 915–946.

Hargreaves, A., & Fullan, M. (2000). Mentoring in the new millennium. *Theory Into Practice, 39*(1), 50–55.

Hassel, E. (2002). *Professional development: Learning from the best.* Naperville, IL: North Central Regional Educational Laboratory.

Hawk, P. (1986–1987). Beginning teacher programs: Benefits for the experienced educator. *Action in Teacher Education, 8*(4), 59–63.

Head, F. A., Reiman, A. J., & Thies-Sprinthall, L. (1992). The reality of mentoring: Complexity in its process and function. In T. M. Bey and C. T. Holmes (Eds.), *Mentoring: Contemporary principles and issues* (pp. 5–24). Reston, VA: Association of Teacher Educators.

Hendrie, C. (2002, June 12). Annenberg Challenge yields lessons for those hoping to change schools. *Education Week,* p. 6.

Hiebert, J., Gallimore, R., & Stigler, J. (2002, June/July). A knowledge base for the teaching profession: What would it look like and how can we get one? *Educational Researcher, 31*(5), 3–15.

Ingersoll, R., & Kralik, J. (2004, February). *The impact of mentoring on teacher retention: What the research says.* Education Commission of the States Report. Document Number: 5036.

Johnson, S. M. (2003, March). *Supporting and retaining the next generation of teachers.* Presented at the national convention of ASCD, Harvard Graduate School of Education, Cambridge, MA. Available at http://www.simulconference.com/ASCD/2003/scs/

Johnson, S., & Birkeland, S. (2003a, Fall). Pursuing a sense of success: New teachers explain their career decisions. *American Educational Research Journal, 40,* 608.

Johnson, S. M., & Birkeland, S. (2003b, May). The schools that teachers choose. *Educational Leadership, 60*(8), 20–24.

Johnson, S. M., & The Project on the Next Generation of Teachers. (2004). *Finders and keepers: Helping new teachers survive and thrive in our schools.* San Francisco: Jossey-Bass.

Kardos, S., & Liu, E. (2003). *New research finds school hiring and support falls short.* Available at http://www.researchmatters.harvard.edu/story.php?article_id=634

Kauffman, D., Johnson, S. M., Kardos, S., Liu, E., & Peske, H. G. (2002, March). Lost at sea: New teachers' experiences with curriculum and assessment. *Teachers College Record, 104*(2), 273–300. Also available at http://www.gse.harvard.edu/~ngt/papers.htm

Laird, S. (1989). Reforming "women's true profession": A case for "feminist pedagogy" in teacher education. *Harvard Education Review, 58*(4), 449–463.

Little, J. (1990). The mentor phenomenon and the social organization of teaching. In C. B. Cazden (Ed.), *Review of research in education* (pp. 297–351). Washington, DC: American Educational Research Association.

Public Education Network. (2004). *The voice of the new teacher.* Washington, DC: Author.

Shields, P. M., Esch, C. E., Humphrey, D. C., Wechsler, M. E., Chang-Ross, C. M., Gallagher, H. A., et al. (2003). The status of the teaching profession 2003. In *Teaching and California's future.* Santa Cruz, CA: Center for the Future of Teaching and Learning.

Waters, T., Marzano, R., & McNulty, B. (2004). *Balanced leadership: What 30 years of research tells us about the effect of leadership on student achievement.* Aurora, CO: Mid-Continent Research for Education and Learning.

WestEd. (2002). *How to support beginning teachers: Looking beyond our borders.* (R&D Alert). San Francisco, CA: Author.

Wong, H. (2002a, March). Induction: The best form of professional development. *Educational Leadership, 59*(6), 52–55. Also available at www.NewTeacher.com

Wong, H. (2002b, September). Play for keeps. In *Principal Leadership.* Available at www.NewTeacher.com

Wong, H. (2003a). *Induction: How to train, support, and retain new teachers.* Paper presented at the National Staff Development Council, December 10, 2003. Available at www.NewTeacher.com

Wong, H. (2003b). Induction programs that keep working. In M. Scherer (Ed.), *Keeping good teachers.* Association of Supervision and Curriculum Development (ASCD). Available at www.NewTeacher.com

Wong, H. (2004a). Collaborating with colleagues to improve student learning. *ENC Focus, 11*(6). Available at www.NewTeacher.com

Wong, H. (2004b). Induction programs that keep new teachers teaching and learning. *NASSP Bulletin, 88,* 43. Available at www.NewTeacher.com

Wong, H. (2004c). Producing educational leaders through induction programs. *Kappa Delta Pi Record, 40*(3), 106–111. Available at www.NewTeacher.com

Wong, H., & Asquith, C. (2002, December). Supporting new teachers. *American School Board Journal, 189,* 26. Available at www.NewTeacher.com

Wong, H., Britton, T., & Ganser, T. (2005). What the world can teach us about new teacher induction. *KAPPAN, 86*(5), January 2005.

Wong, H., & Wong, R. (2004). *The first days of school.* Mountain View, CA: Harry K. Wong.

4

Launching the Next Generation of Teachers

The New Teacher Center's Model for Quality Induction and Mentoring

Ellen Moir

Over the next decade, more than two million new teachers will find themselves facing a full classroom on their first day, charged with the mission of transforming it into a learning community. Most will be full of enthusiasm, bringing years of training and a long-held sense that their new profession is among society's most important. Education is a career that many of these new teachers feel chosen for, a calling they have had since childhood. Some will feel a chill go down their spines when they hear the word *teacher*.

It's easy to forget what it was like to be a beginning teacher, having to acquire curriculum knowledge and classroom strategies while at the same time balancing practical concerns with lofty ideals. Veteran teachers may well ask themselves, "If I were starting my career today, what would most help me develop into an outstanding, caring, and accomplished teacher?" One answer stands out among all the rest: "I can only imagine how much better a teacher I would have been that first year if I'd had a mentor."

dent teaching and preservice training are necessary steps in creating etent and qualified teaching professionals, but they are not enough. tors have an impact on new teachers in ways that no amount of train- can. The real-life classroom presents questions that only real-life experience can answer. Mentors help provide those answers. They give practical, concrete advice, pose important questions to prompt reflection, model teaching techniques in the classroom, observe and offer feedback, and offer another point of view at a time when it's easy to lose all perspective. Their experience helps the novice teacher balance professional development with day-to-day details.

Mentors also decrease the isolation of the new teacher. Their emotional support is essential when the obstacles seem too great and allows the novice to take risks and grow while still keeping the classroom functioning. By developing a specific plan for each new teacher and setting specific performance goals to improve teaching practice, mentors create an environment based on collaboration, exchange of ideas, and professionalism. And, by making them a part of a supportive community of educators, mentors help keep alive the enthusiasm and sense of mission that brought new teachers into the profession in the first place.

A report by the National Commission on Teaching and America's Future (2003) stresses that a successful mentoring program can change the face of that first year of teaching. Take this quote from a new teacher at the end of her first year: "My advisor kind of walked me through the year. She was always there to listen to my ideas, my reflections. I never felt that I was alone, even when she wasn't in the room, because I knew that I had daily access to a person who would listen and respond to my ideas. I trusted her to give me honest feedback on how successfully a strategy worked . . . she met whatever needs I had."

A DECADE AND A HALF OF CHANGE

In the mid-1980s, California found itself facing a crisis, one caused primarily by exceptionally low rates of teacher retention. The problems that would eventually visit the rest of the country came early to California, where the student population was increasing in size as well as becoming more diverse. At the same time the state and many districts were adopting far more complex curricula. Finding and, more important, retaining qualified teachers had become almost impossible for many rural and urban districts.

The new teachers who entered this challenging situation were thrown into the classroom with little support beyond their preservice training. Turnover rates were high, particularly among minority teachers. Although a paucity of research on teacher induction had been published at the time, it was obvious to many of us that the "sink or swim" method had failed.

As the need to change the system became clear, and state funding became available, I was able to oversee the creation of a new program for teacher induction in Santa Cruz County (California). Our design process brought together the entire community of educators: district administrators, principals, union representatives, experienced teachers, new teachers, and Education Department faculty from the University of California, Santa Cruz (UCSC). Together, in 1988, we created a comprehensive new teacher support program, with mentoring at its core. The Santa Cruz New Teacher Project (SCNTP), led by UCSC in partnership with the Santa Cruz County Office of Education and all school districts in the area, began its work with forty-two elementary teachers. Exemplary teachers, released full time, acted as mentors, providing individualized support.

After the initial first three years, funding lapsed, but the success of the statewide effort (California New Teacher Project) and the SCNTP served as models for statewide reform. In 1992, California policymakers enacted SB 1422, which implemented Beginning Teacher Support and Assessment (BTSA) programs, providing funding for mentor-based programs throughout the state. These BTSA programs ultimately have constituted a redesign of the state's credentialing process. The final stages in teacher credentialing, which were previously administered by institutions of higher learning, are now integrated into a comprehensive induction system with mentoring at its core. There are currently 150 BTSA programs in California. In short, the law now assures that all new teachers in California will receive mentoring on their way to becoming fully credentialed teachers.

In 2000, the SCNTP expanded to include the Silicon Valley New Teacher Project, and now serves 760 new teachers in thirty districts. Since 1988 the SCNTP has worked with over 9,000 new K–12 teachers.

Five years ago, the New Teacher Center (NTC) at UCSC became the latest outgrowth of the process that began in 1988. The Center's mission is to give national scope to this work by researching, designing, and advocating high-quality induction programs for new teachers. The SCNTP model is being implemented in the Charlotte-Mecklenburg School District and the Dorchester County public school system in Maryland. We are providing mentor training for 300 mentors for New York City schools. We are also collaborating with districts in Alabama, Alaska, Arizona, Colorado, Georgia, Hawaii, Nevada, Massachusetts, Missouri, New Jersey, Tennessee, Texas, Utah, Virginia, Washington, and Wisconsin.

So, what has this experience taught us about the essential components of an effective induction program and the role of mentors?

Mentor Role and Selection

Too often, mentoring programs are conceived as buddy systems, in which experienced educators are paired with new teachers on an informal basis. In the buddy system model, mentors are neither trained for their new role nor given time to carry out its demands. In other words, new mentors are treated pretty much as new teachers were, allowed to sink or swim, armed with only intuition and good intentions to keep themselves afloat.

Effective induction programs conceive the role of mentor as "teacher of teachers." Mentors use their expertise to help support beginning teacher development in ways that are responsive to the needs of new teachers. This work is complex and different from teaching students. To have a real impact, induction programs must provide the same kind of support to mentors that the mentors are in turn providing to new teachers (Moir & Gless, 2001). Like novice teachers, new mentors need training, guidance, and the support of the entire community of educators. Even exemplary teachers will need to learn new skills in order to effectively pass on their wealth of experience and wisdom.

Not all good teachers make good mentors. Of course, every mentor must have exemplary professional ability—a full knowledge of standards, curriculum, and student assessment. BTSA mentors are required to have taught a minimum of seven years. But mentors must also demonstrate an ability to learn a new set of skills: teaching adults.

At the NTC, we look for veteran teachers who have already developed their interpersonal skills. Experience with coaching, facilitating groups, and other collaborative models is an important indicator of likely success as a mentor. Successful mentors will have keen observational skills, excellent communication skills, and, of course, patience, enthusiasm, and a love of all kinds of learning.

Successful mentors also have to possess a commitment to collaboration. They have to be able to build relationships, both with individuals and among groups. And because so many new teachers are placed in schools that are culturally diverse, often having a high percentage of English language learners (ELL), the NTC pays special attention to hiring mentors who have experience working with diverse student populations. In districts in which a high percentage of students are ELL, ideally all new teachers are paired with mentors who have expertise in first and second language acquisition, literacy, and English language development.

Mentor Training

Mentoring requires new abilities: working with adults, collaboration, and, often most complex, being able to articulate the set of teaching skills that they work with every day. Not all good teachers know how they teach; they experience their teaching practice as second nature. A good mentoring program makes sure mentors have the time and training to reflect on their practice. The strongest induction programs will expend time and resources to prepare mentors for their new roles as communicators of their knowledge and experience. Training mentors is as important as training the novice teachers they will serve.

In the SCNTP, prior to the beginning of the school year, mentor trainees participate in at least two days of initial training called "Foundations in Mentoring." The training covers these five core areas:

1. Role of the new teacher mentor

2. Development of an effective mentoring relationship

3. Identification of new teacher needs

4. Mentoring conversations

5. Formative assessment for new teachers

Training doesn't end when the school year begins, however. Throughout the year, mentors receive additional professional development including a two-day coaching and observation training session. This training focuses on techniques for observing new teachers, collecting classroom performance data, and using data to inform instruction. Mentors also attend weekly forums that give them the opportunity to further develop their mentoring skills; work collaboratively; and share insights, challenges, and successes. In this learning community, mentors develop a shared vision of good teaching, calibrate their classroom observations using videos, and share and analyze evidence of their work. In districts with well-established programs, these forums can help new mentors seek the guidance of those with more experience.

During the first year that a veteran teacher is working as a mentor, the following subjects can be covered to increase a new mentor's grasp on his or her new role:

- Professional teaching standards
- NTC Formative Assessment System
- Lesson planning in content areas
- Analyzing student work
- Differentiating instruction
- Collecting classroom data
- Analyzing classroom data
- Data-based revision of practice
- Effective strategies for working with ELL
- Literacy instruction

In the second year of a program, a new set of topics is introduced in mentor training, helping mentors to expand their roles. As experienced mentors, they are now leaders in the process of creating a vibrant, dynamic, and sustainable program. The following subjects are covered as the school year progresses:

- Mentor professional growth
- Planning for year-two mentoring
- Advanced coaching skills
- Promoting new teacher resiliency
- Tailoring support to second-year teachers
- Content-specific pedagogy
- Developing mentor leadership skills
- Building school-site learning communities
- Becoming a mentor trainer
- Planning for project continuation: goals and implementation plan
- Program evaluation

Many of these second-year topics give mentors a forum to express their concerns and offer the leadership of the mentoring program an opportunity to assess its results informally. A healthy induction system is constantly gathering feedback, using the creativity and experiences of its participants to reshape itself from year to year. Programs that encourage and respond to participant feedback are more likely to sustain themselves over the long term.

Commitment to Quality Induction

Successful induction programs recognize that mentoring is an energy-consuming job, requiring the same kinds of time for preparation and professional development as full-time teaching. Ideally, new teachers should have a mentor in their classroom for at least two hours each week to perform demonstration lessons in the classroom, observe the novice teaching, and assist with curriculum development as well as classroom management and other on-the-job skills. In some districts, to meet this time commitment, mentors are released from their classroom full-time.

Of course, not every district can afford to implement mentoring as a full-time job. Some mentors will have to combine classroom teaching with their mentoring duties. Experience has shown, however, that it is very difficult for teachers to spend the time and effort necessary for successful mentoring without some adjustment in scheduling. As much as possible, they should be teaching the same subjects at the same grade levels. This matching of content area and grade level saves the mentor valuable time and builds opportunities for deeper collaboration.

The caseload for each mentor can be variable, depending on his or her experience, classroom duties, and other support available to new teachers in the district. However, even experienced, full-time mentors should ideally work with no more than fifteen novice teachers at once. (With two hours of classroom work per novice per week, this already represents six hours a day of classroom observation, assistance, and modeling.) Part-time mentors, of course, cannot afford to spread themselves this thin. Without substantive weekly contact, the capacity of a mentor to contribute is greatly reduced. Simply knowing that a mentor will be in their classrooms once a week can sustain beginning teachers facing daily challenges.

Acquiring the new skills and techniques of mentoring also requires a time commitment of a broader sort. In many SCNTP induction programs, mentors work with novice teachers for as long as three years before moving back into teaching or on to the next phase in their career. This extended period gives them a chance to adapt fully to their new leadership role. Just as teachers need time to gain their footing, so do mentors.

Obviously, to implement a program with these levels of support requires resources. A system of quality teacher induction costs money. But compared with the financial expense (and educational cost) of recruiting and training replacements, the cost of effective induction is relatively low. In California, under BTSA, the state provides nearly $3,500 for each new teacher, and districts contribute (ideally) another $2,000. Levels of between $5,000 and $6,000 per teacher have proven adequate for a top-flight system of induction.

With these realities in mind, it is very important that when states mandate induction programs, they also provide adequate funding to help districts meet these mandates. Mentoring is not a cost-free magic bullet to save our schools. It is a proven and effective system that requires a serious commitment of resources at both the state and district levels.

Assessment and Accountability

Induction systems operate best when both mentors and new teachers are working collaboratively toward the same goals. Professional teaching standards should be clearly defined, well articulated, and consistent statewide. In California, the California Standards for the Teaching Profession (California Commission on Teaching Credentialing, 1997) provide a framework, identifying and categorizing a set of abilities and practices that every teacher should master.

But published, statewide standards are only the beginning of a framework for teacher growth and development. The NTC has embedded these standards in its Formative Assessment System (FAS). The FAS helps structure the interactions between mentors and beginning teachers while guiding the beginning teachers' development. Early in their first year, new teachers in SCNTP programs work with their mentors to self-assess on the Continuum of Teacher Development by comparing their strengths and areas for growth against the benchmarks of the Continuum (New Teacher Center at UCSC, 2002). Together they develop an individual learning plan (ILP). To be useful, the process of formative assessment must also involve support for improvement, so the ILP includes a set of professional development activities designed to help the novice progress. The mentor helps the beginning teacher move toward these goals by collecting and discussing in-class observation data, codeveloping lesson plans, making suggestions, and modeling lessons for the novice to observe.

Working together for two years, the mentor and novice use the ILP to share accountability. Both are responsible for maintaining a goal of high-quality teaching, constant professional inquiry, and continuous growth.

The continuity and shared responsibility of this process help the new teacher keep the ups and downs of teaching in perspective. Rather than growing to fear assessment, teachers who work closely with a mentor gain the confidence to accept and implement the suggestions of their colleagues. As one new teacher in an SCNTP program said, "I meet once a week with my advisor to discuss the inevitable highs and lows. . . . She is patient and respectful, and I have learned that most of the time I am not so far off the track. What seems like a total derailment to me is just a minor bump. My confidence has grown."

The basis of the mentor-novice interaction is a formative assessment process that includes an ILP and that incorporates

- Clearly articulated standards and goals
- Guided, continuous self-assessment
- Developmental support linked to all assessment
- Shared accountability between novice and mentor

After two years, the novices (always with help from their mentors) put together a portfolio to document their progress as teachers, including student work, observation data, and lesson plans.

Of equal importance to the assessment value of the portfolio are the benefits of the process itself. Keeping a portfolio compels beginning teachers to focus on the long term and to reflect on what they have learned. It also ensures that they develop self-assessment skills early in their careers. As one NTC-supported new teacher put it, "The portfolio cycle has allowed me to move forward, beyond immediate needs. It has had a major impact on me, on my students, and on my collaborative team. It's the difference between being given a fish by my advisor and being taught to fish. Collaboration with an experienced teacher has enabled me to stay focused, to connect areas of practice and to reflect on my progress."

Assessment is not limited, however, to the individual teachers and mentors. Each program should constantly work to assess its own progress, maintaining a dialog between the leadership, the mentors, and the new teachers who are the "customers" of the enterprise.

The most immediate forms of program assessment are surveys and interviews. The SCNTP typically conducts wide-ranging surveys of program participants at the end of the year—collecting data from new teachers, mentors, and principals. The surveys' results are followed up with interviews of as many participants as possible.

The process of gathering feedback serves two goals. Hearing from participants helps to ensure continuous program development, enabling the leadership to respond to the individual needs of the program's constituents. The feedback process also makes participants into stakeholders. When mentors and teachers have a voice in shaping the system, they gain a sense of ownership and become invested in sustaining the mentoring program in the long term.

Of course, not all program assessment is informal and anecdotal. Long-term statistical studies are also necessary to understand the overall benefits of induction programs. See "The Data on Teacher Retention" below for examples of the statistical work being done by the NTC, documenting the impact of induction systems in California and elsewhere.

Mentoring, Collaboration, and Community

At every step, the mentor is a collaborator, not an overseer. Mentors and new teachers work jointly to assess the new teachers' levels of practice and to develop individual plans to improve their work, including specific training activities and performance goals. But the concept of collaboration goes beyond the mentor-teacher relationship; the practice of reaching out to peers, drawing upon a wide network of support, and building relationships should be inculcated into every new teacher and become a career-long habit.

Whenever possible, mentors should encourage new teachers to become part of the professional community of the school. For the community to truly support them and meet their needs, novices must learn to make their voices heard. They should feel free to suggest curriculum innovations and new uses for technology and present their own solutions to day-to-day teaching challenges. After receiving new training, novices benefit from demonstrating the results to other staff members, in meetings or colloquia. New teachers should open their classrooms to visitors, to gain confidence as presenters and to feel assured that their work matters to the entire school community.

An example of such collaborative success comes from the Starlight Professional Development School, in the Pajaro Valley Unified School District. Starlight students are 90 percent Latino, and two thirds are ELL. To help meet the community-wide need for bilingual materials, one new teacher worked with her SCNTP mentor to create a multicultural literature unit. After sharing the material with the school staff, the new teacher was invited to present her work at a summer biliteracy institute for migrant teachers. This experience of collaboration and communication moved the new teacher to say, "I feel that all of us are being trained at this school to be teacher leaders."

Collaboration among peers is also important. New teachers can meet in small groups throughout the year to brainstorm, problem-solve, and discuss issues of content and curriculum. Monthly seminars, organized at the district level and presented by mentor teachers, give new teachers a space to network with each other.

Mentors can also help new teachers expand the concept of collaboration by training them in community relations. Mentors should be available to observe, assess, and model parent-teacher conferences, showing new teachers the ropes in this important real-world aspect of teaching. Those veteran teachers who have worked in diverse communities can show new teachers how to leverage students' multicultural backgrounds as a learning opportunity. Communities are willing to support their teachers, but activating that support takes experience that new teachers have not yet acquired. Connecting the novice to this dynamic source of assistance is a crucial role of the experienced teacher.

This focus on collaboration and community makes induction a multi-dimensional process. The best induction systems are exactly that: systems. They incorporate input from new teachers, veteran teachers, administrators, unions, parents, preservice programs, and the higher educational institutions that will supply the next generation of educators. Communication among these groups is inherently valuable, allowing all the participants in a child's education to provide feedback and support for the new teachers upon which that education depends. This feedback creates a different cycle, not one of teacher burnout and attrition, but a cycle of ongoing development and support within the community of educators.

The Data on Teacher Retention

The NTC recently conducted a study on retention rates for those new teachers supported by the SCNTP in 1992–1993. The study documented that after seven years, 88 percent of these teachers were still teaching in K–12 classrooms. Four other teachers were on leave but planning to return, and five more were employed in administrative positions in education, meaning that a total of 94 percent were still in the field. Among those interviewed, a quarter indicated that the support they had received from the SCNTP was the most important reason they had remained in the profession (Strong, 2001).

Another study, this one from outside of California, documented the impact of the NTC induction model in the Charlotte-Mecklenburg Schools in North Carolina. Charlotte-Mecklenburg is an urban district with a student body of more than 100,000. The NTC model was implemented in the most high-priority schools in the district, those in which teacher retention rates were even lower than those in the district as a whole. The results of this study document that schools in which beginning teachers received weekly mentoring, using the NTC model, found their teacher drop-out rates cut almost in half. Whereas attrition rates across the school system hit 32 percent, those with intensive mentoring were at 17.5 percent despite the challenging nature of those sites.

However successful, teacher induction programs require resources. They cost money. So what are the economic benefits of increased teacher retention? Do these benefits justify the expense of induction programs? Weighing recruitment and other training costs against those of induction programs suggests that they do.

When a new teacher leaves the profession, the direct financial costs come from many directions: advertising and hiring, short-term vacancy replacement, and training. Of course, the expense of losing a teacher varies, depending on the nature of the individual school. Unfortunately, schools with the highest recruitment costs are those with the highest turnover rates. In wealthy, suburban schools, recruiting is inexpensive (as low as 15 percent of a teacher's salary) and turnover minimal. Urban schools with a diverse population have higher recruiting expenses (generally 50 percent of a teacher's salary, and 200 percent in some extreme cases), and turnover tends to be much higher (Texas Center for Education Research, 2000). For obvious reasons, it is the latter schools that benefit the most from induction programs that boost teacher retention.

With its BTSA commitment of roughly $5,700 per new teacher in the 2002–2003 school year (a combination of state- and district-level support), California spends far more on teacher retention than any other state. So what does it get for its money? In its 2002 study, the California Commission on Teacher Credentialing found that the state has a retention rate of 84 percent after four years, compared with a nationwide rate of 67 percent. To look at the data another way, the nation loses 33 percent of its teachers after four years, California only 16 percent. That is, California has to replace its beginning teachers at only half the rate of the nation as a whole.

The NTC is conducting a survey to establish as precisely as possible the costs and benefits of BTSA programs. The results are preliminary, but they allow for some basic observations. In those districts with the highest recruitment costs (50 percent of teacher salary), the benefits of BTSA teacher induction exceed costs by roughly $2,800 per teacher, based on the 17 percent difference between national and California-wide retention. In districts with low recruitment costs (15 percent), the benefit is much lower, only about $850.

Of course, the above cost-benefit differences are based only on direct expenses of teacher loss. The NTC is currently expanding its analysis to include all the other economic burdens that result when a new teacher walks away from the profession: the state's initial investment in credentialing, the cost of ongoing professional development, and the impact of teacher experience on student achievement. We estimate that these hidden costs of teacher loss are ten times greater than the direct costs of replacing teachers. But the numbers above make one point abundantly clear: Induction programs should be implemented first in those districts where they can have the most immediate impact, those with the highest turnover rates and the highest recruitment costs.

Teacher retention is not the only measure of success, and saving money not the only goal of induction. New teachers supported by induction programs shouldn't just be more satisfied in their jobs, but should be better teachers as well and should become better teachers sooner. So the NTC is also working to document the impact of quality teacher induction on the students themselves.

Currently, NTC researchers are analyzing a three-year span of SAT-9 reading scores in a unified school district which has been an SCNTP participant for fifteen years. The scores are broken down into three groups—the students of beginning teachers, midcareer teachers, and experienced teachers—in order to show the effect of teacher experience on the increase of reading scores over the school year. Early results indicate that students of beginning teachers supported by the NTC show test-score increases similar to increases of students of more experienced teachers. This study is not yet conclusive and is being extended to a larger comparison group. In order to chart the impact of various levels of teacher experience over several years, the analysis of the larger group will incorporate an analytical framework based on the Tennessee Value-Added Assessment System (Sanders & Horn, 1995).

As mentoring programs take root in districts across the country, they should have an effect at all levels: from monetary savings to standardized test scores, from teacher retention to the professional satisfaction of teachers new and experienced. The NTC is working to document these changes in ways that convince state policymakers to fund and sustain quality induction systems.

CORE ELEMENTS OF A QUALITY INDUCTION PROGRAM

Part of the NTC's mission is to work with educational leaders and state policymakers to establish induction programs that work, that are sufficiently funded, and that use tried and tested methodologies. Here is the checklist that we present as containing the core elements of a quality induction program:

- **Full-time program administrators:** Programs should be staffed with innovative, full-time program administrators with the training, time, and resources to establish and run excellent programs.
- **Quality mentoring:** Mentoring should take place during the school day, in class and one-on-one, with sanctioned time for both mentors and beginning teachers.
- **Mentor selection:** Mentors should be selected for their ability to work with adults, their expertise in pedagogy and content areas, their leadership qualities, and their commitment to collaborative work.
- **Mentor development:** Mentors need ongoing training and support to be the most effective "teachers of teachers."
- **Formative assessment for beginning teachers:** New teachers, with help from their mentors, should systematically identify areas for growth, set personal performance goals, and develop the skills needed to attain these goals.

- **Training in data collection and analysis:** New teachers and mentors should be trained to collect classroom data, analyze data, and use the results to guide instruction.
- **Training for site administrators:** Site administrators must understand the needs of beginning teachers, provide them with resources, and learn techniques for evaluation that build teacher practice.
- **Teaching standards:** New teacher guidance and self-assessment must take into account the accepted state standards for what teachers need to know and be able to do.
- **High expectations for new teachers, mentors, and students:** Induction programs should be expected to help teachers excel, not just survive.
- **Training for work with diverse students and English language learners:** Additional support is necessary for areas with minority students and English learners, since beginning teachers are so often placed in schools serving these students.
- **Networking and training opportunities for beginning teachers:** Workshops and training sessions help novices overcome the traditional isolation of teachers.
- **Contractually bargained new teacher placement:** Working with teachers' unions, policymakers should ensure that new teachers are not routinely placed with the hardest-to-serve students in high-priority schools.

This is not a list from which to pick and choose, but a coherent plan for effective change. All of these elements are important, and each has been shown to support the others, creating a well-rounded, robust system that has the capacity to transform the experience of a teacher's first years and to bring the entire community of educators into the process. The multidimensional aspect of this work—incorporating new and veteran teachers, administrators, unions, and parents—is what makes it truly radical, capable of not only solving a crisis in teacher hiring but of transforming the culture of education in our country.

Such a comprehensive induction and mentoring system can sustain and nourish that initial enthusiasm of new teachers on their first days. But it can also reinvigorate veteran teachers and can maintain for entire careers that chill down the spine at the sound of the word *teacher*.

REFLECTIONS AND APPLICATIONS

This chapter contends that the basis of the mentor-novice interaction is a formative assessment process that includes an individual learning plan. Exercise 4.1 asks you to reflect on the extent to which your novice teachers incorporate four specific areas into their plans, and then, based on the material in the chapter, to consider how you might provide the opportunity for novice teachers to more effectively address these areas.

Exercise 4.1   Novice's Individual Learning Plan

Directions: Below, in column 1, are four items that should be part of a novice's individual learning plan (ILP) component. In the box to the right of each component, reflect on how that item is being addressed by novices in your induction and mentoring program. In the next box, speculate how, by applying material from this chapter, you might provide novices with opportunities to apply or enhance each component.

ILP Component	How Addressed	Potential Opportunity to Apply or Enhance
Clearly articulated standards and goals		
Guided, continuous self-assessment		
Developmental support linked to all assessment		
Shared accountability between novice and mentor		

REFERENCES

California Commission on Teaching Credentialing. (1997). *California standards for the teaching profession.* Sacramento, CA: California Department of Education.

Moir, E., & Gless, J. (2001, Winter). Quality induction: An investment in teachers. *Teacher Education Quarterly, 28*(1), 109–114.

National Commission on Teaching and America's Future. (2003, January). *No dream denied.* Washington, DC: Author.

New Teacher Center at UCSC. (2002). *Continuum of teacher development.* Santa Cruz, CA: ToucanEd.

Sanders, W. L., & Horn, S. P. (1995). The Tennessee Value-Added Assessment System (TVAAS): Mixed model methodology in educational assessment. In A. J. Shrinkfield & D. Stufflebeam (Eds.), *Teacher evaluation: Guide to effective practice* (pp. 337–350). Boston: Kluwer.

Strong, M. (2001). *A study of teacher retention: The effects of mentoring for beginning teachers.* Retrieved January 12, 2004, from www.newteachercenter.org

Texas Center for Education Research. (2000). *The cost of teacher turnover.* Prepared for the Texas State Board for Educator Certification, Austin, TX.

5

Embedding Induction and Mentoring Into the School's Culture

Hal Portner

Over the past two decades, many of us involved in new teacher induction and mentoring have gained a number of insights during the course of planning, implementing, and evaluating a variety of programs. Foremost among the lessons I have learned is that although well-conceived and-executed induction and mentoring programs have proven to be fundamental to the development and retention of new teachers, the induction and mentoring process itself must be ingrained into the culture of a school in order for it to continue to serve its purpose over time. It is the application of the following three principles that form the framework for successfully embedding teacher induction and mentoring into the culture of a school or district.

Principle 1: *An embedded induction and mentoring program consists of both internal and external relationships.* Not only do the components within a program interact with each other, but the program itself invariably interacts with a surrounding array of related programs. Application of this principle calls for systems-thinking.

Principle 2: *Leaving the responsibility of inducting and mentoring new teachers to assigned mentors only is shortsighted and a prescription for failure.* There are many other people who need to be actively involved. Application of this principle calls for collaborative-doing.

Principle 3: *An embedded induction and mentoring program thrives on informed dedication and purposeful nurturing.* Resources such as time, money, and people are essential, of course, but more important are motivated and proactive leaders who guide the transformation of their schools' cultures to the point where communal support of induction and professional growth of beginning teachers is the norm. Application of this principle calls for committed-leading.

I will discuss these three principles, describe how their application shaped a unique induction and mentoring program, and then show how the principles formed the basis for embedding induction and mentoring into the school system's culture.

SYSTEMS-THINKING

We typically refer to induction and mentoring as a program. We think of an induction and mentoring program as a collection of components occurring in some sort of sequence over time. For example, we select mentors, train them, and match them with mentees. This concept of *program* is more than a definition; it is a mind-set (Portner, 2001, p. 3). Using programmatic thinking, we plan and treat people, policies, and procedures as discrete items. But Principle 1, *an embedded induction and mentoring program, consists of both internal and external relationships* and calls upon us to see a program through the lens of **systems-thinking.**

In order to understand systems-thinking, we need first to understand systems. A system is a group of interacting, interrelated, and interdependent components that form a complex and unified whole. Variations in state and local budgets, for example, whack us upside the head with the reality of how much everything impacts everything else. "Systems are everywhere," an article posted on the Internet by Pegasus Communications, Inc., points out: " . . . the circulatory system in your body, the predator/prey relationships in nature, the ignition system in your car." The Pegasus Communications article goes on to list several characteristics of systems.

- *Every system has a purpose within a larger system.* Example: One purpose of the induction and mentoring system is to acculturate and nurture new teachers so that they will more likely continue to teach in the district.

- *All of a system's parts must be present for the system to carry out its purpose optimally.* Example: The induction and mentoring system in your school consists of people, policies, and processes. If you remove or ignore any one of these components, this system could no longer function.
- *Systems emphasize wholes rather than parts and stress the role of interconnections.* It is the relationships between and among the parts of an induction and mentoring program, not the parts themselves, that characterize systems-thinking.
- *Systems emphasize circular feedback* (for example, A leads to B, which leads to C, which leads back to A) rather than linear cause and effect (A leads to B, which leads to C, which leads to D, and so on).

Employing systems-thinking helps us see induction and mentoring events and patterns holistically and to respond to them in more broadly focused ways. For example, suppose a mentor and mentee don't get along and break off their relationship. If you respond to this by trying to find a new mentor for that mentee, you're reacting. That is, you have done nothing to prevent similar situations from happening again. If you form a reserve pool of mentors, you're adapting. You still haven't done anything to prevent future mismatches. Now suppose you analyze what caused the event in the first place, adjust your criteria for matching mentees with mentors, and establish and publish a protocol for dealing with contested match-ups in the future. Now you've used feedback to make purposeful changes among interrelated components. You've used systems-thinking.

Systems-thinking involves seeing interconnections and relationships: the whole picture as well as the component parts. It requires awareness of interactions not only between and among local people, policies, and procedures, but also with the surrounding systems of "government, professionals, higher education, . . . mandates, guidelines, and practices . . . that influence and shape the structure of individual elements in a mentoring program" (Portner, 2001, p. 32). Figure 5.1 illustrates this macrosystem concept.

COLLABORATIVE-DOING

When new teacher induction and mentoring became mandated policy in most states—and subsequently a more-or-less common practice—inducting new teachers into the profession was generally left entirely in the hands of assigned mentors. The pervasive attitude of most other educators was, "New teacher induction . . . what does that have to do with me? That's the mentor's responsibility, not mine." But as Principle 2 emphatically states, *an embedded induction and mentoring program involves more people than just*

Figure 5.1   The Education Macrosystem

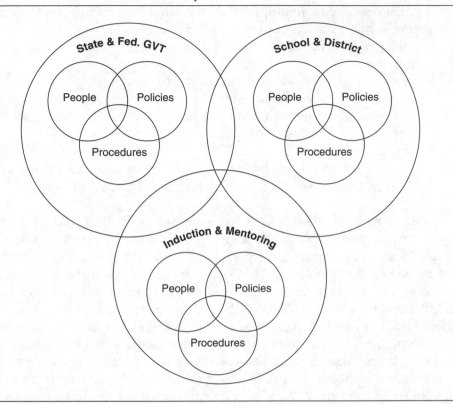

mentors and mentees we have come to learn that the enrichment of the induction and mentoring experience, and the infusion of induction and mentoring into a school's culture, depends on the collaboration of a wide variety of committed people directly and actively participating in the process, that is, **collaborative-doing.**

The operative phrase in the definition of collaborative-doing is *direct and active participation.* People are practicing collaborative-doing when they are directly and actively involved in (1) developing, monitoring, and adjusting their induction and mentoring policies and procedures; (2) interacting directly with new teachers to supplement the efforts of mentors; and (3) supporting mentors and new teachers by providing them with time, facilities, and materials. Collaborative-doing works best when the people involved are committed to and prepared for their roles. Following are brief descriptions of five such models of collaborative-doing.

The Dumont, New Jersey, induction and mentoring philosophy of simultaneous renewal for both new and veteran staff is embedded throughout the district largely because it was spearheaded by individuals who had influence throughout the district: the assistant superintendent and the association president. An example of

Dumont's philosophy in action that incorporates collaborative-doing is the recently established FirstYear Cohort. New teachers meet during common lunch periods with the teacher association president (who is also a mentor trainer), administrators, coordinators, experienced teachers, and university faculty to discuss school procedures and politics and teaching in general.

The University of New Mexico Resident Teacher Program has developed a unique relationship with the Albuquerque School District. The program, in existence since 1984, involves the temporary release (usually for three years) of experienced teachers to work toward graduate degrees in education at the university while at the same time mentoring a caseload of new teachers. The district supports the collaboration by assigning their participating experienced teachers' salaries to the program, which in turn uses the money to cover the teachers' tuitions and to provide them with stipends. The experienced teachers visit new teachers in their schools, work with them in and out of the classroom before and after school, during lunch and recess, during preparation periods, and often in the evening and on weekends. Meanwhile, as part of their graduate program, the experienced teachers receive mentor training and participate in weekly support sessions provided by the university.

Learning Circles is a professional development model of collaboration taking place in California's Bay Area Coalition for Equitable Schools. Small groups of teachers meet regularly to provide an opportunity for mentors and new teachers to build knowledge about content and best practices.

The Teachers' Loft is a newly formed community-based teacher center in Western Massachusetts that supports the region's school-based teacher induction programs by providing resources, facilitating inquiry groups, and offering workshops for beginning teachers. Participating teachers have the opportunity to examine and discuss a variety of teaching and learning models and to gain professional and emotional support while interacting with colleagues from schools and districts other than their own.

Suska is a new first-grade teacher at the Lowell Elementary School in Brainerd, Minnesota. Karen and Sharon, also first-grade teachers at Lowell Elementary, collaborate to mentor Suska. Karen mentors Suska in instruction and Sharon mentors her in school policy and culture and in the use of school and community facilities.

Each of these examples of collaborative-doing share the contention of Helen Regan and colleagues (Regan, Dubea, Anceil, Vailancourt, & Hofmann, 1992) that "we have an obligation to share knowledge, wisdom, and council with our colleagues and to seek such from them in return . . . ." There is power in such collaboration. When we practice collaborative-doing, we share in our program's vision and goals.

COMMITTED-LEADING

It has been said that vision without action is a daydream; action without vision is a nightmare. Committed leaders are those who not only hold and share the vision but also focus the energy of others toward the achievement of that vision. What kind of leadership behaviors characterize such a leader? What do committed leaders do to focus energy on the vision of induction and mentoring as a healthy and effective ingredient of a school's culture? Rick DuFour (2003) reminds us that such leadership "does not happen by chance or by invitation. It happens only when leaders commit to creating the systems that embed collaboration in the routine practice of the school." Committed leaders "plan for (rather than hope for) small wins and . . . celebrate the successes of individual teachers, teams of teachers, and the entire school in very public ways" (DuFour, 2004). DuFour's words speak to the heart of Principle 3: *an embedded induction and mentoring program thrives on informed dedication and purposeful nurturing.*

So what are some specific behaviors of committed-leading? Hank Rubin (2002) offers a litany of principles of effective leadership that can help answer this question. Below are several of Rubin's principles, each followed by my thoughts and observations of how that principle fosters the embedding of induction and mentoring into the culture of a school.

Cultivate a Shared Vision Right From the Start—Even If It's Vague

A shared vision is one that enunciates and reinforces the hopes and goals of all who are and will be committed to a vital induction and mentoring program. A meaningful vision will address the value of collaborative-doing, underscore the effect of induction and mentoring on student achievement, and emphasize teacher development and retention. An induction and mentoring vision or philosophy is made tangible when it is affirmed in writing. For example, the Connecticut State Department of Education Vocational-Technical School System's induction and mentoring program states its collaboratively developed and infused philosophy on the first page of its policy and procedures manual (2003).

> The cornerstone of quality education is what happens between the educator and the student. Therefore, we expect our teachers to have and to continue to develop the skills, knowledge and understanding needed in order for their interactions with students to be highly effective.
>
> We hold these expectations for all our teachers and recognize the need to encourage and support their ongoing professional growth. We especially recognize the need to encourage and support the ongoing professional growth of teachers new to the

profession and new to the system. These teachers will bring with them a strong knowledge base and an eagerness to teach.

However, research and experience suggest that without a program that supports their induction and continuous professional development, some promising beginning teachers will leave the profession after their first year or two. Those who do remain may take longer to reach their full professional potential.

An exemplary professional development program is one which sets system norms for its staff, recognizes officially that learning is a process which never stops, and perceives staff as continuous learners. The basis of *continuous improvement* is a belief that learning about one's work is never finished. Professional development cannot be limited to a few days in the school calendar, but must be ongoing and job-embedded.

The Vocational-Technical School System highly values the teachers new to the system. We consider mentoring by their experienced colleagues to be fundamental to their professional growth and their ability to better serve our students. The Vocational-Technical School System strongly supports the Collaboration for Induction, Mentoring and Support process for beginning teachers delineated in this Policy and Procedures Manual.

Take Care to Recruit the Right Mix to Reach Your Stakeholders and Decision Makers

It may be tempting for one person—usually an assistant superintendent or a professional development coordinator—unilaterally to plan and implement an induction and mentoring program, but experience has shown over and over again that representation from as many areas of the education community as possible should be included in the process if it is to continue to develop over time. If, for example, the building principal is not directly involved or if the teacher's association is kept out of the process, there is little chance that [induction and] mentoring will ever become part of the institutional fabric. (Portner, 2001, p. 23)

What constitutes the "right mix" of visionary leaders? Who are the leaders, real and potential, when it comes to planning, overseeing, evaluating, nurturing, adjusting, and moving their induction and mentoring program forward? The list is straightforward; it includes administrators, instructional supervisors, subject and curriculum coordinators, department chairs, nonmentor veteran teachers, and even the new teachers themselves.

Not to be overlooked is the importance of the visionary and proactive involvement of the local teachers association's leadership. For example, Adam Urbanski, president of the Rochester (New York) City School

District's Teachers Association, is among the district's strongest advocates for its induction and mentoring program. Urbanski carries on the tradition of the association's support of the program since 1988 when it proposed and successfully negotiated an internship program for new teachers.

Another, often overlooked, leadership opportunity is inherent in the role of mentor. These skilled veterans can help schools make the cultural and systemic shifts necessary to build successful learning communities by modeling the mentoring behaviors of professional inquiry, lifelong learning, collaboration, analysis of student data, and professional risk taking.

When it comes to taking the lead in the induction and mentoring process itself, however, the most important role falls to the building principal. Perhaps the most significant way a principal can influence collaboration from staff is to encourage their active participation and then set an example for them to follow. This kind of powerful leadership is exemplified by Brother Thomas Puccio, principal of Malden (Massachusetts) Catholic High School. Several years ago, in an effort to free up some time for his school's mentors and mentees to meet for the amount of time required by policy, Brother Thomas urged his nonmentoring teachers to occasionally volunteer to take over a mentor or mentee's class. He set the example by offering to do so himself and was immediately taken up on his offer, and it wasn't long before others followed his lead.

The potential for following Brother Thomas's example is especially enticing in states like Georgia, where regulations stipulate that

> [f]or (Principal) certificates that expire June 30, 2001, or after, an applicant for renewal must demonstrate that he or she has worked as a teacher in a classroom for not less than five days during each school year beginning on or after July 1, 2000. . . . (Georgia's Professional Standards Commission Teacher Certification—Rules 505-2-.13(9) Standard Renewal Requirements)

What a win-win potential! Imagine, fulfilling the recertification requirement and applying Brother Thomas's visionary-leadership model at the same time.

Become—or Ensure You've Identified—the Institutional Worry

This is the person who will pay unwavering attention to sustaining the momentum, attend to the management details of the collaboration, and address the process needs of each individual partner in the work of the collaboration.

Management of the induction and mentoring program is not a job for a committee. One person (a committee member, perhaps, or an administrator, mentor teacher, or retired former mentor—someone who is available to mentors and who is accountable to the mentoring committee) can efficiently handle day-to-day issues, provided he or she (1) thoroughly understands everyone's roles and responsibilities, (2) is clear about the purpose and goals of the program, (3) is familiar with the many aspects of the local school district, and (4) has the authority and resources to do the job (Portner, 2001, p. 52).

The leader who manages the induction and mentoring program (let's call that person the coordinator) is the person who protects mentors from the burden of administrative duties. Ideally, the coordinator has had experience mentoring as well as dealing with physical arrangements and logistics. The coordinator, among other responsibilities, might schedule the use of meeting rooms; arrange for training, materials, and the use of equipment; monitor activities; keep track of logs, portfolios, journals, and meetings; provide data for program evaluation; and engage in overall problem solving for the good of the program. Carl O'Connell, former mentor program coordinator for the Rochester (New York) City School District, stressed the importance of interpersonal problem solving. He told me that a significant aspect of his role was that of troubleshooter, monitoring relationships among mentors, administrators, and interns.

To the Greatest Extent Possible, Ensure That Each Partner's Individual and Institutional Self-Interests Are Served by Both the Process and the Products of the Collaboration

The National Foundation for the Improvement of Education (NFIE) report, *Creating a Teacher Mentoring Program* (1999), points out how a successful induction and mentoring program can benefit stakeholders' individual and institutional self-interests.

> For school administrators, mentoring aids recruitment and retention; for higher education institutions, it helps to ensure a smooth transition from campus to classroom; for teacher associations, it represents a new way to serve members and guarantee instructional quality; for teachers, it can represent the difference between success and failure; and for parents and students, it means better teaching [and learning].

Recognizing that induction and mentoring addresses their self-interests is a characteristic of leaders committed to embedding the program into their schools. Another characteristic is that their beliefs and values about teaching and learning resonate with those of induction and mentoring. Confidence that their efforts will succeed is also an important attribute of committed leaders. That is why it is important to share models of successful induction and mentoring programs.

Finally, Rubin (2002) reminds us that "cultivating partners shouldn't end once they commit to the partnership. Cultivation of partners' attachment to the collaboration requires ongoing attention, and that effective collaboration happens between people—one person at a time" (p. 106).

CIMS: A CASE IN POINT

Collaborative Induction, Mentoring and Support (CIMS) of Beginning Teachers is the induction and mentoring program recently developed by the Connecticut State Department of Education Vocational-Technical School System Task Force (2003). (The system's name was changed to the "Connecticut Technical High School System" in September 2004.) CIMS was constructed using the conceptual framework described above, and it employs elements of the framework's principles throughout its structure.

Background

The Connecticut system consists of eighteen schools and two satellites and is the largest secondary school system in the state. The Technical High School Committee of the Connecticut State Board of Education serves as the district's board of education. The statewide district has its own superintendent, whose central office staff includes academic and trade subject area consultants, a coordinator for professional development, and a district facilitator of the state's Beginning Educator Support and Training (BEST) program. Each school has its own BEST facilitator.

By state regulation, new teachers participate in the BEST program as a requirement for certification advancement. The BEST program provides a series of professional development workshops geared to the needs of beginning teachers, and BEST-trained mentors provide comprehensive mentoring during the new teachers' first year. During year two, the mentors concentrate on helping new teachers prepare portfolios and videos of classroom performance for review by state-appointed assessors. Beginning trade area teachers, however, are not subject to the portfolio and video requirements, although they, too, are expected to be mentored.

During the 2002–2003 school year, the district, in response to severe budgetary constraints, offered an early retirement option to its teachers. More teachers than anticipated opted for early retirement. The exodus of so many early retirees, combined with the greater-than-usual number of recently hired teachers who announced that they would also be leaving, left the district having to hire an exceptionally large number of new teachers for the 2003–2004 school year. It was evident that the district would be hard-pressed to address the state's BEST regulations in the year to come, given that (1) there would not be enough willing and able experienced teachers available to mentor the unusually large number of new teachers; (2) it would be difficult to match new teachers with mentors certified in the same subject, especially in the trade areas; (3) the perennial problem of providing enough time for mentors and their mentees to interact would be even more pronounced due to the increased number and needs of new teachers coupled with the demands of the No Child Left Behind Act; and (4) the limitations of the anticipated budget would substantially reduce the number of substitute teachers needed to free up time for mentors and mentees to interact.

In response to the dire nature of the situation, meetings took place to discuss how to continue addressing state requirements without compromising the quality of the district's BEST and professional development programs. What began as dialogue around how to patch up a damaged system ended with the realization that along with the crisis came the opportunity to rebuild the system anew.

As you read through the following sections, pay particular attention to how the principles of strategic-thinking, collaborative-doing, and committed-leading not only came into play during the development and implementation of CIMS, but also the way the principles are built into the structure of the program itself.

The Process

A task force was formed consisting of the assistant superintendent, district BEST facilitator, subject area consultants, president of the teachers' association, and a school administrator. The coordinator of professional development chaired the group's meetings and generally managed the process. The task force's charge was to develop policies and procedures that would build on the district's existing professional development and BEST programs by

- Increasing the variety of and opportunities for collegial support and professional growth of beginning teachers
- Acculturating beginning teachers into the vocational-technical school community
- Incorporating individualized personal growth plans as well as group activities designed to address the identified needs of beginning teachers

I was contracted to advise the task force, facilitate its monthly meetings, and consolidate the resulting program's goals, policies, and procedures into an operational manual. Task force members regularly solicited input and data from their constituents.

The task force decided to look at the existing program and its projected constraints through the composite lens of systems-thinking, collaborative-doing, and committed-leading. This approach resulted in mitigating the program's people, time, and money problems through the construction of a mechanism for collaboration. It also provided a detailed yet flexible structure, process, and calendar of procedures. The structure was to be flexible enough to accommodate the unique culture and organization of each school while still maintaining its own integrity throughout the district. The newly developed program, Collaboration for Induction, Mentoring and Support (CIMS) of Beginning Teachers in the Connecticut Vocational-Technical School System, was approved and adopted, and a CIMS policies and procedures manual was produced.

Figure 5.2   The CIMS Framework

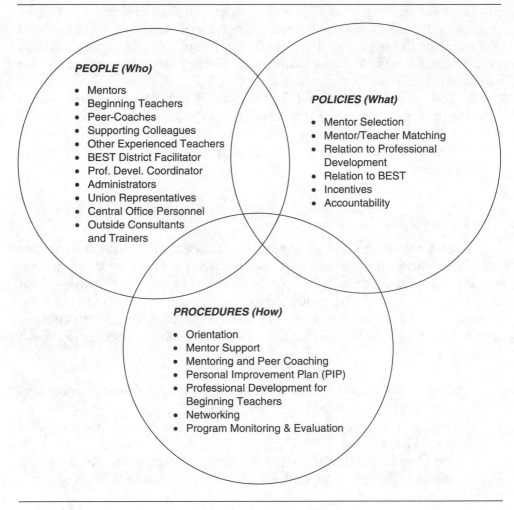

PEOPLE (Who)

- Mentors
- Beginning Teachers
- Peer-Coaches
- Supporting Colleagues
- Other Experienced Teachers
- BEST District Facilitator
- Prof. Devel. Coordinator
- Administrators
- Union Representatives
- Central Office Personnel
- Outside Consultants
  and Trainers

POLICIES (What)

- Mentor Selection
- Mentor/Teacher Matching
- Relation to Professional
  Development
- Relation to BEST
- Incentives
- Accountability

PROCEDURES (How)

- Orientation
- Mentor Support
- Mentoring and Peer Coaching
- Personal Improvement Plan (PIP)
- Professional Development for
  Beginning Teachers
- Networking
- Program Monitoring & Evaluation

The Product

The CIMS manual spells out the program's activities, timelines, and expected outcomes. It is constructed on the framework for embedding teacher induction and mentoring into a school's or district's culture that emphasizes the systematic and empathic relationships among people, policies, and procedures. Figure 5.2 illustrates the CIMS framework.

People, Policies, and Procedures

CIMS is based on the philosophy that experienced educators have an obligation to share knowledge, wisdom, and time with their colleagues new to the profession. The task force recognized in this philosophy the opportunity to address three of the critical issues facing them: the inadequate number of teachers willing and able to be mentors; the inability to match many mentors and mentees by subject area; and the lack of sufficient time available for mentors and mentees to interact. The program's developers utilized systems-thinking to create two new roles that rely on collaborative-doing to address those three issues. Inherent in those roles is the concept that mentoring focuses on both the content and process of teaching. Typically, mentors are assigned to mentees with an eye on matching content. Yet, as one mentor put it, "The commonalities of classroom management extend across disciplines."

Task force members felt that although it is desirable that the mentor and beginning teacher teach the same subject or be members of the same department, in the event this is not possible, the CIMS structure provides the option of peer coach as a supplement to the otherwise comprehensive mentoring function of an assigned mentor. A trained mentor-teacher can effectively help a new teacher address the BEST requirements and support a new teacher's acculturation, lesson planning, and classroom management. Other teachers, the peer coaches, volunteer to be available as needed to share their expertise one-on-one in such areas as content, instructional methodology, and assessment. Peer coaches could also conduct group sessions based on their expertise. It was determined that more experienced teachers would be willing to be mentors under those circumstances. It was also agreed that new trade-area teachers were generally well prepared and up-to-date in the content of their trade but needed mentoring in the non-content aspects of teaching. Teachers and administrators can also become involved in the program as supporting colleagues. Below are descriptions of these two new roles.

Peer Coach: A highly competent and experienced teacher who has no role or responsibility, formal or informal, in the teacher evaluation process and who has volunteered to be available on occasion, at the request of a mentor or beginning teacher, to consult in a specific content or process area.

Supporting Colleague: A certified member of the education community who does not have a formal or designated role in CIMS but who has volunteered to be available on occasion, at the request of a BEST facilitator, mentor, or beginning teacher, to monitor or conduct a class in order to make time for mentors and beginning teachers to engage in mentoring activities. Supporting colleagues meet with the teacher of the class they will teach at least three days prior to taking over the class in order to discuss the class and agree on a lesson plan. Experienced teachers, administrators, and retired personnel may serve as supporting colleagues.

Other roles delineated in the manual are those of beginning teacher, mentor, BEST facilitator, program administrator, professional development committee members, and school and central office staff.

Task force members found that some of the mentoring procedures prescribed by the BEST program were not able to be readily followed in the trade areas. They felt that adherence to BEST requirements and implementation of the new focus on collaborative-doing would be more achievable if a structure geared specifically to the vocational-technical district (as it was called at the time of the development of CIMS) was provided. Therefore, the CIMS manual contains a detailed chart that specifies responsibility, activities, timelines, operational guidelines, and outcomes for each of the program's various roles. Guidelines concerning mentor recruitment and selection, matching mentors with beginning teachers, mentor training and support, incentives, and program evaluation are also included.

Induction begins with an intensive three-day orientation session and continues with a variety of networking and professional development activities that take place periodically until beginning teachers have successfully completed the requirements for more advanced certification (usually two years). CIMS specifies that orientation for the beginning teacher includes four key components:

1. The school's community
2. The state vocational-technical school district's policies and procedures
3. The school and its policies and procedures
4. The curriculum

Looking back over the months of developing CIMS, the induction and mentoring task force recognized that the limitations they faced had actually presented them with the unexpected opportunity to enhance the program. They agreed that by applying the principles of systems-thinking, collaborative-doing, and committed-leading, they had overcome the challenge presented to them.

The Launching

The introduction of CIMS on June 26, 2003, to the district's leaders took place with the principles of systems-thinking, collaborative-doing, and committed-leading consciously in mind. Upwards of seventy administrators, curriculum directors, supervisors, teachers' union representatives, BEST facilitators, and professional development coordinators from the system's eighteen schools, two satellites, and central office gathered for a CIMS presentation and work session.

Copies of the newly printed manual were distributed. The need for increased new teacher support and the role of CIMS in that effort was explained by the superintendent, the district professional development coordinator, the BEST facilitator, and the teachers' union president. The consultant presented the details of CIMS and the presenters answered questions and led discussions. Following a break, participants formed small groups by school affiliation to brainstorm ways to support and implement CIMS in their buildings. The groups shared their ideas before adjourning.

Embedding CIMS into the culture of Connecticut vocational-technical schools will take time, probably two or three years beyond its implementation. Meanwhile, it seems to be heading nicely in that direction. Midway through the first year of its implementation, a member of the CIMS Task Force told me that "people are very excited about CIMS. I believe the manual shows them how serious we are about induction and mentoring. Exciting things are happening. The acting superintendent . . . has totally supported our efforts. . . . So far we have trained fifty teachers as mentors and next week we will provide training to fifty more."

LESSONS LEARNED

A legitimate goal of a well-conceived and executed induction and mentoring program is to ensure its long-term survival so that it can continue to serve its purpose over time. Barry Sweeny (2003), writing about the problem of keeping a mentoring program going once it is instituted, puts it this way:

> If mentoring is perceived as a single, isolated initiative with no relationship to organizational goals, then some day that mentoring program will be "at-risk." In the world of scarce resources, inadequate time, and demands on good people for increased performance, productivity and their time, a culture of competition rather than collaboration can be created. That competition means there will be winners and losers . . . mentoring is often the loser in the competition at budget crunch time.

The lesson is clear and worth repeating: Unless and until induction and mentoring becomes a part of a school's everyday routine—is taken for granted yet highly valued—it runs the all-too-real risk of becoming just another fad of the month. Schools and districts that have successfully embedded induction and mentoring into their everyday routine have done so through the efforts of visionary leaders who understand how components of their programs interact and who provide for and support the active participation of committed people.

State regulations have given impetus to the widespread creation of mentoring programs. Nevertheless, the reason a growing number of schools and districts have embedded induction and mentoring into their cultures is not necessarily because of regulations. Words on paper don't define culture—people and their actions do. The people in schools where induction and mentoring is part of their culture consider induction and mentoring sacrosanct. They place a high priority on the support, development, and retention of their new teachers; are energized by the involvement of their colleagues; and are at ease with the program's structure and processes.

Highlighted by the work of Richard Ingersoll (2001) and others, one of the primary incentives for instituting induction and mentoring programs has become reversing the high rate of new teacher attrition. Michele Israel (2002) cites this comment by Sharon Nemser, a professor of education at Brandeis University: "Mentoring alone cannot stop teacher attrition. It is part of a larger system. It needs to be reinforced by a professional culture that supports teacher learning, collaboration, and experimentation."

The conclusions by Ingersoll and Nemser are echoed by Johnson and Kardos (2002), who found as part of a longitudinal study that "new teachers working in settings with integrated professional cultures remained in their schools and in public school teaching in higher proportions than did their counterparts in veteran oriented or novice-oriented professional cultures. In other words, the professional culture of schools may well affect teacher retention over the long term."

A cautionary note is in order here. Child and Merrill (2003) found in their research that induction and mentoring "was probably unsustainable in the longer term unless more adequate funding enabled [its] development." They also found that even when inadequately funded, induction and mentoring was nevertheless a strong source of "vitality" in schools. They warned, however, that "professional goodwill cannot be assumed to be an endless resource." Another aspect of the money issue is illustrated by the following comment made to me by an experienced mentor. "If they are going to continue to hold mentors accountable for the time and paperwork involved, they had better take the issue of compensation more seriously."

In a recent conversation, Walter Carter, district coordinating teacher for staff development in the Blue Valley School District in Overland Park, Kansas, expressed his belief that "paying mentors to do their job has done a great deal to establish credibility of the program. With pay has come an expectation for mentoring performance."

Finally, we must remember that embedding induction and mentoring into a school's culture takes time, probably a minimum of two or three years beyond the program's implementation. Validation is the key. Induction and mentoring will have been embedded into a school's culture once people have lived through the program and found it to resonate with their beliefs and values, have experienced its success, and have felt that they and their school have grown as a result.

REFLECTIONS AND APPLICATIONS

This chapter discusses four conditions implemented by committed leaders that contribute to embedding induction and mentoring into a school's culture. Exercise 5.1 asks you to reflect on the extent to which these conditions exist in your program. Then, based on the material in the chapter, the exercise asks you to consider how you might more effectively institute or enhance these conditions.

Exercise 5.1 Conditions Implemented by Committed Leaders

Directions: Below, in column 1, are four conditions implemented by committed leaders that contribute to embedding induction and mentoring into a school's culture. In the box to the right of each condition, reflect on how that condition is being addressed in your induction and mentoring program. In the third box, speculate how, by applying material from this chapter, you might implement or enhance the provision of each condition.

Condition	How Addressed	Potential Implementation or Enhancement
Share the vision		
Include a mix of stakeholders and decision makers		
Identify and support the leader who manages the induction and mentoring program		
Ensure that each partner's individual and institutional self-interests are served by both the process and the products		

REFERENCES

Child, A., & Merrill, S. (2003). Professional mentors' perceptions of the contribution of school/HEI partnerships to professional development and school improvement. *Journal of In-Service Education, 29*(2), 315.

Connecticut State Department of Education Vocational-Technical School System Task Force. (2003, August). *Collaboration for induction, mentoring and support (CIMS) of beginning teachers in Connecticut vocational-technical schools.* Middletown, CT: Author.

DuFour, R. (2003). "Collaboration lite" puts student achievement on a starvation diet. *Journal of Staff Development, 24*(4), 63–64.

DuFour, R. (2004). Leading edge: Leadership is an affair of the heart. *Journal of Staff Development, 25*(1), 67–68.

Ingersoll, R. (2001). *A different approach to solving the teacher shortage* (Problem Policy Brief 3). Center for the Study of Teaching and Policy, University of Washington, Seattle.

Israel, M. (2002). Guidance from the get-go: Mentoring new teachers (*Administrator's Desk Newsletter* 3/12/2002). Retrieved March 15, 2002, from Education World: http://www.educationworld.com/a_admin

Johnson, S. M., & Kardos, S. M. (2002). Redesigning professional development: Keeping new teachers in mind. *Educational Leadership, 59*(6), 12–16.

National Foundation for the Improvement of Education. (1999). *Creating a teacher mentoring program.* Report based on the proceedings of the National Foundation for the Improvement of Education Teacher Mentoring Symposium, Los Angeles. Washington, DC: Author.

Pegasus Communications, Inc. (n. d.). *What Are Systems?* Retrieved June 4, 2004, from http://www.pegasuscom.com/aboutst.html

Portner, H. (2001). *Training mentors is not enough: Everything else schools and districts need to do.* Thousand Oaks, CA: Corwin.

Regan, H., Dubea, C., Anceil, M., Vailancourt, R., & Hofmann, J. (1992). *Teacher: A new definition and model for development and evaluation.* Philadelphia: Research for Better Schools.

Rubin, H. (2002). *Collaborative leadership.* Thousand Oaks, CA: Corwin.

Sweeny, B. (2003). *Strategies for sustaining a mentoring program.* Retrieved March 15, 2004, from International Mentoring Association: http://www.mentoring association.org

Note: The CIMS Philosophy and other excerpts that appear in "Collaboration for Induction, Mentoring and Support" (CIMS) are used with permission by Abigail Hughes.

PART II

Mentoring Constructs and Best Practices

6

The Stages of Mentor Development

Jean Casey

Ann Claunch

The idea of mentoring has its origins in classical literature. When Odysseus left for Troy, he charged a wise old man, Mentor, with the care, guidance, and protection of his son, the young Telemachus. Indeed, many times before his father's return, Telemachus sought the advice and counsel of his friend. Mentor listened with a patient ear, provided support and encouragement, and even intervened at one point to protect Telemachus from harm. The concept of mentoring has changed little since the days of Homer, but until recently the term *mentor* was seldom used except as a literary allusion or in reference to a coach who acted as the counselor, teacher, and leader of young athletes. Study and research during the recent past has revived the concept of mentoring, particularly in the context of personal achievement in the corporate world, so that *mentoring* has almost become a household word. Having a mentor is currently viewed as critical to professional success, and institutionally designated mentors are charged with directing the personal growth and development of others.

HISTORY AND CONCEPTUAL FRAMEWORK

Daniel Levinson has provided one of the most contemporary views of mentoring in *The Seasons of a Man's Life* (1978), the study of the personal and professional development of men at midlife transition. According to Levinson, the act of mentoring includes providing a model of adult conduct and involves the acts of giving and receiving. The activities of a mentor are varied, and Levinson asserts that true mentoring is not defined by formal roles but by the character of the relationship. Other researchers, particularly those in business and industry, have characterized the mentoring relationship as having two distinct functions—career functions and psychosocial functions. The career functions of mentoring center on enhancing career development and professional opportunities for the novice. A mentor in this case acts as sponsor, protector, promoter, and guide. The career mentor opens doors for the protégé, challenges, provides opportunities for wider exposure, and introduces the protégé to those with influence and power. The psychosocial functions of mentoring, on the other hand, are aimed at personal development. In this case, the mentor acts as role model, counselor, teacher, supporter, and friend. The protégé receives reinforcement, affirmation, acceptance, and confirmation from the mentor. The mentor's role becomes one of offering opportunities for enhancing self-esteem or self-concept at both the personal and professional levels.

In conceptual models, the levels of mentoring relationships are wide and varied. Some models make the clear distinction between *mentor* and *sponsor*, the latter performing only the career functions. Phillips (1977) proposed the concept of secondary and primary mentors. Secondary mentors are involved in the career development, skills, and advancement of their protégés, while primary mentors perform both career and psychosocial functions in the mentoring relationship. Anderson and Devanna's (1981) model provides a mentoring relationship continuum based on the kinds and levels of mentor-protégé interactions, ranging from *patron* to *sponsor* to *guide* to *peer pal*. Levinson's model is inclusive of all roles, including both career functions and psychosocial functions, and he adds the notion that the mentor and protégé are both connected to achieving a common "dream."

Levinson's work, and that of many others, suggests that mentoring relationships are a function of life cycle changes. There seems to be a natural inclination in youth to seek out mentors. Developmental tasks in early adulthood include the development of life and professional skills, and respected, mature adult role models aid in that process. As a degree of security, confidence, and competence is developed in young adulthood, the tasks shift from the development of self to concern for the development of others. Middle adulthood often brings on the need to lead, teach, counsel, and coach young people. In this way, the development tasks of each life cycle are complementary.

The work of Levinson supports that of Erik Erikson (1963). In Erikson's life stages, the turning point of middle life involves the choice of what he terms "generativity versus stagnation." The choice of stagnation suggests the end of growth and productivity. Generativity is best defined as a concern for the next generation, the desire to guide it and take responsibility for the emerging generation of adults. There is a clear connection between Erikson's and Levinson's models in life transitions when there is the need to realize one's self. This realization is often accomplished through the formation of mentoring relationships and is one way in which older workers may realize their professional contribution and the significance of their lives (Bova & Phillips, 1984). Levinson says that the mentoring relationship is the most important relationship a young person can have, as it provides models of adult behavior and opportunities to enhance skills and self-concept. The mentoring relationship may be equally as important in middle adulthood. Carl Rogers (1961) has said that "the degree to which we can help others grow and develop is a measure of the degree to which we ourselves have grown" (p. 65). Mentoring offers an alternative to stagnation and allows adults to confirm the value of their own lives.

Teacher induction programs as they are currently conceived and structured may be viewed as a specific application of the mentoring concept. Mentor teachers are charged with the professional and personal development of novices. The needs of new teachers have been clearly identified in numerous studies and summarized by Simon Veenman (1984), who suggested that the problems encountered by beginning teachers are predictable, yet individual needs remain person-specific and situation-specific. However, induction programs and mentoring efforts that focus narrowly on new teachers' unmet needs, either general or specific, may be successful in reducing stress levels and addressing immediate problems, but they may fail to promote professional development and the improvement of teaching and learning that should be the larger goals of mentoring (Feiman-Nemser, 2001).

In examining the relationship between mentor and protégé in teacher induction programs, the stages of teacher development and the stages of the mentoring relationship are helpful. Francis Fuller (1969) and others have identified several stages of teacher development, including survival, competence, confidence, autonomy, and commitment. During these stages, concerns of the new teacher shift from self to students to other teachers to the profession as a whole. O'Neil (1981) has identified comparable stages in the formation of mentoring relationships: entry, trust building, encouragement or risk taking, the teaching of skills, and concern for professional standards. These two stage models are complementary, and a combination of them is found in Kram's (1983) discussion of mentoring as a series of phases. The first phase, *initiation*, involves introductions and trust building. The second phase, *cultivation*, requires risk taking and the teaching of new skills for reaching desired levels of competence. The third phase, *separation*, occurs when the new teacher has achieved a level of competence and autonomy and is no longer in need of mentoring support. The final phase is *redefinition*, in which the mentor and protégé teachers become peers and share in the common concerns of their profession. Understanding the stages of teacher development as well as how mentoring relationships unfold is important in the growth of effective mentor teachers.

TRANSITION TO MENTORING

Educational research and writing from the past twenty years provides a strong rationale for induction programs, definitions of mentor roles and responsibilities, training models for mentors, survival guides for beginning teachers, examination of the effects of mentoring activities, and a plethora of program descriptions (Portner, 1998; Daloz, 1999; Boreen, Johnson, Niday, & Potts, 2000; Odell & Huling, 2000; Villani, 2002). Understandably, the spotlight has shone almost exclusively on the growth and retention of new teachers, and little attention has been paid to the effects of mentoring initiatives on the lives and careers of mentors themselves. Our twenty years of experience in a mentoring program supported by a long-standing school-university partnership has led to our assertion that the growth and development of mentors is as complex and important as is the growth of their protégés.

In spite of recent attention, mentoring remains a fledgling initiative in education. While mature, comprehensive, and successful programs exist in some states and large school districts, the mentoring of beginning teachers has not been fully institutionalized in public education. For most practicing teachers, the only models for adult-to-adult interactions in a classroom are educational assistant relationships, clinical supervision as part of preservice training or personnel evaluation, or long-ago memories of team teaching. The what and how of mentoring remains uncomfortable for many. Added to this general lack of familiarity with mentoring roles and relationships is the erroneous assumption that every excellent classroom teacher will make an equally excellent mentor. The knowledge and skills needed for working with adults differs from those required for educating young students. Mentoring knowledge and "best practices" are now recognized as necessary for an effective induction and mentoring program.

The effort to embrace mentoring as part of entry into the profession is further inhibited by the fact that most new teachers are so intent on seeking professional autonomy that in their first year of teaching they purposely *do not* seek assistance from experienced educators. At the same time, experienced teachers are reluctant, for a variety of reasons, to interfere with the struggle of a beginning teacher, creating a "double bind" that widens the gulf between new and veteran teachers. Dan Lortie (1975) described teacher autonomy and isolation as additional barriers in the professional development of both new and experienced teachers. In the typical school setting, there is little time for interaction and exchange between adults, a condition that inhibits mentoring relationships when one of the most important functions of the mentor teacher is breaking down the walls of isolation for the new teacher.

The transition to mentoring as a common practice in schools is paralleled by the transition that experienced teachers must make when they accept a mentoring role. Moving from being a classroom teacher to becoming a mentor of novice teachers is a learning process. It is not smooth and has been described as "walking on sponges." The mentor is required to build a knowledge base on adult learning that is flexible and adaptable to the variables of human interactions. Layered onto the new knowledge base is the need to distill a lifetime of knowledge of teaching, learning, and pedagogy into clear messages that give new teachers information that will enhance their growth.

For mentor teachers, the knowledge base in daily practice changes from content curriculum to professional competence, which includes adult learning theory. Communication in the form of telling and teaching shifts to listening and reflecting. Mentors focus on the adult's knowledge and extend that knowledge through professional conversations. There is a curriculum content that is brought to the classroom context by the teacher that implies that learning revolves around what the teacher knows. In the classroom there is also a strong control of the learning design as the teacher maps out the curriculum in systematic and purposeful ways. As a teacher moves into the role of mentor, that control of the learning design is lost. The mentor is not the single agent who designs the learning context for the beginning teacher. A young teacher draws from many resources—university training, varied life experiences, professional readings, and advice from other adults. The mentor's job, then, is not to deliver the teaching curriculum to the new teacher, but rather to interpret what the teacher already knows and mediate that knowledge in practice.

STAGES OF MENTOR GROWTH

Several distinct stages have been observed and identified by mentor teachers as they reflect on their growth as mentors. Each stage represents a different level of growth as teachers transition to mentoring roles. This model is grounded in the literature on adult education and teacher learning and through documentation of experiences of mentors over a twenty-year period. The five stages include *predisposition, disequilibrium, transition, confidence,* and *efficacy* (Figure 6.1). Although individuals experience professional learning in a variety of ways, each stage of learning to mentor has identifiable attributes or characteristics. The mentors often reveal their developmental stage through the language they use to describe their work. The following descriptions of each stage are illustrated by written feedback and reflection from mentor teachers at different levels of mentoring experience.

Figure 6.1   Stages of Mentor Growth

Predisposition	• Seeks professional growth • Desires to assist and nurture others • Challenges self to improve • Practices effective interpersonal skills • Is open-minded and flexible
Disequilibrium	• Applies skills of time management and organization • Strengthens procedural knowledge • Shifts professional paradigm from teaching students to teaching adults • Has doubts, fears, and unclear expectations about mentoring roles • Has little self-confidence as a mentor • Experiences the "impostor phenomenon"
Transition	• Expands the understanding of mentoring roles • Expands knowledge base and new vocabulary • Develops individualized mentor strategies • Develops better questioning skills • Replaces personal agendas with the new teacher's agenda • Develops trusting relationship with colleagues • Reflects on and clarifies personal philosophy and beliefs
Confidence	• Understands job expectations • Continues the development of mentoring strategies • Refines listening and questioning • Begins to dissociate from the protégé's success • Finds a renewed sense of professionalism that includes collaboration, collegiality, and articulation • Trusts in his or her own beliefs • Begins to advocate for beginning teachers
Efficacy	• Develops a personal mentoring style • Continues to reflect on and adjust multiple strategies • Recognizes personal strengths as a mentor • Makes emotional shift to detachment and minimal response • Deepens the understanding of effective teaching • Moves from intuitive to intentional practice

Predisposition

A question often asked of new mentors is "Why would teachers who are successful in the classroom seek to disrupt their success and become teachers of teachers?" To answer this question, we look to the literature of psychosocial development. Not every classroom teacher desires to work with novice teachers, but many career educators choose to honor their life-long commitment to students by continuing to serve the profession in alternative roles (Steffy, Wolfe, Pasch, & Enz, 2000) and extend their own learning by sharing what they know with others. The successful classroom teacher who chooses to move from the classroom into a mentoring role may be responding to the need for generativity. A veteran teacher with the predisposition to share professional knowledge and expertise

- Seeks professional growth
- Desires to assist and nurture others
- Challenges self to improve
- Practices effective interpersonal skills
- Is open-minded and flexible

Reaching a certain level of expertise in teaching is often an impetus for professional change. Excellent teachers continually challenge themselves, and becoming a mentor is one way to meet that challenge. One new mentor wrote, "I have been working for fifteen years in the classroom and I have loved working with the children, but I want something to offer new teachers and would like to work with adults." Another mature and experienced teacher described his motivation by explaining, "I want to be a mentor because my enthusiasm for learning and for ongoing professional development and my ability to work well with others would serve to make me an effective addition to the [mentoring] team. I would also welcome the opportunity to extend my own personal and professional growth during this time." Both of these teachers have arrived at a point in their personal and professional lives when they are ready to share their expertise and at the same time move on to another level of professional challenge. Such predispositions support their readiness to mentor.

Our experience has demonstrated that teachers at midcareer or at middle adult stages become strong mentors. While younger, less experienced teachers can do an excellent job at helping beginners develop technical teaching skills, their predisposition to mentor often does not include commitment to or understanding of the psychosocial dimensions of mentoring. The predisposition stage of mentor development is not unlike the idealistic stage of development seen in first-year teachers. Both the mentor and the new teacher enter into the new learning context with some assumptions and idealism, without full comprehension of the cognitive shift that is to occur. This professional naïveté on the part of even the most experienced teacher results in the disequilibrium experienced in the second stage of mentor growth.

Disequilibrium

The second stage of development in mentoring is the stage of disequilibrium as the realities of being a mentor become evident to the teacher. The teacher has just left a context in which he or she was recognized as successful and now is placed in a situation that is unfamiliar. Previous assumptions about being a mentor must be revised, and second-year mentors are able to reflect on their initial assumptions: "I thought I would be working with curriculum and students, which I did, but the job of being a mentor is much more complex than telling first-year teachers what you know." At the stage of disequilibrium, a mentor

- Applies skills of time management and organization
- Strengthens procedural knowledge
- Shifts his or her professional paradigm from teaching students to teaching adults
- Has doubts, fears, and unclear expectations about mentoring roles
- Has little self-confidence as a mentor
- Experiences the "impostor phenomenon"

After several weeks, most mentors confess to their initial confusion and uncertainty about where they fit into the lives of new teachers. For some, success in the classroom and beliefs in the value of mentoring are challenged early in the year: "Coming into this job, I had a vague notion of what I was supposed to do and that I could make a difference for new teachers. I had been told I would be good at this by my principal and several teachers. I found my [new] teachers and introduced myself to them with varying reactions from 'I don't need any help' to 'I'm dying already!' At this point I became lost." This mentor's professional confidence was shaken by the degrees to which new teachers both accepted and rejected her offers of help, and she had little notion of what to do next.

When mentors begin meeting their new teachers, they discover the difference between building relationships with students and establishing working relationships with adults. The resistance of some new teachers bewilders new mentors. "I was visiting all the schools assigned to me and was not really sure of what I was doing—it was a confidence thing. I wanted to help these new teachers do well, and my assumption was that they would welcome any help. Much to my dismay, most of the teachers that were not at the Jump Start [orientation meeting] in August seemed to feel threatened by my presence." Understanding the new teacher's need to be autonomous and perceived as competent helps mentors to cope with resistance.

The Imposter Phenomenon

A lack of strategies for assisting adults, initial resistance from new teachers, and role confusion create disequilibrium. Mentors are challenged to learn a new set of skills. They may sense failure, and at this point may experience the impostor phenomenon, a self-imposed feeling of inadequacy and a fear that others may discover how little they really know (Clance, 1985). The syndrome is recognized as a natural process that is experienced when a job change is introduced into successful professional lives, but it is amplified in correlation with how successful the teacher was in the classroom. Feelings of confusion and inadequacy may return often for mentors as they encounter the unexpected array of problems experienced by new teachers. New mentors approached these challenges by responding in ways that had helped them become effective classroom teachers. "After a year and a half, I still don't know what best practice for this job is. I think everything is fine, and then something happens that makes me examine what I am doing. This is good, except I feel as though I am in a state of disequilibrium most of the time. . . . I visualize and work with the first-year teachers as I did my students: recognize their strengths, build on them, and help them to go where they want to go while paving the way with some basics. . . . I'm still wondering how I can most effectively facilitate their growth while I feel that I have made little growth myself toward competence in this role." Reliance on skills learned in the classroom, coupled with questions about adult learning relationships, helps the new mentor devise more effective supporting strategies.

The stage of disequilibrium causes many to rethink their decision to become a mentor. The mentor's own survival stage is discomforting. "I don't get the same effect I am used to receiving as when I'm working with children. (This seems to be a recurring theme with me.) I wonder whether it is because I am out of my comfort zone. I am not too different from the first-year teachers I'm trying to help." Some react to this discomfort by magnifying their organizational skills. Others control the mental and emotional chaos by becoming list makers. Some develop complex schedules and feedback questionnaires. Visitation logs and anecdotal notes substitute for the effectiveness once felt in the classroom. Disequilibrium at this stage is of great value to mentors because it demands that they seek new paradigms, new knowledge, and new understandings.

Transition

Moving from the stage of disequilibrium requires a realization that the expert classroom teacher is a novice teacher of teachers. This transition stage could also be renamed the quiet stage. Just as second language learners experience a silent stage as they are acquiring their new language, mentors go through a stage in which they read professional literature more purposefully and listen more carefully to acquire the language and skills of mentoring. Consequently, the new mentor may do more listening then sharing. In the transition stage, a mentor

- Expands the understanding of mentoring roles
- Expands knowledge base and new vocabulary
- Develops individualized mentor strategies

- Develops better questioning skills
- Replaces personal agendas with the new teacher's agenda
- Develops trusting relationships with colleagues
- Reflects on and clarifies personal philosophy and beliefs

Mentors at this stage of development have accepted that they are novice adult educators and focus their energy on building a new knowledge base. "I recognize that my efficacy is currently in a low cycle. It is obvious that I need to learn a new vocabulary, develop a new attitude and identity." In the transition stage, mentors are ready to explore the theories of adult learning, teacher development, and mentoring models.

During this transition stage, mentors also give up the idea of being in control. One wrote, "When I started this job I thought my role was to 'hand out answers' to first-year teachers. After all, I was the one with all those years of classroom experience! I quickly learned that [teachers] did not need to be given answers, but needed to be guided to their own answers." At this point an important epiphany occurs. As revealed in her written reflection, this mentor's transition to becoming an effective mentor began when she realized that mentoring was more about the new teacher than it was about herself. She continued, "I backed off on my agenda and started having them [new teachers] reflect on what they were doing. I answered a lot of questions about procedures or methods of doing particular things and gave my opinion when asked. I still asked them to think about using different strategies, but I quit talking to them about it unless they asked, and I praised them when they told me about something new they tried."

Confidence

As mentors build their knowledge base in the transition stage of growth, they begin to apply their new information and experience success with their first-year teachers. This success improves their confidence. A mentor with confidence

- Understands job expectations
- Continues the development of mentoring strategies
- Refines listening and questioning
- Begins to dissociate from the protégé's success
- Finds a renewed sense of professionalism that includes collaboration, collegiality, and articulation
- Trusts in his or her own beliefs
- Begins to advocate for beginning teachers

The confident mentor teacher is learning to measure growth by the new teacher's standards rather than by the mentor teacher's expectations. This signals a change from "teller of information" to "facilitator of understanding." Mentors experience a paradigm shift from giving answers to posing questions. One mentor wrote, "I am feeling more comfortable in the job of mentor. I am able to ask better questions and accept the answers as a jumping-off point rather than trying to convert the speaker to my answers."

Confident mentors have also learned that entering a classroom with a powerful question is better than providing answers. This discovery was particularly important to one: "'A conversation is only as good as the question it entertains.' This [line] from *The Courage to Teach* [Palmer, 1998] makes me ponder the sheer power of asking the right question to initiate growth—how a carefully posed question should encourage deeper and more analytical thinking and very possibly reflection which carries the potential to bring about transformation and growth."

Mentors in the confidence stage not only see growth in their teachers but also see growth in themselves. "I am so much more comfortable in the role of mentor, and my ability to really help has increased so much, even over last year. I can now suggest strategies and techniques I've been learning for the past two years without having to stumble around trying to remember. . . . These ideas roll effortlessly from my mouth, and I sit amazed afterward." After struggling with role definition and relationship building, this mentor began to employ strategies she had studied or shared. Her confidence came from recognizing the changes in herself.

Efficacy

"Seeing such growth in a teacher and knowing that I was instrumental in helping bring about the change is rewarding. I gave her the push, supported her through it, and she was successful. As a support teacher, I can see that I have made a tangible, positive difference." Mentors in the efficacy stage know that they make a difference and take great pride in their accomplishments. At the same time, mentors who have a sense of efficacy also can detach themselves from the failures and successes of their new teachers. Seasoned mentors understand that it is their job to create the conditions for learning but not to have expectations about what learning will take place. A mentor in the efficacy stage

- Develops a personal mentoring style
- Continues to reflect on and adjust multiple strategies
- Recognizes personal strengths as a mentor
- Makes emotional shift to detachment and minimal response
- Deepens the understanding of effective teaching
- Moves from intuitive to intentional practice

As veteran teachers transition into the role of mentor, they often lament the loss of being able to touch the lives of children. A mentor in the efficacy stage is satisfied with touching the lives of novice teachers. In thinking over her experience as a mentor, one wrote, "I am feeling comfortable in my skin. I have less hesitation as I go into rooms. I am able to offer materials and not feel bad or take it personally if they are not used. I feel confident that I can do the job and know what I am doing. I am no longer measuring my worth or exacting satisfaction from the students in the first-year teacher's classroom who would hug me. I feel a sense of [accomplishment] in just working with the teachers."

Experienced mentors understand that while they are in a helping role, there is also profound learning that comes from the process of giving. Mentoring no longer means saving young teachers from themselves. It also encompasses receiving as mentors cultivate in themselves a new sense of professionalism and competence. One teacher sums it up after a year of fighting to define her new role: "Perhaps I have learned more, grown more from working in this position this year than have the teachers I have been supporting. Perhaps in approaching every encounter from the perspective that 'it is all about the teacher with whom I work' rather than being about me, has indeed created a most unexpected learning experience for ME!"

CONCLUSION

Acknowledging that mentors develop in ways not unlike those of new teachers is important for educators committed to effective induction programs. Those who would serve as MoMs or "mentors of mentors" will carefully consider their role in the development of a strategic mentoring culture (Sweeny, 2001) in which the learning of the mentor is as carefully tended to as that of the novice. Meeting the needs of mentors will enhance their effectiveness in meeting the needs of classroom teachers. In such an environment, mentors can use their knowledge and expertise in teaching and learning to instruct new teachers while encouraging personal growth.

In that long-ago story from Homer, Mentor played many roles—a trusted counselor, friend, teacher, and more. "The first mentor is a surrogate parent, who manages to do an exemplary job of giving his young charge a modicum of knowledge, skills and wisdom. However, Telemachus . . . [also] lacks a degree of courage; he is hesitant to act. The goddess Athene disguises herself as the trusted Mentor in order to persuade Telemachus that he is no longer a child; he must set out, on his own. . . . Homer's *two* Mentors (the sage old man and the wily goddess) capture the need for great mentors" (T. Keyes, personal communication, December 2003) who can guide others and transform themselves at the same time.

REFLECTIONS AND APPLICATIONS

This chapter contends that mentors often reveal their developmental stage through the language they use to describe their work. Exercise 6.1 asks you to reflect on the extent to which your program provides opportunities for mentors to grow through these stages and to consider how you might provide or extend such opportunities.

Exercise 6.1 Empowering Mentor Growth

Directions: Below, in column 1, are the five developmental stages of mentors. In column 2, reflect on how your induction and mentoring program provides opportunities for mentors to grow through these stages. In the third column, speculate how you might provide or enhance such opportunities.

Developmental Stage	Opportunities Provided	Potential Applications or Enhancements
Predisposition		
Disequilibrium		
Transition		
Confidence		
Efficacy		

REFERENCES

Anderson, C., & Devanna, M. (1981). Mentors: Can they help women get ahead? *Career Development Bulletin, 2,* 5–8.

Boreen, J., Johnson, M., Niday, D., & Potts, J. (2000). *Mentoring beginning teachers.* Portland, ME: Stenhouse Press.

Bova, B., & Phillips, R. (1984). Mentoring as a learning experience for adults. *Journal of Teacher Education, 35*(3), 16–20.

Clance, P. (1985). *The impostor phenomenon.* Atlanta, GA: Peachtree.

Daloz, L. (1999). *Mentoring.* San Francisco: Jossey-Bass.

Erikson, E. (1963). *Childhood and society.* New York: Norton.

Feiman-Nemser, S. (2001, December). From preparation to practice: Designing a continuum to strengthen and sustain teaching. *Teachers College Record, 103*(6), 1013–1055.

Fuller, F. (1969). Concerns of teachers: A developmental conceptualization. *American Educational Research Journal, 6*(2), 207–226.

Kram, K. (1983). Phases of the mentoring relationship. *Academy of Management Journal, 26,* 608–625.

Levinson, D. (1978). *The seasons of a man's life.* New York: Knopf.

Lortie, D. (1975). *Schoolteacher: A sociological study.* Chicago: University of Chicago Press.

Odell, S., & Huling, L. (2000). *Quality mentoring for novice teachers.* Indianapolis, IN: Kappa Delta Pi.

O'Neil, J. (1981). Toward a theory and practice of mentoring in psychology. In J. H. O'Neil & L. S. Wrightsman (Eds.), *Mentoring: Psychological, person and career implications.* Symposium at the annual meeting of the American Psychological Association.

Palmer, P. (1998). *The courage to teach: Exploring the inner landscape of a teacher's life.* San Francisco: Jossey-Bass.

Phillips, L. (1977). *Mentors and protégés: A study of the career development of women managers and executives in business and industry.* Unpublished doctoral dissertation, University of California, Los Angeles.

Portner, H. (1998). *Mentoring new teachers.* Thousand Oaks, CA: Corwin.

Rogers, C. (1961). *On becoming a person: A therapist's view of psychotherapy.* Boston: Houghton Mifflin.

Steffy, B., Wolfe, M., Pasch, S., & Enz, B. (2000). *Life cycle of the career teacher.* Thousand Oaks, CA: Corwin.

Sweeny, B. (2001). *Best practices in new teacher mentoring and induction.* Wheaton, IL: Best Practice Resources.

Veenman, S. (1984). Perceived problems of beginning teachers. *Review of Educational Research, 54*(2), 143–178.

Villani, S. (2002). *Mentoring programs for beginning teachers.* Thousand Oaks, CA: Corwin.

7

Mentor Teachers as Instructional Coaches

James Rowley

One of the problems that have consistently complicated efforts to build quality, mentor-based, entry-year programs has been the failure to clearly define the various roles that a quality mentor should play in the life of a beginning teacher. Failure to thoughtfully define those roles leads to confusion about the very purpose of the work of mentor teachers, often resulting in compromised relationships and negative political dynamics. In no area of mentor performance is this truer than with the role of the mentor as an instructional coach.

QUALITIES OF THE GOOD MENTOR

In 1999, after a decade of training mentor teachers and helping school districts develop entry-year programs, I endeavored to articulate the qualities of good mentor teachers by developing a framework to clearly define the diverse roles they play. The result of that effort was a framework for defining the high-performing mentor teacher with regard to six essential qualities (Rowley, 1999). Those qualities included

1. Committing to the roles and responsibilities of mentoring

2. Accepting the beginning teacher as a developing person and professional

3. Reflecting on interpersonal communications

4. Coaching for classroom success

5. Modeling personal and professional growth

6. Communicating hope and optimism for the future

Each of these qualities was conceptualized as a personal or professional belief realized in the form of a set of congruent behaviors. For example, good mentor teachers not only personally accept beginning teachers as developing persons and professionals, they overtly communicate that acceptance to the novice teachers they are supporting. For example, they accept beginning teachers having relatively low skills in many areas of professional practice as a normal condition that characterizes beginning professionals in many other fields where skill development is largely a function of experience. Consequently, good mentors employ appropriate coaching strategies to help novice teachers acquire the relevant knowledge and skill. Importantly, they do so in ways that do not imply deficiency or incompetence on the part of the persons they are seeking to help.

The Most Challenging Mentor Quality

Over the past five years, I have frequently asked prospective and practicing mentor teachers which of the six qualities of the good mentor they believe to be the most challenging. While this question has often prompted divergent responses and lively debate, my personal perspective is less ambivalent. While compelling arguments can be made for any of the six qualities, it is preparing mentor teachers to coach for classroom success that has proved the most challenging for this writer. In many ways, I believe this challenge has largely been a function of the evolution of mentor programming in the context of specific aspects of school culture characteristic of many U.S. schools. Those aspects of school culture often include a conception of classroom teaching as a largely private enterprise in which teachers in many schools work in isolation from their peers. A second important factor is related to the fact that most classroom teachers tend to view *observation, evaluation,* and *supervision* as synonymous terms. This is understandable because for many veteran teachers the only adult ever to observe their teaching was their principal, who was there in a supervisory capacity to evaluate their performance. To complicate matters even further, professional associations and local bargaining units for many years failed to support peer observation for fear that it would lead to peer evaluation.

THE HISTORICAL DEVELOPMENT OF THE ROLE

Before describing the future of the mentor teacher's role as an instructional coach, a brief review of the historical context from which that role has emerged seems warranted. The mentoring of beginning teachers in

American schools was largely an informal, hit-or-miss process until the early 1980s. Personal interviews with hundreds of veteran teachers who began their teaching careers in the 1960s and 1970s have consistently revealed that approximately 50 percent of such teachers felt informally supported during their first year of teaching. In contrast, the remaining 50 percent report that their first year of teaching was a lonely, frustrating experience in which no one stepped forward to provide technical or social-emotional support.

Beginning in the late 1970s and early 1980s some school districts began recognizing the need for more formalized approaches to supporting beginning teachers. In some states, recognition of this need was supported by state departments of education, some of which provided funding to support mentor-based, entry-year initiatives. The majority of these programs placed an understandably strong emphasis on providing social-emotional and logistical support focused on helping beginning teachers navigate the challenges of being socialized in a specific school culture. During this time period, school districts and state departments of education worked to develop model *induction* or *entry-year* programs and to address a variety of essential questions such as these: How should mentors be selected? How should they be matched with beginning teachers? What should they do? How should they be trained? And should they be compensated? Many important experiments in mentoring and entry-year programming took place during this time and helped set the foundation upon which subsequent programs would be built.

In the late 1980s and throughout the 1990s entry-year programming began to change in a couple of significant ways. First, there was an emerging sense that beginning teachers would be better served by formal programs of entry-year support that included a focus on mentor teachers serving as instructional coaches for beginning teachers. This shift was likely driven by the increasing emphasis on the standardized testing of K–12 students and on the development of new licensing standards for beginning teachers. Whatever the causes, this was the beginning of a continuing focus on the need to shift from historical models of informal mentoring, often characterized as "buddy models," to formalized "coaching models."

A false dichotomy was created as proponents of the new model often denigrated the earlier model as being weak or misguided. This phenomenon was unfortunate because it tended to devalue the role of mentor teachers as agents of social-emotional support, suggesting that such a role required little or no training because veteran teachers were already well schooled in terms of their helping relationship skills. Unfortunately, the critics of the old and proponents of the new had a blind spot. This blind spot was a failure to recognize that providing social-emotional support to elementary and secondary school students is substantively different than providing such support to young or midlife adults entering a new profession. This is problematic because any instructional coaching process, no matter how clinical or scientific its approach, is limited by the interpersonal skill of the coach. The ability to provide specific feedback in a caring way that communicates the intentionality of the coach to be a helpful force is where the process flourishes or fails.

With the historical context established, one might ask, Where are we today? And where are we going in the years ahead with regard to the role of mentor teachers as instructional coaches?

WHERE WE ARE TODAY

Any discussion of the state of mentoring beginning teachers in U.S. schools must begin with the simple acknowledgment that we are in many different places at the same time. While the majority of states currently require entry-year programs and mentor teachers to support beginning teachers, there is no single model dominating the educational landscape. Simply put, there is significant diversity in entry-year programming from state to state and from school district to school district within any given state.

Five Critical Questions

Given this diversity, I pose the following five questions to provoke reflection on where your state or school district program is at the present time.

1. Has your entry-year program clarified the relationship between mentoring and coaching?

2. Has your entry-year program clarified the purpose of instructional coaching with regard to formative and summative assessment?

3. Does your entry-year program require mentors to complete a formal mentor training program that includes a focus on specific instructional coaching strategies?

4. Has your entry-year program selected a performance-based framework to focus the instructional coaching process?

5. Does your entry-year program encourage mentors to coach beginning teachers to employ developmentally appropriate and subject-specific pedagogies tied to the local or state standards for student performance?

These questions are specifically focused on the relationship between mentoring and instructional coaching and were not crafted to promote examination of the many other program qualities that could be explored. After restating each question I will describe how the question may serve as a place to begin thinking about contemporary practices as well as current trends and future trends.

Question 1. Has Your Entry-Year Program Clarified the Relationship Between Mentoring and Coaching?

For many people, coaching is a word that can carry considerable baggage. Depending on one's own experience as a coach, or as one who has been coached, that history may be positive or negative. For example, I often encounter prospective or practicing mentors who do not like to think of themselves as coaches because they view coaching as being an essentially directive process wherein someone in a position of authority tells a performer what to do or not to do. "It is not my job to tell a beginning teacher how to teach," they argue. Instead, they might add, "It is my job as a mentor to help them find their own way." Such perspectives often emerge from personal interpretations of the word *coach* and its relationship to the word *mentor*.

From my perspective, the very best mentors are good coaches, and the very best coaches are good mentors. I differentiate the two terms in the following way. To mentor another is to provide the help necessary for the protégé to find satisfaction and success in the field to which he or she aspires. To coach someone, in contrast, is to help the protégé acquire and refine the knowledge and skills required for enhanced performance in that field. To state it a different way, I might argue that the work of the mentor is more concerned with the holistic needs of the beginning teacher including social-emotional needs and personal concerns, while coaches are more concerned with technical proficiency. Anyone who has ever mentored, however, is likely to take issue with this distinction, arguing that good mentors must focus on helping novice teachers acquire technical proficiency. Similarly, anyone who has ever coached an athlete, actor, or musician will argue convincingly that good coaches must also be excellent motivators who know how to read and meet the personal needs and concerns of individual performers.

If you find the preceding discussion of the relationship between mentoring and coaching tedious or unnecessary, it may be because you have already struggled with these issues at a personal or program level. If that is the case, you have done some important work that hopefully has influenced your personal performance as a mentor or the direction and focus of your entry-year program. In contrast, if you found the discussion interesting or provocative it may suggest that there is still work to be done to clarify the roles and responsibilities of mentor teachers in your entry-year program. By the way, if it occurred to you that the very best classroom teachers mentor and coach their students every day, it may bring new and important insight to the word *mentor teacher*. This is one way to help resolve the dichotomy that I may have unintentionally created by proposing alternative definitions of *mentor* and *coach*.

In many ways, this same dichotomy is beautifully reconciled in the writings of Costa and Garmston (1994) and their work on cognitive coaching. In cognitive coaching the word *coach* does not mean "telling someone what to do" but instead refers to coaching as a "means of conveyance" or a manner of helping someone move from one place to another. In such an approach to coaching, the role of the mentor is to facilitate such movement by helping the valued person acquire the reflective skills and dispositions necessary for self-directed professional growth.

Definitions aside, a second problem that can seriously constrain mentor teachers in their role as instructional coaches is a failure to value observation as part of the coaching process. Imagine, if you will, a varsity volleyball coach who decides that the best way to help her players build their skills is to never watch them practice and never watch them play. Instead, she commits to a new coaching strategy she calls "locker room coaching." With this new approach, she meets daily with her team to give them instructions for practice and then waits for them to return to the locker room to report on their progress. She then uses these self-reports to plan strategy for the upcoming match. On game day, she gives a motivational talk in the locker room and describes what the team should do based on the information she has received after practices and on her own past experiences as a player. As the young women head out to the gym floor, she remains in the locker room anxiously waiting for the first game to end so that she can help the team make the necessary adjustments.

Unfortunately, this story too closely describes the work of many mentor teachers who limit themselves to a similar strategy I call "workroom coaching." Simply put, they rarely, if ever, see their beginning teachers perform. Instead, they rely on self-reports from the beginning teachers or on informal reports from colleagues. How can we help people improve their technical skills if we never see them perform in realistic conditions? The answer—obvious as it may be—reminds us of the importance of mentors placing themselves in authentic situations where they can observe their beginning teachers working under all of the conditions that make classroom teaching the complex enterprise that it is.

> Significant Trend: Over the next decade entry-year programs will place increasing emphasis on the role of mentors as instructional coaches, alleviating the current condition in many programs where mentors are not committed to, or prepared to, serve in such a capacity.

Question 2. Has Your Entry-Year Program Clarified the Purpose of Instructional Coaching With Regard to Formative and Summative Assessment?

Once a school or district commits to having mentor teachers serve as instructional coaches, it is imperative that program leaders work with mentor teachers to clarify the purpose of the coaching process. This is important because failure to clearly communicate that purpose inevitably leads to confusion at best and conflict at worst. The problem stems from the fact that once mentors fully commit to serving as instructional coaches and begin observing their beginning teachers in action, they naturally become involved in the assessment dimension of coaching. The potential for confusion and conflict increases in direct proportion to the lack of clarity mentors have about the differences between formative and summative assessment. For example, in a confidential helping-relationship program model, mentors must understand that any assessment data they collect are strictly formative in nature and are to be shared only with the beginning teacher in the context of the mentor relationship. In contrast, in a peer assistance and review program model, mentors and beginning teachers should both understand that performance assessment data collected in the coaching process can be both formative and summative and consequently may be used to inform decisions about retention or nonrenewal. The point here is not to suggest that one program model is preferable to another, but only to suggest that whatever the model is, it is essential that all parties involved, especially the beginning teacher, are fully informed as to how, with whom, and for what purposes information will be communicated. I share the following story to illustrate this point.

Consider the case of a first-year teacher named Ellen and her mentor Karen. Ellen and Karen are both middle school teachers who work in a district that recently established a formal mentor program that requires mentors to conduct quarterly observations of their beginning teachers. The guidelines for the new program place mentor teachers in the role of formative coaches who carry out their work in a confidential, helping relationship. The previous mentoring program was an informal one in which there was no requirement for conducting classroom observations of beginning teachers.

During the summer Karen attended a mentor training workshop now required by the district as part of their new program. Karen, like many of the other veteran teachers in attendance, had reservations about the new quarterly observation requirement, many of which were raised during the workshop. Because she was not comfortable with her new role as an instructional coach, and definitely not confident of her newly acquired classroom observation skills, Karen kept delaying her first visit to Ellen's classroom.

As the deadline for the first observation approached, she reluctantly informed Ellen that she needed to visit her classroom to conduct an *observation*. Within minutes of being informed of the impending observation, Ellen was hurriedly contacting other first-year teachers to find out if their mentors had been in to *evaluate* them. "Yes," they all reported with varying degrees of enthusiasm. Two of the entry-year teachers told Ellen not to worry, that it was just like when the principal evaluated them. This only made matters worse since Ellen had been very anxious during that experience. A large part of her anxiety stemmed from the fact that she was not comfortable with managing her students' behavior and feared her principal would rate her unsatisfactory in this performance area. Now she would have to repeat the experience with her mentor and possibly risk losing her respect. Ellen's only consolation as she prepared for Karen's visit was something she was pretty sure she heard during the new teacher orientation. She thought she remembered someone say that the relationship between the mentor and an entry-year teacher was confidential. This helped her relax somewhat because she felt like she had a new opportunity to make a fresh impression with Karen.

Unfortunately, on the day of Karen's observation things did not go well. Several students were not only rude and disrespectful of their classmates; they failed to respond to Ellen's efforts to alter their behavior. In the postobservation conference Karen was almost as nervous as Ellen but steadied herself by sticking with the conferencing strategies she had learned in the summer workshop. To both Karen's and Ellen's surprise, the conversation went well. Karen was pleased that Ellen was able to reflect on the class, acknowledge the problems, and openly seek suggestions for improvement. Ellen was pleased because she felt Karen accepted the issues she was facing as a normal part of the first-year experience. And she especially appreciated a self-disclosure by Karen about her own first-year struggles and a couple of solid suggestions for new strategies to try.

Later that afternoon, Karen had an impromptu hallway conversation with Mrs. Johnson, the building principal, in which she expressed relief that she had completed her first observation. When the principal asked what her impressions were, Karen promptly reported that she found Ellen to be a thoughtful planner and an organized manager of classroom resources and materials. "The main issue is discipline," she added. "I gave her a couple of new ideas to try and we agreed to meet after she tries them for a day or two."

The next morning, Ellen arrived at school feeling energized by her conference with Karen and ready to try out the new discipline strategies. Just as she was about to close her classroom door, however, she noticed Mrs. Johnson doing her morning walkabout and decided to delay for a few seconds to say good morning. After a quick and cordial exchange of greetings, Ellen started to close her door when Mrs. Johnson quickly added, "Good luck with those new behavior management ideas. I wish I had thought of them. They should help." Closing the door and facing her class, Ellen felt a rush of mixed emotions. Was she supposed to feel encouraged by Mrs. Johnson's final comments? If so, why instead was she feeling so discouraged and betrayed? The answers to these questions did not come easily to Ellen. All she knew was that Karen and Mrs. Johnson had been talking about her problems and that she could never trust Karen again.

Karen spent the next few months trying to figure out what happened to Ellen. She knew something had changed in their relationship. Ellen seemed cold, distant, and difficult to reach. Scheduling the next three conferences was like "pulling teeth," she complained to a fellow mentor who quickly agreed that the classroom observation thing was a bad idea. And if scheduling the observations was tough, the postconference dialogue was painfully strained. When Ellen failed to respond to Karen's reflective prompts she began to feel awkward and unsure of what to do. In the end, she found herself arriving at two conclusions. First, she was increasingly convinced that Ellen "wasn't cut out for teaching." Second, she decided that this would be her last experience as a mentor, at least as long as the district kept the quarterly observation requirement.

What is sad about the above story is not only that is it true but that it happens far more frequently than it should. By the way, I hope you agree that there were no villains here. Karen did not intend to provide Mrs. Johnson with a negative report on Ellen. And Mrs. Johnson was only trying to encourage Ellen with her hallway remarks. As for Ellen, she was only guilty of being a first-year teacher with strong needs for approval from authority and acceptance by her peers. The problem was, as is so often the case, not a failure to communicate but a failure to communicate clearly about the nature and purpose of the conversations that occur between mentors, entry-year teachers, and building principals working in a specific program context.

The purpose of the preceding story is not to suggest that mentors and principals should never communicate about the beginning teachers they are both seeking to support. This may or may not be appropriate depending on the program context. For example, in some programs beginning teachers are supported by a team of mentors that includes a building level and central office administrator. In such settings, beginning teachers are made aware that conversations about their progress will occur and can and likely will influence their summative assessment. Just as classroom teachers teach in a complex context, mentors carry out their mentoring and coaching efforts in an equally complex context. Good mentors understand that context and behave accordingly.

As a final note, I periodically hear mentor teachers complain that their beginning teachers do not understand how the entry-year program works with regard to such issues as were involved in the preceding case. Typically, they want to know why the director of human resources, or the building principal, or the head of the entry-year program has failed to communicate this information to the beginning teachers they are seeking to support. My response to such complaints is simple and consistent. No one is in a better or more opportune position to do this work than the mentor teacher. Yes, it would be most helpful if other members of the school community would speak with a common and clear voice, and ideally they will. Nonetheless, it is one of the first and most basic responsibilities of the mentor to make sure that beginning teachers clearly understand the nature and purpose of the mentoring relationships they are about to enter. The earlier this is done in the relationship, the better. While it is important for mentors to craft their own approach to this initial conversation, consider the following message that Karen might have communicated to Ellen in one of their first meetings. Perhaps such a message would have served Karen as much as Ellen, helping her to remember a promise to maintain the confidential nature of their relationship:

> Ellen, I am really excited about having the opportunity to work with you. This is my first time being a formal mentor so we are both going to be learning a lot this year. Before we get started, I want you to understand a couple of important things. First, I want you to know that I am not going to be evaluating you. That is not my job. That is the principal's job and I am going to leave that job to her. Please know that I will not be talking to her about you. In fact, I won't even be sharing the positive things that I am sure I will want to share with her. Anything that you and I talk about will be confidential, OK? Second, I want you to know how much I am looking forward to having good conversations with you about teaching and learning. In fact, I hope that together we can be students of teaching and learning this year.

Significant Trend: Over the next decade, entry-year programs will remain diverse with regard to the role of mentor teachers as formative coaches or summative assessors. The vast majority of programs, however, will focus on formative coaching in the context of a one-to-one or team-based mentoring model.

Question 3. Does Your Entry-Year Program Require Mentors to Complete a Formal Mentor Training Program That Includes a Focus on Specific Instructional Coaching Strategies?

Schools or school districts that encourage or require mentor teachers to serve as instructional coaches have a responsibility to provide relevant professional development experiences to support that role. Prior to becoming a university professor in the early 1990s, I was a high school teacher for eighteen years. During that time, the progressive and respected school district in which I taught had no mentoring program. This is not a criticism, but simply a reminder of where many school districts were during that time period. During those years as a high school teacher, I supervised many student teachers from local universities. As I look back on those experiences, I realize that I was performing that role with virtually no relevant training. I had no understanding of supervisory theories or processes, no training in effective feedback and conferencing methods, and certainly no knowledge of alternate methods of classroom observation.

Instead, I flew by the seat of my proverbial pants, relying primarily on my interpersonal intuition and my own beliefs about what constituted good teaching. I am not going to denigrate myself here with comments about how I hope I did no harm to those young teachers. In reality, I probably did an adequate job.

What is clear now is that I could have done a much better job if I had some preparation for the role. For example, I wish that I understood then the relationship between description, interpretation, and judgment in the coaching process. My observation strategy was crude at best and was created with no consideration of the important differences between those processes. My approach was to draw a vertical line down a piece of paper creating two columns, one which I labeled with a plus sign and the other with a minus sign. Observing student teachers, I would record their teaching behaviors in what I thought was the appropriate column. In general, the things that went in the plus column were those things I liked and would likely do myself. In contrast, the minus column was reserved for behaviors I did not like and wouldn't employ in my own teaching. Of course, after collecting and organizing such data, I immediately worried about how I would communicate any bad news. Typically, I reverted to what I later heard someone describe as the "positive, positive, BUT negative feedback model." Using this model, my feedback might have sounded something like this: "Well, Jerry, you seem to have established good rapport with the class and I was impressed with how well behaved the students were, *BUT* you need to work on giving clear instructions, as some students didn't seem to understand the assignment."

Again, one might argue that there is nothing wrong with this approach. After all, I was a veteran teacher supervising a student teacher, not mentoring a first-year teacher. And, after all, as a veteran teacher I should have a good sense of what works and doesn't work in the classroom. Again, I don't reject such thinking as much as I now see the limitations of the approach. For example, such an approach places the primary responsibility for thinking about the quality of the lesson on the observer rather than on the novice teacher. In addition, my two-column data collection method caused me to leap to interpretation and judgment because I wasn't describing what I saw but rather was categorizing it as positive or negative. As Glickman (1985) points out, I was falling into the "interpretation trap." To make matters worse, I wasn't even aware I had fallen.

Most of us can remember being in a situation where someone was providing us with feedback on our performance and we quickly began to feel that we were being unfairly judged based on that person's own sense of what he or she considered to be good teaching. Perhaps you can remember how quickly you may have found yourself going into a defensive position from which you felt a need to provide counter-evidence or personal interpretations. Once again, calling on the work of Glickman, I had no framework for thinking about the developmental nature of the coaching process and how I, as a supervising teacher, could adjust my communication behaviors to meet the developmental needs of the student teacher I was endeavoring to help. From my perspective, asking mentor teachers to serve as instructional coaches for beginning teachers without introducing them to the prerequisite theories, models, and best practices that inform the coaching process is unfair at best, and malpractice at worst.

In the preceding paragraphs I discussed the coaching process in a way that may have left the impression that the primary and preferred method of coaching a new teacher involves formal observation of the beginning teacher's classroom. In fact, that is not the case. For example, I believe that some of the most powerful coaching opportunities occur in the context of a shared experience in which both mentor and beginning teacher engage in collaborative planning and teaching. Such experiences have the effect of placing mentors in a position where they can engage simultaneously in the process of observing and coaching. Consequently, mentoring teams should be strongly encouraged to engage in some kind of collaborative teaching experience. Coaching in a coteaching context is especially powerful because dialogue is often more focused on student learning than on teacher performance. In addition, such experiences can go a long way toward building a positive mentoring relationship based on open communication and mutual respect. This is particularly true if mentors allow their beginning teachers to be full and contributing partners in the planning and instructional processes.

Unfortunately, far too many beginning teachers are not provided with such opportunities because mentors are not encouraged or supported to employ this method of coaching. Even when they are encouraged, many mentors typically resist the idea, pointing out that their beginning teacher does not teach the same subject matter or grade level or, more frequently, that they do not have the time for such an initiative. Regarding time, it is hard to imagine a better use of a mentor's time. Regarding the grade level or subject matter excuse, a creative disposition is required. Why, for example, can't a sixth-grade mentor engage his students in studying a topic or conducting a project with a beginning teacher's fourth-grade class? For that matter, why can't a beginning high school social studies teacher and her English department mentor develop an integrated unit on some topic of common interest or importance?

Significant Trend: Over the next decade many entry-year programs will require mentor teachers to complete a formal mentor training program that introduces diverse methods of instructional coaching that include opportunities for mentors and beginning teachers to work in collaborative planning and teaching environments.

Question 4. Has Your Entry-Year Program
Selected a Performance-Based Framework
to Focus the Instructional Coaching Process?

One of the most helpful decisions the leaders of a school-based or districtwide mentoring program can make is to adopt a framework to focus the coaching process. Such frameworks clearly define good teaching with rubrics grounded in the effective teaching and best practices research. In a state where new standards for licensing beginning teachers have been established, such standards might logically provide the framework. For example, the INTASC Principles (Interstate New Teacher Assessment and Support Consortium, 1992), PRAXIS III Classroom Performance Criteria (Educational Testing Service, 2001), and Enhancing Professional Practice Components (Danielson, 1996) represent excellent examples of such frameworks.

Training mentor teachers to focus their coaching efforts on a standards-based framework has numerous advantages. First, when mentors collect and share data on a specific dimension of teaching articulated as a performance standard in a state or national framework, beginning teachers are less likely to feel that mentors are focusing on arbitrary topics of personal interest or preference. Second, using such standards has the effect of helping veteran and beginning teachers build a common professional language to guide their reflections and communications. Third, and perhaps most important, using such a framework encourages mentors and beginning teachers to focus on specific aspects of teaching that are empirically tied to student learning.

In training mentor teachers, I frequently use a list of "100 Things a Mentor Teacher Might Do" (Rowley, 2000, pp. 51–53) to promote reflection and dialogue on the work of mentor teachers. I give the prospective mentors approximately five minutes to scan the list and then circle any items that they do not understand or do not agree with. One of the ideas I wrote for the list simply says "use research-based findings on effective teaching to guide classroom observation." In almost every workshop this item makes the top-five list of circled items. In many cases, this occurs in a state that has adopted standards for the licensing of beginning teachers. Unfortunately, it is not clear to many mentors that such standards are based on research findings that constitute the knowledge base for their profession.

Over the past decade, several states have developed new protocols for the licensing of beginning teachers and created complementary entry-year programs specifically designed to support new teachers in successfully completing the licensure process. Such programs represent a significant opportunity for focusing the coaching process on research-based understandings of what constitutes effective teaching. The state of Ohio, for example, has adopted the PRAXIS III Beginning Teacher Assessment Program as the licensure test and simultaneously developed a statewide entry-year program model as well. In this case, every beginning teacher is required to be supported by a trained mentor who has developed in-depth knowledge of the nineteen PRAXIS III performance standards and specific skill in coaching beginning teachers. This initiative has had a profound impact on the quality of entry-year programs across the state. Not only has it significantly advanced the conception of the role of mentor as instructional coach, but it has focused the coaching process on a four-domain framework for teaching that helps beginning teachers develop a cognitive map to guide their personal reflections and mentoring conversations.

Having supported numerous school districts in preparing for the new Ohio Entry-Year Program, which became operational in the 2002–2003 academic year, I felt that I learned quite a lot about the potential of the program to impact the performance of beginning teachers. Nothing, however, made the power of the program as clear as the personal experience with my son Jon, who at the time of this writing was completing his first year as a third-grade teacher. As the school year progressed, I tried, on a couple of occasions, to initiate a conversation about how he was feeling about the PRAXIS III assessment. Did he feel prepared? Was his mentor being helpful? Was there anything Dad could do to help? None of these conversations really got off the ground, and they usually ended with a "Thanks Dad, but it's not that big a deal." Not that big a deal? It seemed pretty big to me, who silently worried if my own son was going to fall victim to the overconfidence factor that I had warned so many other beginning and mentor teachers about.

One day in early March, I received a call from Jon, who wanted to let me know that his state assessor had called, and that the date for his assessment visit had been set. He also wanted to know if we could talk sometime. "Sure," I said, relieved that there was some evidence he was beginning to feel the pressure. When we did meet a couple of days later, I discovered that he really did not need my help at all. Well, maybe like most first-year teachers he needed some additional affirmation. The truth was, he was ready. He knew the PRAXIS III framework, which he had studied and reflected on throughout his university preparation, and he was applying that knowledge in his daily practice. His student teaching evaluation had been based on the same framework, and his mentor teacher had been using it to guide her coaching as well. As we sat at the kitchen table that night and talked about teaching and learning using the common language we both had acquired through our respective studies of the PRAXIS III framework, I could not avoid one stark realization. He was far more sophisticated in his professional thinking than I had been in my own first year of teaching. But then, he had a powerful conceptual framework to guide his thinking and a caring and committed mentor dedicated to her role as an instructional coach.

Significant Trend: Over the next decade, entry-year programs will increasingly focus the work of mentors and beginning teachers on a framework for teaching that includes clearly articulated rubrics for defining effective practices.

Question 5. Does Your Entry-Year Program Encourage Mentors to Coach Beginning Teachers to Employ Developmentally Appropriate and Subject-Specific Pedagogies Tied to the Local or State Standards for Student Performance?

One of the most significant changes in educational policy and practice over the past twenty years has been the emphasis on utilizing standardized tests as a measure of student achievement and school improvement. Today, most states have developed competency-based curriculum models that clearly define student performance standards by grade level and subject matter. In many of those states, there are high-stakes implications for both poorly performing and high-performing districts. Consequently, school administrators, teachers, and curriculum leaders are dedicating significant resources in an effort to help teachers acquire or refine specific teaching strategies and practices that are positively linked to student learning. Mentor teachers can and should play a major role in such efforts by focusing their coaching efforts on helping beginning teachers develop their skill in using such practices. Engaging mentor teachers in this effort presents both an opportunity and a challenge. The inherent opportunity is the chance to help mentoring programs reach their fullest potential by assisting novice teachers in providing the best possible instruction for their students. At the same time, fulfilling that dream is challenging because it requires mentors to fully embrace the role of instructional coach. For schools and districts where instructional coaching has been a part of the school culture, the challenge will be more easily met. Those that lack such a history will have a longer and more difficult road to travel. This insight was made especially clear as I recently had the opportunity to observe two entry-year programs at opposite ends of this continuum.

In the first district, which had a long history of quality entry-year programming, I sat in on a mentor committee meeting where the topic of conversation was how to improve the quarterly meetings that all beginning and mentor teachers were required to attend as part of their entry-year experience. Historically, these meetings had focused on the common problems and concerns of beginning teachers, covering such diverse topics as classroom management, student motivation, and parent conferencing. The sessions were typically presented to all beginning teachers from across the district. Because the audience was so diverse, presenters frequently struggled to make the content meaningful to all of the teachers. Nonetheless, the sessions were generally well received and continued in their original format for nearly a decade.

Now, a new proposal was on the table. The suggestion was to replace dealing with the traditional generic topics for a pre-K–12 audience with separate meetings for elementary, middle, and high school teachers. Those meetings would focus on specific instructional strategies presented by teachers with a history of successfully implementing them in their class-rooms. The more generic topics, it was argued, while still important, could be dealt with more effectively by mentors and beginning teachers working in their personal relationship and addressing issues on an as-needed basis. After some thoughtful dialogue, the new proposal was adopted and plan-ning for the new program format initiated. In the end, what carried the day and was most impressive to me was that the decision was made because the participating mentors and administrators agreed that this was an opportunity for veteran and beginning teachers to be engaged in a shared learning experience where the focus was on student learning. This was not an indictment of past practices, but rather an affirmation that programs, like people, grow and change with time.

In contrast, consider my experience consulting with a newly formed mentor committee that, while well intentioned, was focused on a far dif-ferent set of issues. In this meeting, teachers and administrators struggled with a host of program issues. Clearly, however, the most contentious issue was whether mentors should be required to observe their beginning teachers. This new responsibility being promoted by the district's curricu-lum director was meeting with significant opposition by a couple of veteran teachers who argued passionately that mentors should not be involved in the evaluation of beginning teachers. When I explained that mentors would conduct the classroom observations only to provide for-mative help, and would not be involved in the summative evaluation process, I was asked, who would make sure that policy was enforced. Clearly, there was much work to be done.

> Significant Trend: Over the next decade, quality entry-year programs will increasingly focus the instructional coaching of mentor teachers on helping beginning teachers develop competency in employing the generic and subject-specific pedagogies most clearly tied to student learning.

WHERE WE ARE GOING AND WHY

Hopefully, the five questions just posed and discussed have been helpful tools for analyzing the current state of your personal practice as a mentor teacher, or for reflecting on your entry-year program that provides the context in which mentor and beginning teachers carry our their important work. In closing, I would like to share a few additional thoughts based on my own sense of where we are going and why with regard to the mentoring and coaching of beginning teachers.

First, I believe that the next decade will see increased uniformity in entry-year programs as more and more schools, school districts, and states fully embrace the role of mentor teachers as instructional coaches. In other words, ten years from now I hope that a review of the five questions posed in this chapter might more often serve as affirmations of progress made than as guideposts for change.

Second, I am hopeful that the current discussions of schools as learning communities will lead to transformative changes that transcend the rhetoric to be actualized in the form of true communities of practice in which all teachers share the responsibility for the mentoring and coaching of beginning teachers.

Several years ago, Brother Raymond Fitz, then president of the University of Dayton, made a speech to the faculty that I found particularly memorable. In that speech he spoke of the idea of the university as a conversation. By this he meant that, at its best, a university is defined by the quality of dialogue between and among professors and students in common pursuit of the answers to life's most compelling questions and humankind's most troubling problems. Similarly, the quality of a mentoring relationship can only be as good as the quality of the conversation that connects the mentor and beginning teacher. If the conversation is superficial and focused on the trivial, so likely will be the relationship. If, by contrast, the conversation is deep and focused on the meaningful, so likely will be the relationship. A mentoring relationship or program, at its best, finds mentor and beginning teachers in common pursuit of answers to our profession's most compelling questions and solutions to its most troubling problems. These, of course, are the questions and problems that inevitably focus on student learning and what we as teachers can do to motivate and support that learning. Perhaps the most significant challenge for any mentor teacher is to help beginning teachers join that conversation, which hopefully will sustain and inspire them throughout their teaching lives. To meet that challenge, we will need dedicated veteran teachers who fully embrace the complementary roles of caring mentor and committed coach.

REFLECTIONS AND APPLICATIONS

This chapter asks and proposes answers to five questions that define the role of mentor teacher as instructional coach. Exercise 7.1 asks you to reflect on how your mentoring program addresses these critical issues, and then, how applying the material in the chapter might improve your program.

Exercise 7.1 Five Critical Coaching Issues

Directions: Below, in column 1, are the five issues posed as questions in this chapter. In the box to the right of each item, reflect on how that question is addressed in your mentoring program. In the next box, speculate how, by applying material from this chapter, you might be able to provide a more meaningful answer to each question in the future.

Critical Issue	How Applied	Potential Enhancement
Clear relationship between mentoring and coaching		
Clear purpose of instructional coaching with regard to formative and summative assessment		
Mentor training program that includes a focus on specific instructional coaching strategies		
Performance-based framework to focus the instructional coaching process		
Beginning teachers coached to employ developmentally appropriate and subject-specific pedagogies tied to the local or state standards for student performance		

REFERENCES

Costa, A., & Garmston, R. (1994). *Cognitive coaching: A foundation for renaissance schools.* Norwood, MA: Christopher-Gordon.

Danielson, C. (1996). *Enhancing professional practice: A framework for teaching.* Alexandria, VA: Association for Supervision and Curriculum Development.

Educational Testing Service. (2001). *Praxis III: Classroom performance assessments orientation guide.* Princeton, NJ: Author.

Glickman, C. (1985). *Supervision of instruction: A developmental approach.* Boston: Allyn & Bacon.

Interstate New Teacher Assessment and Support Consortium. (1992). *Model standards for beginning teacher licensing, assessment and development: A resource for state dialogue.* Washington, DC: Council of Chief State School Officers.

Rowley, J. B. (1999). The good mentor. *Educational Leadership, 56*(8), 20–22.

Rowley, J. B. (2000). *High-performance mentoring: A multimedia program for training mentor teachers.* Thousand Oaks, CA: Corwin.

8

Mentoring

A Matter of Time and Timing

Barry Sweeny

Fundamentally, effective induction and mentoring are subversive activities. This is true because such teacher support activities are really about improving the professional practices of all teachers, increasing the resulting levels of student learning and success, and transforming the nature and extent of professional dialogue among educators about teacher and student performance. When induction and mentoring are effective, these three results are achieved and the prior norms and behaviors of staff and students in a school are changed.

If the people who lead and participate in induction and mentoring programs are to succeed in bringing about these desired improvements, they must consciously understand their work as seeking the transformation of the current culture to a new, more collaborative one, and of redefining the use of professional time. These are completely interdependent issues because collaboration takes time. In a traditional school, almost all the time is focused on students. In an improving school and a true learning community, the time available is shared between teacher and student learning because the former is understood as a prerequisite to the latter. The induction and mentoring work must be consciously planned as a counterculture effort because the prevailing culture and practices within a school will resist, even sabotage, programs and behaviors which run counter to the norm. If understood as subversive, induction and mentoring efforts can be designed to be "magnetic" and attractive to others because they enable a staff and students to succeed at the very things for which they come to school.

Effective induction and mentoring efforts recognize these ideas. Given that teacher development is a necessary prerequisite to improved student development, rather than trying to just find the time among all the other demands of the school day and year, effective programs will intentionally take on the challenges of providing the time and appropriate timing for powerful professional support of teacher learning and growth. The program's activities will be designed to make the time available and not leave it to teachers to steal time from kids whenever they can. Essentially, induction and mentoring will not be just an effort to help new teachers. Mentoring and induction will also be used to support the cultural changes educators know are needed for increased teacher and student performance to occur. This means that induction and mentoring will be designed and conducted as integral strategies which are aligned with the school's improvement goals and plans. When that happens, no one will perceive induction and mentoring as a frill which is nice to include when we can find the resources and time. The resources and time are made available because mentoring is viewed as critical to achieving the school's vision.

On the other hand, induction and mentoring programs which do not understand the subversive nature of the task will probably leave undone those things that are necessary to succeed in a countercultural activity. This includes things such as training mentors in how to respond positively to negative statements which can be made by those not in the program. When not viewed as a counterculture effort, the powerful potential of the program will likely be held hostage by the other demands for professional time, and the extended time needed for effective developmental efforts will not be made available. When that happens, time-intensive, developmental programs like effective mentoring will be less than effective and can become victims of budget cutting or other negative forces.

Helping readers avoid such an outcome is the purpose of this chapter. In it you will learn both strategies to make the time for effective mentoring and how to time the mentoring and induction support so they are as effective as possible.

THE BASIC COMMITMENT TO EFFECTIVENESS

The root of success in the challenges laid out in this chapter's introduction is a commitment to effectiveness in induction and mentoring program activities rather than merely conducting those activities. As an example, program leaders and trainers should not be content with providing mentor training. The goal should be the ongoing development and improvement of mentor training, such that mentors are increasingly more effective and report greater success in the use of the small amount of time they can give to mentoring. In other words, mentor training should effectively function as a strategy for accomplishment of the program's purpose.

To increase mentor effectiveness and mentor feelings that time invested is productive, mentor training must

- Train mentors in how to most effectively use the mentoring time they can give
- Provide sufficient time for guided, coached practice of essential mentoring strategies
- Be provided at a time when mentors are ready to learn what the training offers
- Include sufficient time for follow-up support and problem-solving activities, in both individual and group contexts

At its most general level, effectiveness is about providing the time learning takes and timing the provision of the help to the developmental readiness of the learner.

Essentially, then, the time and timing issues are about a commitment to conducting the program according to those practices of effective human development which we all know are needed for growth to occur. I have heard it said that we need to be careful if we want mentoring in the worst way, since we might compromise too much and get it that way. Instead, we must commit to doing induction activities, including mentoring, according to the principles of effective staff development, or, I suggest, we should consider not doing them at all.

Providing mentoring and induction which are less than what we know to be effective

- Inadequately prepares and supports people during the necessary transitions in practice
- Results in little or no improvement since it leaves people to struggle on their own to grow and change
- Will be perceived as not worth the time it takes
- Risks loss of teacher and administrator commitment and good will toward the program
- Presents mentoring and induction as just like all other ill-conceived, unrealistic, and inadequately supported staff development activities

Conversely, using effective practices which provide sufficient time, adequate preparation and support in effectively using that time, and a model of and training in how to assess the timing for providing induction and mentoring support will result in greater transformation of practice and results. In short, the fastest way for induction and mentoring to deliver increased teacher and student performance is to do mentoring and induction right the first time.

Deciding the Timing of the Assistance

Humans are complex, which is why teaching them well is complex. Therefore, learning how to teach well is also complex. Since these statements are true, we can assume that teaching others how to teach in ways that result in high levels of student performance cannot be very simple. Why then would we expect effective induction and mentoring of novice teachers to be simple? It is not. It is a rich and complex professional practice with its own knowledge base and best practices.

One of those best practices is selecting when to provide assistance and knowing what assistance to provide. Just like in teaching, effective induction and mentoring support is a matter of timing. Doing effective practices at the wrong time is not effective. In effective induction programs, mentors match the extent and nature of their support to each protégé's needs and professional maturity.

How does a mentor or mentoring and induction program learn how to provide just what is needed exactly when it is needed?

1. Make the initial program decisions using the guidance of a mentoring expert.

2. Provide support which is aligned with the developmental stages of novice teachers.

3. Treat individuals individually.

Strategy 1

The best solution initially is to access and rely on the induction and mentoring knowledge base and guidance available from expert practitioners—mentoring for induction and mentor programs and leaders. Such an expert can help you plan activities that are designed more strategically to deliver what is needed and to achieve these results sooner than is possible by trial-and-error learning. An expert can also help you assess needs, plan programs to effectively address those needs, and avoid the many pitfalls inherent in such a complex and sophisticated process. I serve in this role frequently and have seen many times the differences in program and mentoring effectiveness that can be attained when programs and mentors are themselves mentored (Sweeny, 2001). However, eventually, you have to become expert enough to do these things independently and effectively.

Strategy 2

Provide support and guidance which are aligned with the developmental stages of novice teachers. There is a clear need for induction programs and mentoring practices to be designed and delivered based on a conceptual framework for novice teacher development. It makes sense. If your program aims to develop teachers, what teacher development model is the basis for your planning and action? The model of teacher development I recommend is the Stages of Concern portion of the concerns-based adoption model (CBAM). I have used this model to guide all kinds of mentoring and induction planning as well as other forms of staff development since 1987. It is the most effective model for such planning that I have seen.

Essentially, the Stages of Concern are eight phases through which developing people (protégés, mentors, students, etc.) must move. These stages are as follows:

8. Refocusing

7. Collaboration

6. Consequence

5. Routine management

4. Mechanical management

3. Personal

2. Information

1. Awareness

Although a thorough discussion of the CBAM is not appropriate for this chapter, readers with such an interest can access that information in a great little book, *Taking Charge of Change* (Hord, Rutherford, Huling-Austin, & Hall, 1987). Application of this model for assessing and addressing new teacher needs includes both the induction program level and the mentoring practice level.

At the induction and mentoring program level, the Stages of Concern are used to

1. Frame items for a novice teacher or mentor needs-assessment instrument for topics in which the program expects training will be needed

2. Display needs assessment data to reveal which topics are perceived as needed (readiness to learn)

3. Display needs assessment data to reveal the level of prior knowledge and experience or skill for each of the possible training topics

4. Reach conclusions about the varied needs of individuals for learning in the topic

5. Reach conclusions about the design of training and other staff development for clusters of participants with similar needs

6. Assess the extent of growth on the Stages of Concern model attained after and as a result of the training

7. Plan the follow-up activities after training such as support and problem-solving groups

An example of this application of the CBAM is its use as a new teacher classroom management training strategy. A very quick, one-response, one-page survey, such as the following example, is sent to protégés in advance of the training or given to them at a previous training session or meeting.

When you think about your knowledge and skill in classroom management, which ONE response below best indicates your most immediate concern or need?

1. I am not sure what effective classroom management really is.

2. I need to know more about the factors that lead to effective classroom management.

3. I need to know how to plan for more effective class management in my room.

4. I need help solving class management problems so I can become a more effective teacher.

5. I have good class management on most days but I wonder if what I do can be improved so kids can accomplish and learn more.

6. I'd like to share what I know and learn from a teacher who is very good at class management.

One caution: The data from such a survey indicate novice teacher perceptions of their needs. Remember, however, that there are things they don't yet know they don't know.

The responses reflect each of the CBAM Stages of Concern so that program planners can easily determine how many of the participants are at each of the stages. As an example, the trainers decide that two training sessions need to be offered since the data show learners are in two groups: one group is at a stage where information and personal planning are the focus of needs has and the other group has greater experience and only needs to problem solve specific situations and seek the advice of colleagues.

At the end of the training sessions, the trainers give back each participant's survey and they each re-mark them, showing the level of concern they have at the end of the training and their need for any ongoing training, follow-up, or support. Finally, the program uses the pre-post data to demonstrate the amount of growth the program causes, to guide program revisions, and to assess increased impact when program changes are made.

The Stages of Concern are also used at the level of individual mentoring practice. (Note the parallels to the program applications.)

1. Frame questions for a novice teacher to allow the mentor to assess protégé needs for learning in specific topics.

2. Provide the mentor with data about what the protégé perceives are needed topics for learning (readiness).

3. Provide the mentor with data about the level of the protégé's prior knowledge and experience or skill for each of the possible mentoring topics.

4. Guide the mentor in designing mentoring that is appropriate to the protégé's development and readiness to learn.

5. Help a mentor assess the extent of protégé growth attained as a result of mentoring.

6. Guide the mentor in the design and planning of the timing for follow-up support activities.

7. Alert the mentor to protégé readiness for new challenges and learning in new areas.

An example of this CBAM application is a mentor whose protégé has just attended the induction program training on class management. The trainers provide the mentor with the posttraining data on the protégé's stage of concern for the topic so the mentor can provide individualized follow-up support. Data may show, for example, the protégé is ready to move from the personal level (planning for implementation) to the lower of the two management levels, that of mechanical practice.

The mentor analyzes this data and realizes the protégé will be struggling to implement strategies which will take time to master and perform consistently. The mentor meets with the protégé to review the class management plan the protégé developed in the induction program training.

The mentor's questions help the protégé anticipate potential stumbling blocks in implementing the plan, consider alternative actions for use if elements of the plan are not successful, and plan how to assess in-process whether the class management plan is working and when to shift to the alternative strategies. Essentially, the mentor's experience frames the questions and models for the novice the kinds of questions that expert teachers ask themselves. The open-ended nature of the questions allows the protégé to make the analysis and decisions, to do all the learning, and to own the alternative plan.

By using the CBAM Stages of Concern to guide the mentoring, the mentor's actions target exactly what the protégé needs to learn, the protégé grows, and the success of the implementation of plans is increased. Minimum time is needed to act so effectively, and teacher time is respected, not wasted. Although not specifically about time, these are both examples of how effective practices by induction programs and mentors can actually address and reduce protégé and mentor concerns about the time needed for effective novice teacher support.

In fact, when most people express concerns about the time needed for induction and mentoring, what they are really saying is that they do not perceive that the activities are worth the time they take. In both of the previous examples, the timing of support targets readiness to learn because it is based on assessment of prior knowledge and experience. This is crucial because providing effective support saves time by making the best use of the time that is available. Not only are participants effectively helped, but they also discover the program's commitment to respect their time by making sure that training and mentoring are on-target and worth attending.

Strategy 3

This strategy asserts that differentiated learning strategies be used to design and deliver staff development. Primarily, it is necessary for induction and mentoring programs and practices to be based on differentiated learning strategies because they work. People are individual and can only grow when their individual needs are met and learning assistance is designed for them as individuals. The research on which the CBAM Stages of Concern was based indicates that individuals must move at their own rate of learning, must adapt practices to their own unique strengths and settings, and must have individual coaching and mentoring to help them through and hold them accountable for that process of adaptation. We need to treat individuals individually because that is how learning works.

However, we do not always need to provide individual, one-on-one support to treat individuals individually. For example, an individual protégé's level of development is not necessarily unique. If we have the data to clearly show where in a process of development a person is, and other persons are at that same stage, we can provide group training, or a mentor can provide group mentoring and still give all involved exactly what they need. The only caution is to provide support at the group level when we are sure that everyone in the group has the same needs and readiness for learning in a given topic. If we use the applications of the Stages of Concern described above, we will have the data we need to determine just what is appropriate, when it is appropriate, and how to provide what is most effective.

We also need to use differentiated learning strategies in staff development because programs and mentors need to model exactly what it is we expect novice teachers to do in their classrooms. We need to provide such models

- So novices can see exactly what excellent practice looks like.
- So the training and support we provide is the best it can be, saving rather than wasting time.
- So the mentoring and induction programs have the credibility and moral authority to expect novices to meet expectations for individualizing student instruction and support. How can we ask novices to use practices which we have not held ourselves accountable to use?

FINDING OR MAKING THE TIME FOR INDUCTION AND MENTORING

An earlier statement in this chapter asserted that effective mentoring and induction programs make time for mentoring and aren't content to just try and find the time needed. Of course, both making time and finding time are useful strategies.

Making Time for Mentoring

The first step in every effective problem-solving process is identifying the real problem to be solved. When it comes to the challenge of providing the time for effective induction and mentoring, the true problem is often really not the lack of time. When the challenge of time for induction and mentoring is discussed, we discover the real problem is usually unstated or unconsciously held priorities for what people do with the time they already have. The competition for scarce time creates the challenge. An example of this is a mentor who professes to value observation, data collection, and coaching for the instructional improvement of novice teachers but who rarely schedules the time to provide a novice with that support.

It may be that the mentor conceptually accepts instructional coaching but has never received any coaching and so has never had the opportunity to personally discover the impact of effective coaching. In such a case, the profession of support for coaching suggests a priority, but the lack of making the time to actually coach suggests that the mentor's own instruction of children has a higher priority. There are two approaches for dealing with such conflicts of priorities.

Approach A: Collection and Discussion of Research Which Demonstrates the Greater Impact of the Innovation Over the Traditional Method

This approach works especially well if one can present specific local data rather than general data or data from elsewhere. Therefore, an excellent follow-up to the discussion of research on more effective practice is an invitation and opportunity to try the innovation so that local data can be collected and the innovation proven or disproven in the local setting. An example of this is a mentor who begins to provide increased time for coaching of a protégé after colleagues report how much fun and how valuable coaching has been for themselves and their protégés.

Approach B: Provide the Mentor With a Personal Experience of Benefiting From the Innovation and Then a Facilitated Opportunity to Debrief What Was Learned, Why It Was Learned, and How That Learning Could Benefit Others

An example of this method is mentors who receive mentoring from the coordinator of a mentoring program. Not only will the mentors gain a better understanding of just what effective mentoring is like and how to do it, but the debriefing of that experience can also prompt the mentors to plan how to provide such a powerful learning experience for their own protégés.

Of these two approaches, the latter is more personal, and therefore more powerful a force for revision of priorities. Both approaches work because they take away a person's excuses for not doing the better practice.

Finding the Funding to Make the Time

One often-used excuse for the lack of time for induction and mentoring is the lack of funding to pay substitutes and create release time for mentors and protégés to meet during the school day. Be cautious here, for this excuse can mask the real issue, which may be the belief that children's learning time is more important than adult learning time. Why else do teachers feel guilty when away from school at professional growth activities? The statement made earlier that teacher learning is the prerequisite for improved student learning is the best answer for this concern.

When lack of funds to buy mentoring time is really the problem, there are several highly effective strategies that can be adopted.

Strategy 1: Use local data to demonstrate that it costs less to provide adequate time for mentoring than it does to provide inadequate mentoring time.

Strategy 2: Describe for decision makers the nonfinancial costs of teacher attrition.

Strategy 3: Use the money saved by Strategy 1 for more productive and cost-effective methods of making time.

Strategy 4: Think outside the "time box."

Strategy 5: Assemble several funding pieces from other staff development budgets to create a new full-time mentoring role.

Strategy 6: Demonstrate that providing the time for effective mentoring is worth it.

Here are the details for implementing each of these strategies:

Strategy 1: Use Local Teacher Attrition Data to Demonstrate That It Costs Less to Provide Adequate Time for Mentoring Support Than It Does to Provide Inadequate Mentoring Time

This strategy involves determining your local district's real cost of teacher attrition, which is a hidden, annual waste of money, and then providing proof that, when adequately funded, your mentoring and induction program can and does save the largest part of that money by dramatically reducing teacher attrition. Here are the steps:

1. Start by working with your director of human relations or personnel to chart the actual number of teachers who left the school district, for whatever reason, over at least the last three to five years. Build a chart that presents these numbers categorized by reason, such as retirement, spouse got a different job requiring a move, better salary elsewhere, difficulty with supervisor, left teaching career, and so on.

2. Total up the people who left for reasons which the school district cannot control, such as retirement and spouse getting a new job.

3. Total up those who left for reasons the district might have been able to influence.

4. Estimate the percentage of each of these two groups from the total of all those who left.

5. List all the costs to the district for recruiting, signing, orienting, and training new employees for their first year of employment.

6. Divide the costs to the district by the number of people leaving found in Step 3 to arrive at the cost per teacher of attrition after the first year.

7. Estimate the current cost per novice teacher for your mentoring and induction program. Then estimate the cost of the programs if you were able to provide the time and other effectiveness elements you'd like to provide your new teachers.

8. Compare the costs of teacher attrition per person with the per person cost of effective mentoring and induction support. You may be surprised. Usually the cost of adequately supporting people (doing it right) is far less than the cost of teacher attrition (doing it wrong).

9. Seek funding to conduct a teacher retention experiment. Ask for adequate funding for support of new teachers for two to three years, or for a segment of the new teachers you hire, such as two or three each from elementary, middle, and high school. Document what it takes to provide appropriate levels of new teacher support and collect the data on what happens to the levels of teacher retention each year in those places. Keep in mind that 100 percent retention is not desirable, as not all persons who go into teaching should be teachers. A very attainable goal, however, is 95 to 96 percent retention.

If you'd like an example of this strategy in action, read the Texas State Board for Educator Certification (2000) "Cost of Attrition" research study. Essentially, this study found that the state of Texas was spending much more on replacing teachers than a good statewide induction and mentoring effort would have cost. The conclusion is, "It costs less to do it right!" My analysis of this suggests that every district already has and spends the money on teacher attrition each year that it should invest in teacher retention through adequate induction and mentoring programming. Your district does have more than the money you need to provide the program your novice teachers deserve.

Strategy 2: Describe the Nonfinancial Costs of Teacher Attrition as Well

Though it is hard to place a dollar value on them, there are a number of other costs of teachers leaving after one to three years, which are very significant. An example is the cost of administrative time required for supervision of novice teachers. I have written more about these on my Web site (Sweeny, 2002).

Strategy 3: Use the Money Saved From Attrition for More Productive and Cost-Effective Methods of Making Time

Some examples to broaden your perspective can include

- Full-time mentors—perhaps using a ratio of fifteen novices to one mentor.
- Stipends for "buddy" teachers to orient and generally support novices by providing instructional improvement coaching for approximately half a day each month.
- Subs for released time for mentors to allow coaching (be sure to first provide excellent training).
- Reduced load for mentors. At the secondary level, buy one period a day release. At the elementary level, buy one day a week release and contract with a top-notch teacher to serve as the sub with five mentors, one each day of the week. Expect mentors and the regular sub to plan jointly, so instructional continuity is maintained.
- Reduced load for new teachers. Create the time new teachers deserve to learn the new skills and strategies you want them to master, observe expert teachers at work, work on a regular basis with their mentors, develop longer-term unit and lesson plans (under mentor guidance), attend district-led new teacher seminars and support groups, and so on.
- Dedicated program leadership time. If a program leader does not exist, or if the time to do the task is very limited, create a full-time induction and mentor program coordinator role. Design the role to include at least seeking an increase in the effectiveness of mentors by ensuring that mentoring of mentors occurs on a regular basis (Sweeny, 2001). If such a role already exists, expand it to include adequate mentoring of mentors.

The bottom line here is that as a district increases its expectations for improved results from mentoring, it must also increase its commitment of time and other resources for the support of mentors, the induction and mentoring program, and the novice teachers. It can be argued that only after such a commitment has been made would it be logical to expect increased results.

Strategy 4: Thinking Outside the Time Box

Our conception and assumptions about the use of professional time in schools are blinded by what we know and what we usually have done.

One approach to discovering new ways to create the needed professional time for mentoring is to think outside the boundaries of those assumptions and to dream of what might be, rather than what is already. Here are a few examples.

- Employ recently retired teachers as mentors. They have the time to give and the experience we need to honor and tap as a resource. The only challenge in this strategy is to invite these retired staff to district staff development so they stay current in their fields. A codicil: Having trouble getting good retired teachers to substitute? Well . . . they are retired for a reason. They want to live the life they envisioned, but they still have lots to give back to their lifelong profession. Interview a few of these folks and ask what they want to avoid in subbing and what they would be willing to do. Then create a system of professional development for subs with those features and invite the retired teachers to join. Be sure to market the benefits. For example, commit to never call them before 9 a.m., to never call them for ordinary subbing, and to only call them for professional development reasons that can be easily scheduled days in advance. Then, honor those commitments and sign up the retired teachers you need.
- Sign up with your local university for administrative interns. Use the interns to do some of the more routine tasks to free up your regular administrators to assume more instructionally critical roles, like substituting for new teachers and mentors so they can meet more often for an extended time or for coaching.
- Utilize grade level teams of teachers in more creative ways. For example, combine classes of four teachers for activities that three teachers can easily supervise, and free the fourth person to work as a mentor one period a day, or two or three periods a week.

Strategy 5: Assemble Several Funding Pieces From Other Staff Development Budgets to Create Sufficient Support for a Half- or Full-Time Mentor in Each School

For example, chances are your school has or could get a grant for reading improvement, increasing student success in math and science, or increasing the use of technology as a curricular tool. Without a doubt, each of those grants will support professional development, and some may even specifically state they allow mentoring. Instead of thinking of these pieces as separate fragments of the curriculum, look for ways to access part of each of those grants and pool the resources to buy dedicated teacher time for mentoring and coaching.

In this way each school could have a full-time mentor whose role includes both the support of all teachers in mastering and implementing reading, math, science, and technology strategies into their teaching and specifically supporting novice teachers in these same ways. Couple this assistance with buddy teachers who are assigned individual novices to orient and support, and you'll have a team of experienced teachers who together can give the kind of time and levels of expertise that new teachers deserve.

Strategy 6: Demonstrate That Providing the Time for Effective Mentoring Is Worth It

- Work with a program evaluation expert from outside your district to design an effective mentoring and induction program evaluation system. Collect data that will help you document and improve the impact your program has on new and mentor teachers. Dedicate the time that is needed for this person to lead a study group and to collect the data needed to show that your program is worth the investment. Couple this effort with several of the earlier mentioned strategies (like determining the cost of attrition and using mentoring to improve retention) and you will be well positioned to market induction and mentoring to decision makers.
- Provide mentoring to new board of education members and all new administrators. Demonstrate to them the value of adequate support for people in changing or new challenges. Frame what you offer them as mentoring and prepare their mentors with training and support so they can access what is known about doing effective mentoring at those levels. Then, the next time their peers raise a question about the value of new teacher mentoring, you won't have to answer that question. Stand back and smile as these new decision makers tell their colleagues why mentoring is important and should be adequately supported.

FINDING TIME FOR MENTORING

There are a number of well-known, almost traditional ideas for finding the time for mentoring. This chapter does not need to re-present these since a simple search of the literature will reveal them. All of these methods should be explored and utilized where appropriate. What is less well understood is the use of the Internet and e-mail to create "asynchronous" time for mentoring.

A major impediment to adequate time for any professional development activity is the lack of time and space in the school day. Now, technology supports can be created which make these two impediments a thing of the past. With technology-based solutions, new teachers, mentors, administrators, and anyone with an interest in induction and mentoring can access ideas, resources, solutions to problems, schedules, maps, and so on whenever they need these things and from anywhere they can access the Web.

On vacation during the summer or a break? No problem. Left your induction binder at home? No problem. The program has also placed the information you need on the district induction Web site. Can't arrange a common time to meet with your mentor this week? No problem. Stay in touch through e-mail until you can meet again face-to-face. Can't find a time when all protégés can meet? Use a district mentor hot line which makes each mentor available "on call" one night a month to help any protégé. Use a novice teacher e-zine, an e-mail-based newsletter to send out monthly ideas you have collected, lists of links and other resources, program reminders, and testimonials. Even ideas learned by one protégé can easily be collected and shared with them all.

Now, you don't always need a shared time or a specific place set aside to get your mentoring work done. Sadly, the use of technology for mentor and novice teacher support is still vastly underutilized in most school districts. Review the ideas just shared and then pick just one or two to implement in your program this year.

MONITORING MENTORING TIME

One time-related tool that is often used is a time and activity log for mentoring. Typically, this is a one-page chart on which the program asks mentors to log what they do, how often they have done it, and with whom they have done it. The logs are submitted to the program leadership once a quarter or at some other regular interval. Frequently, these logs are used out of an interest in holding mentors accountable for good use of their mentoring time or the released time we arrange for them. Unfortunately, while these tools can be valuable program data sources, they are often perceived as a demonstration of mistrust of mentors. In other words, mentors perceive the log for what it is, an accountability system. If you use or are considering the use of such a log, here are some things to consider which can help you make this tool a process valued by everyone involved.

- How could you communicate to mentors what they need to hear to value the log as much as the program might?
- What do mentors need to know and believe for them to come to value the logs more?
- What could be done to remove the objections mentors might have concerning the log?
- What does the program do with the log data it collects? How could that data be put to use to benefit the program? Mentors? Protégés?

Let's consider some of the potential of the log and how best to capture that potential to benefit all involved. If you suspect that mentors are not giving the time they should to mentoring and protégés are not getting the support they need, consider the following:

- Edward Deming (the quality guru) once told us (and I believe it) that 95 percent of all people problems are a result of organizational-level problems. The implication of this is that if mentors are not giving adequate time to mentoring, it is a program problem, not a mentor problem. Only one of the reasons for a lack of mentoring time commitment may be that they are poor, uncommitted mentors. Rather, and more likely, the reasons are that the mentors do not know how to be effective mentors. The proof of that is that the bottom line for mentors and protégés is that teachers don't invest time in activities which feel ineffective and unproductive. Their time is too precious to waste.
- If we assume that mentors are doing the best they can and only give time to mentoring when they know it will be well spent and productive, then the program needs to ask itself and its mentors what the mentor training needs to become so that mentors are more adequately prepared to use their mentoring time productively.
- The program needs to consider providing mentoring of mentors so that the mentors personally experience what quality mentoring is like and then receive support in planning how to apply their personal learning in their own mentoring relationships with protégés.
- If your program is going to use a mentoring time and activity log,

  - Let mentors know that you understand they can only give limited time to mentoring because they have full-time jobs as teachers as well.

  - Explain that the log is not used out of mistrust or to pressure mentors to give more time to mentoring.

  - Confess, instead (it's true, isn't it?), that the district has not yet been able to make available to mentors the kind of time that highly effective mentoring probably requires.

  - Ask mentors to think for a minute about what data might help the district decide that greater time for mentoring is needed (see below).

  - Thank mentors for the time they can give to mentoring and the professionalism that their time commitment represents.

  - Inform the mentors that the data they provide in the log will be used to determine what the program can do to better support mentors and protégés.

- Let mentors know that the data collected in the logs is as much to learn what mentors cannot do, given the pressures of their other work, as it is to find out what mentors can do to make time for mentoring.

- Let mentors know, finally, that the program will use the data about the time they are able to give, along with the results that limited mentoring time produces, to create a picture of what is reasonable to expect from mentoring when the time given to it must be limited. Think ahead to a day when your program may present these data and ask the administration and board for greater support for time to mentor because the results they seek from mentoring require greater time than it is currently possible for mentors to give.

It is easy to allow the current structure of traditional schools and the traditional use of professional time to blind us to the possibilities we need to see and to the new schools and uses of professional time we must create when teacher and student performance are to be significantly increased. May the ideas and insights of this chapter inspire and guide you as you seek to create the new realities we need for schools to truly serve as learning communities.

REFLECTIONS AND APPLICATIONS

How does an induction and mentoring program provide just what is needed exactly when it is needed? Exercise 8.1 asks you to reflect on how your induction and mentoring program addresses three of the many related strategies presented in this chapter that answer that question and then to speculate on how, when, and where these strategies might effectively be applied in your program.

Exercise 8.1   Three Timely and Effective Strategies

Directions: Below, in column 1, are three strategies for providing an induction and mentoring program with just what is needed exactly when it is needed. In the box to the right of each item, reflect on how that strategy is addressed in your induction and mentoring program. In the next box, speculate how, by applying material from this chapter, you might be able to provide a more meaningful application of each strategy in the future.

Strategy	How Applied Now	Potential Enhancement
Make the initial program decisions using the guidance available from expert practitioners.		
Provide support and guidance which are aligned with the developmental stages of novice teachers.		
Treat individuals individually.		

REFERENCES

Hord, S., Rutherford, W., Huling-Austin, L., & Hall, G. (1987). *Taking charge of change.* Alexandria, VA: Association for Supervision and Curriculum Development.

Sweeny, B. W. (2001). *Mentoring of mentors: How leaders ensure high impact mentoring.* Wheaton, IL: Best Practice Resources. Retrieved from http://teachermentors .com/NewAbtBWS/MOM.Descrp.html

Sweeny, B. W. (2002). *The non financial costs of teacher attrition.* Wheaton, IL: Best Practice Resources. Retrieved from http://teachermentors.com/RSOD% 20Site/AskMOM.html

Texas State Board for Educator Certification. (2000). *Cost of teacher attrition.* Austin, TX: Author. Retrieved from http://www.sbec.state.tx.us/SBECOnline/txbess/ turnoverrpt.pdf

9

Cultivating Learning-Focused Relationships Between Mentors and Their Protégés

Laura Lipton

Bruce Wellman

Novice teachers learn to teach; they learn from their teaching; and with guidance and modeling, they teach from that learning. Developing the patterns and practices of skillful teaching, and lifelong commitments to professional growth, begins with learning-focused mentoring relationships (Lipton & Wellman, 2003). For the mentor, this process requires developing an identity as a growth agent who builds the capacities in others to be effective problem solvers and decision makers. For novice teachers, this process requires a willingness to learn and to be a learner within the relationship. The ultimate goal of learning-focused mentoring is to create colleagues who can fully participate in the professional life of the school. With clear understandings of expectations and intentions, mentors and protégés can shape their interactions to balance mutual goals and needs with their personalities and preferred approaches to adult learning.

This chapter defines the three functions of learning-focused relationships that distinguish them from other types of possible interactions; it goes on to present a continuum of learning-focused interaction that includes methods for navigating across three stances—consulting, collaborating, and coaching—to increase the effectiveness and productivity of the mentor-protégé relationship. The chapter concludes with an exploration of mentoring practice to support transitions from novice to more expert forms of teaching, along with indicators of those transitions.

FUNCTIONS OF LEARNING-FOCUSED RELATIONSHIPS

Relationships matter. Who a mentor is and how mentors interact with the novices that they support conveys as strong a message as does the content of the interaction. Skillful mentors balance three functions as they cultivate and enrich learning-focused relationships (Daloz, 1999):

1. Offering support

2. Creating challenge

3. Facilitating a professional vision

Like the classic vaudeville act in which the performer balances rotating plates on flexible wands, each of these functions is given a spin when and if additional energy needs to be supplied to keep that plate in motion. Each of these arenas can operate independently from the others, but in the greater context, to sustain learning and growth, they must interact with each other for maximum effect. Support alone provides comfort but may encourage complacency or dependency. Challenge without support increases anxiety and may develop a fear of failure within the protégé. And support and challenge without vision leaves the novice wandering on the journey of learning to teach looking only at the ground beneath but not the road ahead.

Offering Support

New teachers typically require four types of support: emotional, physical, instructional, and institutional.

1. *Emotional support* comes in many forms, ranging from a shoulder to cry on to a hug or smile to help celebrate a small victory or major breakthrough. Support is the safety zone created by the mentor's willingness to listen and be fully present with the protégé. Within the listening space, the mentor nonverbally and verbally acknowledges the feelings, concerns, and questions of that day, making it

OK not to know but not OK to not work toward the knowing. Emotional support that is timely and appropriate bolsters the novice's confidence and helps to normalize the hard work of the moment by providing both practical approaches and a sense of not being in it alone.

2. *Physical support* from the mentor provides both energy relief and the practical how-to knowledge drawn from experience. It might include helping with room arrangements and furniture moving, setting up the first science lab activity and offering expert commentary on the needed safety procedures and logistics of that lab experience, or even helping to cart books from the library to support a thematic unit.

3. *Instructional support* includes such things as sharing specific content area resources and helping the novice to make connections between the curriculum materials and learning standards for each course. It also includes offering appropriate and timely tips on child development as they relate to classroom management and the cognitive and emotional challenges students might be facing within particular units of study. At its most basic, instructional support means helping novice teachers establish productive routines and patterns within their classrooms that are time efficient, developmentally appropriate, and sustainable for both the teacher and students.

4. *Institutional support* helps new teachers navigate the procedures and policies of the school and the district. It includes such things as reminders of important deadlines and details, staff evaluation procedures, how to order materials, sick leave policies and obtaining substitute coverage, hall monitoring, before- and afterschool duties, and all the myriad other particulars that consume the time and attention of newcomers to the organization.

As skillful mentors spin the support plate, there are also opportunities to energize the plates of creating challenge and facilitating professional vision. For instance, while providing physical support such as helping to set up a science lab or art activity, the mentor might also inquire into the novice's sense of the outcomes for that lesson (challenge) and how this lesson fits with what the novice teacher believes is valuable for students to know and be able to do (vision). In this way, openings develop to create cognitive challenges that enlarge the protégé's thinking beyond that activity and to consider the values and beliefs that are driving their professional practice.

Creating Challenge

Support alone, while emotionally satisfying to both the novice and the mentor, is an insufficient resource for promoting patterns of professional thinking, learning, and growth. When mentors balance support with appropriate levels of cognitive challenge, protégés learn to take responsibility for their own professional practice and to embrace the work of becoming a teacher.

To grow personally and professionally, beginners need to develop the capacity to apply and adapt expert information within the context of their own classrooms. By making meaning of new information and experiences, they are then able to apply, refine, and create alternative strategies to match their students' needs and to support curricular outcomes.

To be learning focused, the mentor-protégé relationship must be infused with appropriate levels of challenge. Within the safety of the supportive relationship, the growth-oriented mentor produces what psychologist Leon Festinger (1957) termed "cognitive dissonance." This dissonance is the gap between current understanding and the emerging awareness of that gap on the part of the learner. Skillful mentors paraphrase their protégé's thinking and inquire or offer tips and principles of practice to help novices refine and extend their worldviews and practical knowledge of learning and teaching. Problem finding, problem framing, and problem solving are essential ingredients of professional life. It is through these activities that mentors help beginners develop increasingly effective ways of thinking about and reflecting upon their practice.

Within learning-focused relationships, there are many opportunities to meld support with challenge. Planning, problem solving, and reflecting conversations, whether planned or occurring spontaneously, provide forums for the thoughtful examination of practice. By clarifying goals and success criteria and reflecting on the degree of outcome achievement, the novice teacher learns some of the essential cognitive skills of teaching. A focus on student products and performances establishes an important third point for conversations. Within this focus the mentor can inquire, invite observations from the protégé, and offer expert commentary that is informed by experience and professional knowledge. In this way, theory bridges to practice and outcomes connect to actions.

Facilitating a Professional Vision

The immediacy of the classroom and the pressures of the moment presented by student needs, curricular demands, and institutional requirements can easily consume and at times overwhelm novice teachers. At the beginning of the professional journey, there are few reference points for charting student or personal progress. Taking things one day at a time gets you down the road and through the calendar but does not increase awareness of the surroundings or of the pleasures and value in the travel.

Thoughtful mentors are both guides and models of a professional way of being. As they support and constructively challenge their protégés, they enlarge the view, offering a variety of maps to the territory that help the novice plot a course through the terrain of their own and their students' learning needs. Modeling is as important as advice. Mindful mentors purposely display their own habits as thinkers and problem solvers. They also model their own "informed uncertainties" as they consider the options and opportunities within the choice points of classroom practice.

In learning-focused relationships, mentors facilitate an expanding professional vision by helping the novice set high yet achievable expectations for themselves. The Interstate New Teachers Assessment and Support Consortium (INTASC) beginning teacher standards (1995) are a clear example of a level of performance expectations to which growth-oriented novice teachers might aspire. These standards and locally developed teaching standards also provide a third point for focusing learning-focused conversations for goal setting and for structuring reflections on practice.

Mentors enhance professional vision by supporting protégés in clarifying learning outcomes that are broader than one lesson or unit of study. This bigger picture includes seeking opportunities for content integration that connect content area learning to real-world applications. During planning and problem-solving activities with the novice, the skillful mentor continues to enlarge the professional landscape by helping to prioritize tasks and identifying the various types of resources needed to support goal achievement.

By facilitating a professional vision, skillful mentors support novice teachers in clarifying and articulating the values and beliefs that drive their practice. The skills of professional collaboration, learning to think together with colleagues and finding oneself within those relationships, emerge from both the activities themselves and the purposeful reflection on those activities. To break the bindings of isolation for the novice and at times within the culture of the school, these early lessons in professional dialogue and discourse, done well, provide novice teachers with both images of and expectations for a professional career in education.

A Continuum of Learning-Focused Interaction

Skilled mentors continually attend to both relationship and learning in their work with protégés. Versatility across the continuum of interaction depicted in Figure 9.1 supports response patterns that are developmentally and contextually appropriate for serving the learning needs of novices. Within learning-focused conversations, accomplished mentors shift as needed between consulting, collaborating, and coaching stances to develop their protégés' capacities to reflect upon practice, generate ideas, and increase personal and professional self-awareness.

The ultimate aims of each of these stances and their cumulative effect is to support self-directed learning on the part of protégés and to enhance the protégé's capacity for engaging in productive collegial relationships.

Figure 9.1   Weighted Continuum of Interaction

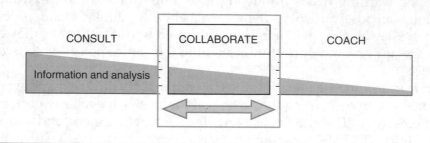

At times, it may be most appropriate to take a consulting stance. The mentor-as-consultant offers counsel and advice about processes, protocols, choices, and actions. By drawing from a stored repertoire of experiences and expertise, the mentor advocates and offers perspectives and options. At other times, a more collaborative stance may be most appropriate. The mentor-as-collaborator participates as an equal with the protégé in planning, reflecting, and problem solving. In this stance, the mentor and protégé share idea generation and analysis. At yet other times, a coaching stance may be the most effective. The mentor-as-coach engages in the nonjudgmental mediation of thinking and decision making to support the protégé's emotional and cognitive development as a teaching professional.

Two attributes ultimately define the stance that a mentor is taking in any learning-focused conversation. One defining trait is the way that information emerges during the interaction. The other defining trait is the source of gap analysis related to differences between planned goals and actual results, or learning standards and student performance. In the consulting stance, the mentor supplies information and identifies and offers expert analysis of any gaps. In the collaborative stance, the mentor and protégé codevelop ideas and analysis. And in the coaching stance, the protégé produces information and analysis as the mentor paraphrases and inquires to increase awareness, enlarge perspectives, and clarify details.

Consulting

The consulting mentor shares essential information about learning and learners, curriculum and content, policies, procedures, standards, and effective practices. Beyond this technical information, a thoughtful mentor also shares principles of practice—the "why" of actions and options. By offering, "Here's what I pay attention to" and "Here's why that matters" and "Here are some options," skilled mentors intentionally think aloud, displaying habits of mind to model professional practice at the highest levels. As novice teachers internalize principles of teaching and learning, these expert lenses become mental resources for independently generating approaches and solutions. A useful template to guide mentoring practice is a pattern of sharing the "what," "why," and "how" of an idea or suggestion.

The consulting stance tends to be the natural stance for many mentors. The apparent and pressing needs of most novice teachers motivate the desire to help, share information, and reduce the burdens of the struggling protégé. Yet context-rich learning opportunities may be missed if advice is the only resource offered. While information and problem solutions are useful supports to offer, if overdone, they rob novices of opportunities to learn from experience. Consultation that is learning focused within a caring relationship offers the novice both immediate support and the thinking tools for tackling future problems with greater independence. The intention to support learning and growth must always be clear to both parties, especially if the potential of a "learning moment" is to be fully appreciated.

Collaborating

The collaborating mentor codevelops ideas and information with the protégé once a problem has been framed or clarified and it is time to develop a set of possible approaches or solutions. This stance usually arises spontaneously as an outgrowth of interacting within a consulting or coaching stance to help frame a problem or to structure a planning task. The mentor's purposeful pausing and paraphrasing opens up the emotional and cognitive space for collaborative productivity. The use of inclusive pronouns, such as *us, our,* and *we,* enhances the invitation to the protégé to contribute ideas.

The collaborative stance signals respect and the expectation of participation in a collegial relationship. Mentors need to resist their own impulse to jump in and do the bulk of the analysis and thinking. Pausing to allow time to think and prompting and encouraging idea production communicates a belief in the personal and professional capacities of the protégé.

Coaching

The coaching mentor supports the protégé's thinking, problem solving, and goal clarification. The outcomes of this stance are to increase the emerging colleague's expertise in planning, reflecting on practice, and instructional decision making. The cognitive coaching model (Costa & Garmston, 2002) defines this stance by addressing the underlying thinking that drives the observable behaviors of teaching.

By inquiring, paraphrasing, pausing, and probing for details, the mentor supports both idea production and exploration of the "whys" and "hows" of choices, possibilities, and connections. This meditative pattern, applied over time, enlarges the frame, developing the protégé's ever-increasing capacity for expert thinking and practice. The ultimate aim of this stance is to develop novices' internal resources for self-coaching so that over time, their own more sophisticated inner voices guide their professional self-talk. Table 9.1 summarizes these three mentoring stances.

Table 9.1 Three Mentoring Stances (From Lipton & Wellman, 2003)

Consulting	Collaborating	Coaching
Intentions: • To share information, advice, and technical resources about policies and procedures, learning and learners, curriculum and content, and effective practices. • To establish standards for professional practice.	**Intentions:** • To co-develop information, ideas, and approaches to problems. • To model a collegial relationship as a standard for professional practice.	**Intentions:** • To support the protégé's idea production, instructional decision-making, and ability to reflect on practice. • To increase the protégé's ability to self-coach and become a self-directed learner.
Actions: • Providing resource materials and references to research. • Demonstrating processes and procedures informally and through model lessons. • Offering a menu of options to consider. • Providing introductions to building and district resource people as needed. • Offering expert commentary on student work samples. • Sharing principles of practice by elaborating the "what," "why," and "how" of proposed ways of thinking about issues, proposed solutions, and choice points.	**Actions:** • Brainstorming ideas and options. • Co-planning and co-teaching lessons. • Sharing and exchanging resource materials. • Planning experiments to try simultaneously in each of your classrooms, and comparing notes on results. • Jointly analyzing student work samples. • Joining the protégé to offer support and "translate" when building and district resource are present to provide technical assistance. • Jointly noting problem frames and generating alternative ways to think about issues and concerns. • Alternating paraphrasing and summarizing oneself with encouraging the protégé to paraphrase and summarize developing ideas and understandings.	**Actions:** • Maintaining a nonjudgmental stance with full attention to the emotional and mental processes of the protégé. • Inquiring, paraphrasing, and probing for specificity to surface the protégé's perspectives, perceptions, issues, and concerns. • Inquiring, paraphrasing, and probing for specificity to support the protégé's planning, problem solving, and reflecting on practice. • Inquiring, paraphrasing, and probing for specificity to support the protégé's analysis of student work. • Inquiring, paraphrasing, and probing for specificity to increase the protégé's self-knowledge and awareness as a teacher, colleague, and professional educator.

Table 9.1 (Continued)

Consulting	Collaborating	Coaching
• Framing presenting problems within wider contexts and providing expert ways to approach issues and concerns.	• Alternating offering ideas with encouraging the protégé to contribute ideas.	
Cues: • Using a credible voice. • Sitting up straighter or leaning back a bit from the table. • Using the pronoun "I" as in, "Here's how I think about issues like that." • Using bookmarking phrases for emphasis, such as "It's important to . . . ," "keep in mind . . . ," "pay attention to . . ."	**Cues:** • Using a confident, approachable voice. • Sitting side-by-side, focused on the common problem or issue. • Using the pronouns "we" and "us." • Using phrases like "Let's think about . . . ," "Let's generate . . . ," "How might we . . . ?"	**Cues:** • Using an approachable voice. • Attending fully and maintaining eye contact. • Using the pronoun "you" as in, "So, you're concerned about . . ." • When responding, using a pattern of pausing, paraphrasing, and inquiring to open thinking; or probing for specificity to focus thinking. • Framing invitational questions to support thinking such as "What might be some ways to . . . ? "What are some options that you are considering?" and "What are some of the connections you are making between . . . ?"
Cautions: • If overused, the consulting stance can build dependency on the mentor for problem solving. Advice, without explanation of the underlying choice points and guiding principles, usually does not develop protégés' abilities to transfer learning to new settings or to generate novel solutions on their own.	**Cautions:** • Mentors need to carefully monitor their own actions when they enter the collaborative stance. Their own enthusiasm and excitement for the topic or issues may override the intention to co-create ideas and possibilities. False collaboration then becomes disguised consultation.	**Cautions:** • The coaching stance assumes that the other party has resources for idea generation. If this is not the case, pursuing this stance can lead to frustration on the part of protégés. You cannot coach out of someone what is not in them.

157

Mentoring From Novice to More Expert Teaching

Learning-focused mentors attend to the verbal and nonverbal signals of their protégés to determine growth strategies in the moment and over time. Nonverbal cues include intonational patterns, postural and gestural positioning, inflection, word emphasis and repetition, and the length and frequency of pauses. Verbal cues include length, degree of detail, source of ideas, and specific language of descriptions and responses to questions. These signals are developmental indicators, as well as indications of present emotional state and cognitive resourcefulness.

Acuity to these signals supports mentors in making effective choices regarding their own verbal and nonverbal responses, as well as their choice of stance. By observing the protégé's verbal and nonverbal behaviors, skillful mentors can monitor and calibrate the effectiveness of a given stance and determine whether and where to shift along the continuum.

Planning and reflecting conversations afford an opportunity to monitor growth. The following dimensions serve as an index for assessing professional development. The skillful mentor, attending fully, makes choices that balance support with challenge and move the novice toward increasing levels of expertise. The questions generated as a result of the mentor's assessments become tools for producing increased awareness and self-directed learning for new teachers. That is, questions purposefully crafted by skillful mentors illuminate the larger principles of practice that produce skillful teaching. In all cases, depending on the confidence and completeness of the protégé's response, these coaching questions might be followed by a shift to a consultative or collaborative stance.

Learning-focused mentors attend to

- The language of the teacher's goals for lessons and units
- The details and level of sophistication of strategies
- The depth of content knowledge
- The ability to recognize and generate choice points
- The sophistication and depth of evidence and data cited

THE LANGUAGE OF THE TEACHER'S GOALS FOR LESSONS AND UNITS

As expertise develops, teachers move from strict adherence to the teachers' guide or other external sources, to their own understanding of the content and students' needs in order to determine learning goals. The confident marriage of source materials with professional experience when setting goals is a developmental indicator.

In addition, setting learning goals that nest short-term objectives with longer-term outcomes, connecting the specific lesson or unit to the broader conceptual understandings of the curriculum or content area, are hallmarks of growing expertise. So, too, are goals that include specific thinking skills, or clusters of thinking skills, such as problem solving or decision making, and social skills, such as listening to other points of view or engaging productively in a group task.

MENTORING MOVES FOR WORKING WITH GOALS

When goals are established primarily from printed materials, the mentor might ask,

> "In addition to this goal, what else might you expect students to take away from this lesson or unit?" Or, "In addition to the content goal, what are some social skills that can be introduced or reinforced during this lesson?" Or, "Given what you've been working on in this content area, how does this lesson fit with the larger picture for this year?"

When goals are limited to content objectives, the mentor might ask,

> "In addition to the content objectives, what other outcomes do you want your students to take away from this lesson?" Or, "As you consider the ways that you want your students to process this information, what are some specific thinking skills goals you might build into your lesson?"

Choosing Stance

If the response to these questions is still limited, navigating to a consultative stance might be appropriate. In this case, the mentor might offer a framework; for example,

> "In addition to a content goal or goals, there are other objectives that can be taught during a lesson or unit. For example, one might build in a social skill like taking turns, or working productively in a group. As I understand your design for this lesson, it seems to me that it lends itself very nicely to explicit instruction in working productively with a partner." At this point, the mentor might stay in the consultative stance, offering a menu of several instructional strategies that would move learners toward this goal, or shift to a more collaborative stance and say, "Let's think about a variety of

instructional strategies that would accomplish both the content and the social skill goal."

Note the use of pronouns related to each stance: *you* and *your* from a coaching stance, *me* and *I* from a consultative stance, and *we* and *let's* from a collaborative stance. These subtle verbal cues increase clarity for both the mentor and the novice regarding the intention of the interaction.

This process of asking first and then assessing the most effective learning-focused stance for the interaction is also applicable to all of the indices described below.

THE DETAILS AND LEVEL OF SOPHISTICATION OF STRATEGIES

Designing strategies to meet specific outcomes, and modifying them to differentiate for individual learners, is an expert skill. A mindful mentor listens to determine whether there is a strategic application of instructional methods or simply activity thinking. The former is a purposeful application, based on the assessment of learner needs; the latter is something found in a teaching journal, sourcebook, or the classroom next door that seems interesting.

MENTORING MOVES FOR WORKING WITH STRATEGIES

When instructional strategies are planned based on an idea found in a journal, or because the students like them, without relationship to desired learning outcomes, assessment of student readiness, and appropriate fit for the content being explored, the mentor might ask,

"In what ways will these strategies support your students in achieving the goals for this lesson?" Or, "Given what you know about your students at this point, how will this strategy build on their present knowledge and skills?" Or, "What are some criteria you use to decide which instructional strategies will be most effective?"

THE DEPTH OF CONTENT KNOWLEDGE

Expert practitioners have deep knowledge of the structure of the discipline, or disciplines, they teach. They are able to sort the nice from the necessary when developing and applying curricular outcomes to daily instruction. They make critical choices when time is short regarding these distinctions. Lesson plans demonstrate a relationship between what has already been learned and what is expected in future lessons. Skillful teachers also know where to emphasize important and recurring concepts that are foundational to further learning. Expertise in this area includes the ability to articulate connections between large ideas in the curriculum and to support students in making those connections.

MENTORING MOVES FOR WORKING WITH CONTENT KNOWLEDGE

When content is viewed as something to "cover," and lesson plans are replicated from teacher guides without regard to building conceptual connections, assessment of students' present understanding, or contingencies for time constraints, need for review, or opportunities for acceleration, the mentor might ask,

> "What are some connections between the content of this lesson and the larger concepts you want students to understand?" Or, "In this lesson, what are the most critical content understandings you are striving to develop?" Or, "If time runs short, which are the most vital objectives in this unit of study?" Or, "How might you sort the foundational outcomes in this unit of study from ones that you might consider extensions or enhancements?"

THE ABILITY TO RECOGNIZE AND GENERATE CHOICE POINTS

For skillful teachers, clear intentions regarding learning outcomes drive instructional choices. As proactive planners, these teachers incorporate if-then thinking to build potential contingencies into a given lesson or unit of study. As planned choices, which include instructional objectives, learning materials, interaction and grouping patterns, and time management, are being implemented, these teachers consistently monitor their effectiveness, making adjustments to meet the immediate needs of the learners, while being mindful of the larger instructional picture. The ability to draw from repertoire to make in-the-moment refinements or revisions to the initial plan is a hallmark of expertise.

Mentoring Moves for Working With Choice Points

While planning, if the sequence of instruction leaves little room for flexibility, or if the beginning teacher has not considered any (or few) "what if" scenarios, the mentor might ask,

"As you implement your plan, what are some things you'll pay attention to, to determine its effectiveness?" Followed by, "If things are not going as planned, what are some alternatives you might try?" Or, "If your less successful learners (or more proficient learners) are not engaged in this strategy, how might you refine the plan to increase their success?"

While reflecting, if there is little mention of potential reconsiderations, or envisioning or other possibilities, the mentor might ask,

"Given your reflections on this lesson, what are some elements you would be sure to incorporate in future lessons? What are some things you might refine or rethink?"

THE SOPHISTICATION AND DEPTH OF EVIDENCE AND DATA CITED

Effective teaching requires the application of day-to-day and moment-to-moment assessment of student learning to inform future action. Expert teachers draw on a wide range of data sources for planning and reflecting on learning. Possibilities include text-based inventories, student work products, teacher-made tests, classroom observation of student behaviors, and learner interviews and inventories, all of which are rich resources for determining short- and long-term next steps—for individual students, groups of students, and the class as a whole.

MENTORING MOVES FOR WORKING WITH EVIDENCE AND DATA

If it appears that the beginning teacher's plans do not include specific methods for determining student progress, or if the novice has a limited repertoire of sources of data used to determine next steps, the mentor might ask,

"What are some ways to determine students' progress that you are building in to this lesson?" Or, "How might the work your students will be producing in this lesson be used to assess next steps for instruction?" Or, "As you visualize this lesson in progress, what are some things you will pay attention to that might be used for determining students' understanding?" Or, "In addition to the end-of-unit tests, what can you build in to this unit to assess your students' readiness to move on?" Or, "What types of student work can you combine with in-class observations to increase your confidence that all your students are progressing?"

Again, in all cases, the quality of the novice's responses determines the mentor's choice of stance. If responses seem partially complete, or if the mentor has specific information to add, a collaborative stance will facilitate the generation of rich information built upon the novice's presenting knowledge base. When the response indicates a lack of knowledge or information, a consultative stance, which includes the key principles of practice related to the issue, a framework for thinking about the topic, a think-aloud that makes the mentor's expert processing visible to the novice, or a menu of suggestions, will fill the immediate gaps and support future learning.

WHEN MENTORING MATTERS

The plates keep spinning on their fragile wands as mentors offer support, create challenge, and facilitate an ever-expanding professional vision for the colleagues in their care. As the opening days of school flow into weeks and months and lessons connect into units and marking periods become semesters, beginning teachers who are fortunate to work in schools with carefully constructed mentoring programs become increasingly confident novice professionals. They become educators with the knowledge and dispositions for what it means to acquire and hone the knowledge and dispositions of skillful practice as teachers, as colleagues, and as members of the school community.

REFLECTIONS AND APPLICATIONS

This chapter discusses five growth strategies to which skillful, learning-focused mentors attend. Exercise 9.1 asks you to reflect on how well mentors in your program address these critical strategies and then to consider how you might provide the opportunity for them to further enhance their ability to do so.

Exercise 9.1 Five Growth Strategies for Learning-Focused Mentors

Directions: Below, in column 1, are five growth strategies to which skillful, learning-focused mentors attend. In the box to the right of each item, reflect on how that strategy is addressed by mentors in your program. In the next box, speculate how, by applying material from this chapter, you might be able to provide them with opportunities to enhance the ways they apply those strategies.

Growth Strategy Attended To	How Addressed	Potential Enhancement
The language of the teacher's goals for lessons and units		
The details and level of sophistication of strategies		
The depth of content knowledge		
The ability to recognize and generate choice points		
The sophistication and depth of evidence and data cited		

REFERENCES

Costa, A., & Garmston, R. (2002). *Cognitive coaching: A foundation for renaissance schools.* Norwood, MA: Christopher-Gordon.

Daloz, L. A. (1999). *Mentor: Guiding the journey of adult learners.* San Francisco: Jossey-Bass.

Festinger, L. A. (1957). *A theory of cognitive dissonance.* Stanford, CA: Stanford University Press.

Interstate New Teachers Assessment and Support Consortium. (1995). INTASC core standards. http://develop.ccsso.cybercentral.com/intasc.htm

Lipton, L., & Wellman, B. (2003). *Mentoring matters: A practical guide to learning-focused relationships.* Sherman, CT: Miravia.

PART III

Connecting Mentoring and Induction to Broader Issues

10

Mentoring Promotes Teacher Leadership

Susan Villani

Everyone is watching me. The students are waiting to see what I do, and I bet some of the teachers aren't sure I'll manage it. I feel like my every move is observed. My legs are shaking—can they see how nervous I am? I've worked hard to get here, and now that I am, I'm not sure I'll be able to pull it off.

These might well be the thoughts of a new teacher. However, they are what went through my mind when I was on a 60-foot-high ropes course. As the principal, I always accompanied our fifth graders on a three-day outdoor challenge. I was very nervous as I decided to try one of the ropes courses. Though I had watched others move across the ropes, and focused on their approach, I wasn't confident in my capability. The reason I even took this risk was that I trusted a colleague to keep me safely on belay. He was on the ground, securely holding a rope that went through the harness I was wearing.

Mentoring a new teacher is like belaying a high-ropes-course climber. Mentors provide new teachers with safety and are readily available to answer questions, give ideas, and help the teachers plan their next moves. As I started to climb the tree that led to the ropes, I faltered. He helped me strategize. "Look for the next foothold on your right, and then step up.

Then what will you do?" Mentors can help even the most uncertain novices take their first steps.

When experienced teachers move beyond their own classrooms to mentor others, they are extending their zone of proficiency and trying something new. They need the support of other experienced teachers and the administration. Just as new teachers need mentors, mentors need support, as well.

My belayer worked with me every step of the way. Though he was on the ground as I was walking on the ropes, he couldn't get too far in front of me or the belay wouldn't work. Success required that he follow my lead. He kept me grounded and safe, and yet he didn't impose his ideas on me. When I was ready, he was there to help me reflect on what happened and how I might improve.

We are facing a crisis in education. Over the next decade, we must hire, train, and retain huge numbers of new teachers and administrators. The NEA projects that 943,000 teachers will be retiring between 2000 and 2010, which is a 50 percent increase over the number of teachers who retired in the previous decade. When this number is combined with growth, 200,000 teachers will need to be hired annually for the next ten years.

The picture is no less bleak for administrators. For example, 40 percent of elementary principals will be retiring in the next ten years, more than half of them the moment they are eligible (Ferrandino, 2000). Furthermore, superintendents describe a decreasing pool of qualified candidates.

We cannot afford to lose so many of our much-needed new teachers and administrators. To provide the best possible educational community, we will want to ask ourselves how we can provide the leadership in schools that will help new teachers be effective with students and remain in the profession. Teachers and administrators must work together to create structures that support, sustain, and retain new teachers, veteran teachers, and administrators. We must be willing to explore new models of leadership and better ways to use the resources and skills of our experienced faculty.

The concept of parallel leadership is worthy of consideration because it capitalizes on the talent and experience of current educators. "Parallel leadership is a process whereby teacher leaders and their principals engage in collective action to build school capacity. It embodies mutual respect, shared purpose, and allowance for individual expression" (Crowther, Kaagan, Ferguson, & Hann, 2002, p. 38). We all know of classroom teachers who so enjoy working with students that they decline opportunities to become administrators. Rather than having to make a choice between teaching or administration, let's capitalize on the leadership of our best teachers, without forcing them to leave the classroom in order to get the respect and resources they need to improve the quality of education all students receive.

Steve DeAngelis, a teacher who came to the profession after being a scientist in the private sector, says that he has already been promoted as much as he wants. "I already have the highest prestige job in the school in my mind. I get to teach physics."

TEACHER LEADERSHIP OPPORTUNITIES ABOUND

Teacher leadership takes many forms. It may mean chairing a grade level or department in a school or coordinating a grant for school improvement. Serving on school councils, working with the community to hire a superintendent, and working on curriculum development committees are other examples of teacher leadership.

Brian Lord and Barbara Miller (2000, p. 3) have categorized the work of teacher leaders as collaborating with

- Individual teachers in classroom settings
- Groups of teachers in workshop or comparable professional development settings
- Teachers, administrators, community members, or students on issues or programs that indirectly support classroom teaching and learning experiences
- Various constituents on the task *du jour*

Mentoring

> Mentoring young teachers provides a window of opportunity to develop and model teacher-leadership concepts. (Crowther et al., 2002, p. 143)

Teacher leadership is acknowledged as having the potential to significantly contribute to school change and heightened school effectiveness. Many educators realize the necessity of teachers having a voice in priorities and goal setting, as well as being involved in decision making about school initiatives and policies (Barth, 1990). Skilled mentors are teacher leaders whose service to new teachers can affect the entire school community.

Let's examine the work and hear the voices of four teacher leaders who impact the professionalism and capability of a large number of teachers through mentoring. These teacher leaders are

- Steve DeAngelis, physics teacher, National Board Certified Teacher, Northern New England Co-mentoring Network mentor (NNECN)
- Colleen Ezzo, instructional specialist, coordinator of mentor coaches

- Judy Klein, English teacher on leave, former codirector of a middle school mentoring program for new teachers
- Ted Niboli, retired science teacher and department chair, Project ACROSS (Alternative Certification Routes with Ongoing Support System) mentor of three teachers seeking alternative certification

When Ted began teaching, he was hired to teach general science and biology and never received any help. Most of the teachers who started with him were fired.

> I resented that I kept thinking that people have to be helped to come on. After my first two or three years, when new teachers came, particularly in the science department, I gave them a lot of help. I gave them my lesson plans and labs. That was in the sixties. No one was doing that at the time.

Steve began teaching after several years as an engineer. Like Ted, Steve didn't have any teacher preparation or student teaching experience.

> I had no clue what was reasonable to expect of students. I went by the textbook. It was a question of sequencing and how to get it [content] across. What is the mix of how much time to do experiments and lecture? I lectured way more then than I do now.

Luckily, Steve had a good department chair who was very helpful. Steve reflects on the new teachers in his current setting.

> Almost all of them, no matter how good they are or how hard they try, live, breath, and sleep teaching. I cannot imagine any first-year teacher I've seen not working eighty hours a week. It is all-consuming, the intensity of it.

Colleen believes that teachers are self-focused their first year. She heard that a new teacher once said to a colleague, "I didn't realize there were kids here until the second year." Survival is a huge issue, and for many new teachers, it is an essential preoccupation.

Colleen had very positive experiences as a new teacher and modeled her mentoring, to some extent, on the mentoring and coaching she received. Colleen first became a teacher in Florida, a state that had mandated mentoring for beginning teachers. Colleen's mentor was paid to work with her. They met at least once or twice a week and whenever Colleen needed help. Colleen went to her mentor's house, which was particularly important to Colleen because she had moved to a city in which she didn't know anyone.

She talked with me about meeting parents and what to do and say. She helped me come up with ways to manage reading instruction that didn't burn me out. During that year, Colleen worked with seven other teachers at the same grade level. They were available to me. They shared lessons and discipline strategies.

Judy also modeled her mentoring after the positive models from her first year in teaching. Her first teaching position, in the early 1970s, was in the same district where she had been a reading tutor. She was assigned to an open classroom in which all the content areas were integrated and the students were taught by team teachers.

I was in the same room with three other teachers all day. Being in the same room with other teachers was very instructive. I felt much more support than first-year teachers ever dream of feeling. That was my benchmark for working with other teachers. The person who had the single most influence on me throughout my career was one of those teachers.

While these teachers each have had very different first-year experiences, they all came to realize how important it is to have a mentor's support and coaching. They have chosen to move beyond their own classrooms in different ways to pursue mentoring initiatives for this new generation of teachers.

Teacher leaders emerge in different ways and offer their school communities different attributes. Judy reflected on the interpersonal skills that are vital if teacher leaders want to be accepted as leaders. The integrity of those people is critical. The traits Judy identified are

- Ability to listen
- Ability to reflect back to a colleague without judging
- Perspective on yourself and your craft that includes humor
- Humility

EMERGING LEADERS SUPPORT NEW AND VETERAN TEACHERS

To support the growth of new teachers in their schools, Steve, Colleen, Judy, and Ted use their talents, initiative, energy, and influence to:

Create and Nurture a Sense of Belonging

When Ted headed the New Teacher Program at his school, he helped teachers find homes, showed them around town, and gave advice about where to go for entertainment. Ted now mentors three new teachers through Project ACROSS. This is a pilot program in New Hampshire designed to support alternative certification–route candidates and their mentors throughout the state. Ted coaches the new teachers, discussing pedagogy and curriculum, as well as observing them teach. Every month Ted cooks for the three teachers at his home as they talk about whatever they deem relevant. He comments, "They can't wait to come."

Coach

As cocreators and directors of their school's mentoring program, Judy and Martin, a colleague, worked with a mentor and new teacher pair who were not having a positive mentoring experience. Instead of giving the new teacher a "no-fault" reassignment, Judy coached the mentor and Martin worked with the new teacher. As a result, the mentor and the new teacher continued their mentoring relationship with each other throughout the school year. Judy and Martin pioneered a different way of dealing with difficulties between partners. Reassignment may be an appropriate and time-saving solution in some cases. However, the investment that Judy and Martin made to coaching the new teacher and mentor may have made a significant difference in the mentor's ability to coach in the future and in the new teacher's understanding of her rights and responsibilities in the relationship.

Create Opportunities for Professional Dialogue and Problem Solving With Colleagues

Several years ago, as new teacher coordinator, Ted organized monthly wine and cheese gatherings at his home. He invited master teachers from the school to join the new teachers and discuss teaching, answer questions, and help new teachers problem solve. Ted believes that it is important to involve master teachers in the development of new teachers. Ted specifically didn't invite administrators to the sessions at his home, thinking that the teachers would be more candid about their questions and concerns if their supervisors were not present.

Offer Professional Development to Colleagues

As codirectors of the Dover-Sherborn Mentoring Program, Judy and Martin provided professional development for new teachers at monthly after-school meetings. They surveyed the new teachers to determine their needs, and topics were chosen accordingly. Martin started asking veteran colleagues who weren't mentors if they would be willing to let him videotape them in their classrooms for a brief period of time, to exemplify classroom practices such as how to begin class and making transitions during a lesson. Though they were unsure at first, the teachers were complimented by Martin's request, and they started welcoming new teachers who had seen the videos into their classrooms.

Model Community Membership and Respect for Colleagues

Steve organized an event at his school to thank custodial and office staff who worked many unpaid hours to move the school from one building to another. Teachers volunteered to use their preparation periods to do the jobs of the custodians and office staff so that they could have a day off. Steve's idea was concrete as well as symbolic, and it was an important way to honor the staff as well as to convey the high esteem the teachers had for their commitment to the school.

> Teacher leadership is facilitated principled action to achieve whole-school success. It applies the distinctive power of teaching to shape meaning for children, youth, and adults. And it contributes to long-term, enhanced quality of community life. (Crowther et al., 2002, p. 143)

Model Lifelong Learning

Steve chose to become involved in the NNECN after participating in the Governor's Academy. He was continually seeking opportunities to deepen his own practice and work with science and mathematics teachers in a quest to be even more effective with students.

TEACHER LEADERS FACE SPECIAL CHALLENGES

In any of these aspects of teacher leadership, there are potential pitfalls and challenges that may dissuade some teachers from assuming leadership roles and dishearten some who have expanded their vision of their role in the school to include aspects of leadership beyond the classroom.

Collegial Opposition

Everyone in schools can become dispirited when they hear veteran teachers say, "That's not a good idea," "That won't work here," "You shouldn't be using your preparation time that way," and "That's the principal's job."

Teacher leaders are in a unique position to influence their colleagues, either directly or indirectly, to look at issues differently. For example, mentoring can have a positive effect on school culture. Mentoring programs and the professional development for mentors and new teachers often promote collaboration and heightened respect for colleagues. One of the things that the school administration in the Dover-Sherborn School District did to support mentoring was to provide a substitute once a month to free mentors and new teachers to observe in each other's classrooms. However, at first teachers didn't always sign up for the substitute's time. Judy and Martin decided to coordinate the time slots, and went to mentors and new teachers with the schedule, thereby assuring that they would take advantage of the opportunity. After a while, veteran teachers started requesting unused substitute time so that they could visit other teachers' classrooms. The principal of the school regarded the mentoring program as the impetus for the school culture becoming more collaborative.

Veteran teachers who are not mentors can play an important role in supporting new teachers. They can

- Welcome new teachers to observe in their classrooms
- Talk with new teachers about the curriculum and their practice
- Respect the confidential relationship that new teachers need to have with their mentors in order to feel safe to share their uncertainties and needs
- Help the school committee understand the need and value of a proposed line item in the budget for a mentoring program

Administrator Ambivalence or Resistance

Administrators may not welcome teachers' wishes to participate in leadership roles. Some may be reluctant to promote or support teacher leadership for fear of losing control of school policies and practices. Others may be resistant because the idea is new to them. In addition, there may be factors that are not evident, even to those working in the school. Building principals may be getting spoken or unspoken messages from the central office to "keep the lid on" their schools, to minimize anything that would threaten the status quo and draw the attention of school committee members. Administrators may be uncertain of teacher support. Will teachers be warm to the ideas but cool to the realities such as budget and bureaucracy? Will teachers portray administrators as trying to avoid responsibility or get someone else to do their job? Teachers and administrators need to work through these issues and learn to collaborate.

Teacher leaders can have a profoundly positive effect on their colleagues' thinking. Teacher leaders often have an ability to see issues from different perspectives. Sharing this with other teachers can be instrumental in teachers and administrators working together to achieve common goals. In these ways and others, teacher leaders can promote dialogue and discussion that is focused on students. They can unite teachers and administrators in these endeavors, rather than pit them against each other in the pursuit of their own ideas and endeavors.

> Professional learning communities are . . . bringing teachers together to talk about how they can improve the learning of all students as they challenge and question each other's practice in spirited and optimistic ways. (Andy Hargreaves, quoted in Sparks, 2004, p. 48)

Conflicting Needs for Time

Mentors can feel torn between the needs of new teachers, their own students and students' families, and their lives outside of school. Steve noted that if he could give five times as much time to the people he mentors, they would be delighted. Yet Steve, like so many other talented and committed teachers, is a teacher who is heavily involved in his school community. For example, in addition to mentoring, Steve has been a lead negotiator for two teacher contracts, the school's grievance officer for the association, and a coach for many youth sports programs. Similarly, Colleen organized school math fairs, created a math club, was on two textbook adoption committees, was a grade level chair, conducted parent workshop presentations, and team taught to help colleagues with math instruction. Steve has found one way of dealing with these multiple roles and responsibilities: he operates on four hours of sleep a night. That is a solution that is not viable for many of us. While Steve and Colleen exemplify the height of teacher leadership, it is not necessary for all teacher leaders to embark on so many endeavors. Teachers may choose to make a contribution to one aspect of their school's objectives, so that they can balance the multiple demands on their time and their other interests.

Some school systems have recognized that mentoring and coordination of a mentoring program are very time-consuming. As a result, they have created part-time or full-time mentoring positions so that teacher leaders wouldn't be torn between equally important priorities. For example, the Glendale Union Regional High School in Arizona, and the Rochester City Schools in New York, structured their programs so teachers could teach half-time and mentor half-time (Villani, 2002).

Advantages of supporting part-time mentoring positions include the following

- Part-time mentors can work with more beginning teachers.
- Teachers have increased flexibility to observe and meet during release time.

- Part-time mentors are actively working with new teachers in ways that are visible to the school community, which can evoke great buy-in.
- Mentors are able to offer the opportunity for teachers to observe model lessons.
- Mentors' teaching skills typically improve. Some school systems have created full-time mentoring positions by adding these salaries to their budget, finding creative ways to utilize staff time or partnering with a university.

The following (adapted from Meckel & Rolland, 2000) are advantages of having full-time mentors:

- A flexible schedule without teaching duties for the mentor makes it easier to observe and meet with beginning teachers.
- Work is entirely focused on beginning teachers and their needs.
- A highly skilled group of mentors usually emerges.
- Time is available for mentor training and ongoing support during the day.
- If mentors return to the classroom, their teaching practice is typically improved.
- There is no substitute teacher expense for providing time for mentors to work with new teachers.

Will this cost money? Yes. But there is currently a huge expense both in dollars and in learning from the exodus of so many of our new teachers. Furthermore, the exodus may well be contributing to burnout of experienced educators.

Figure 10.1 (Developing Effective Mentoring Programs; Dunne & Villani, 2005) The following are components of mentoring programs and criteria for their success:

- Involvement of key shareholders
- Selection criteria and process for mentor teachers
- Mentor and new teacher matches
- Training and support
- Supporting policies and procedures
- Mentor program evaluation

These rubrics are particularly useful when considering ways that systems can support mentoring and teacher leadership, as well as supporting new teachers.

(Text continues on page 183)

Figure 10.1 Developing Effective Mentoring Programs

Criteria for Success	1 Inadequate	2 Basic	3 Proficient	4 Sustainable
Involvement of Key Stakeholders	Mentor program is designed and planned by a few individuals. Could be top-down or bottom-up.	Teachers and administrators work together to design the mentor program.	Teachers and administrators representing all grade levels, school committee members, parents, and students involved in designing and planning the mentor program.	Teachers and administrators representing all grade levels, school committee members, parents, and students are involved in designing and planning the mentor program. There is a multi-representative design team that continually assesses the program, identifies what's working and not working, and makes changes along the way.
Selection Criteria and Process for Mentor Teachers	No criteria exist. Building principals handpick mentor teachers.	Mentors volunteer and are selected by a mentor program committee. No criteria exist.	Criteria for selecting mentor teachers are identified. A mentor program committee selects mentors with input from the building principal.	Criteria for selecting mentor teachers are identified. A mentor program committee selects mentors with input from the building principal. Potential mentors complete an application including recommendations from colleagues.

(Continued)

Figure 10.1 (Continued)

Criteria for Success	1 Inadequate	2 Basic	3 Proficient	4 Sustainable
Mentor and New Teacher Matches	Mentors and new teachers are matched without consideration of grade level, content area, or geographic location.	Mentors and new teachers are matched (to the degree possible) according to grade-level and content area.	Mentors and new teachers are matched (to the degree possible) according to grade-level and content area. Building principals contribute to the matching process by considering the compatibility of individual styles of the mentors and new teachers.	Mentors and new teachers are matched (to the degree possible) according to grade-level and content area. Building principals contribute to the matching process by considering the compatibility of individual styles of the mentors and new teachers. A procedure exists that, in the event matches do not work, both parties are held harmless and a new match is made.
Training and Support	Training consists of disseminating and walking through the new teacher handbook.	An orientation session is held for mentors outlining roles and responsibilities.	An orientation session is held for mentors and new teachers outlining roles and responsibilities.	An orientation session is held for mentors and new teachers outlining roles and responsibilities.

Figure 10.1 (Continued)

Criteria for Success	1 Inadequate	2 Basic	3 Proficient	4 Sustainable
			Three to four days of mentor training is provided to all mentor teachers. Training includes qualities of effective mentors, needs of new teachers, active listening and questioning skills, cognitive coaching, and data collection techniques.	Three to four days of mentor training is provided to all mentor teachers. Training includes qualities of effective mentors, needs of new teachers, active listening and questioning skills, cognitive coaching, and data collection techniques. Mentor and new teacher pairs are provided with on-site coaching and support throughout the year.
Supporting Policies and Procedures	There are no policies in place to support the mentor program. However, the district has decided to implement a mentor program of some sort.	A set of guidelines is developed to support the mentor program. Incentives are provided for mentor teachers. Training dates are set. Mentors and new teachers have to "catch as catch can" regarding finding time to meet.	A set of guidelines is developed to support the mentor program. Incentives are provided for mentor teachers. Structures are in place to provide mentors and new teachers with time during the school day to meet and visit each other's classroom.	A set of guidelines is developed to support the mentor program. Incentives are provided for mentor teachers. Structures are in place to provide mentors and new teachers with time during the school day to meet and visit each other's classroom.

Figure 10.1 (Continued)

Criteria for Success	1 Inadequate	2 Basic	3 Proficient	4 Sustainable
				The school schedule provides regular professional development time during the school day for all teachers allowing new teachers to link with and learn from other colleagues.
Mentor Program Evaluation	There is no evaluation of the mentor program.	Evaluation of the mentor program focuses only participant satisfaction and enjoyment.	The impact of mentor training on supporting mentors to successfully fill their roles is assessed. A survey of new teachers' needs is conducted and used to evaluate how well the mentor program serves those needs.	The impact of mentor training on supporting mentors to successfully fill their roles is assessed. A survey of new teachers' needs is conducted and used to evaluate how well the mentor program serves those needs. Mentor teachers conduct self-assessment around their performance as a mentor teacher. New teachers conduct self-assessment of their teaching against clearly defined teaching competencies. A rubric identifying criteria for success of a mentor program is developed and used to assess the efficacy of the mentor program.

Dunne, K. & Villani, S. (forthcoming 2005). *Mentoring: A resource & training guide for educators*. Woburn, MA: Learning Innovations at WestEd.

COACHING THE COACHES: THE NEED FOR ADMINISTRATOR SUPPORT OF TEACHER LEADERS

Just as new teachers need support from mentors, mentors need support as they assume a new role with beginning colleagues. When experienced teachers step out of their classrooms to mentor new colleagues, they are extending their influence beyond their own students and their students' families. To be successful, they need acknowledgment of their role by school personnel and students' families; they need training, resources, and help from other teachers and administrators.

Coaching is one of the most important aspects of a mentor's role with new teachers. Training is necessary for mentors to become effective coaches. Neufeld and Roper (2003) suggest that professional development for coaches should

- Develop a strong, focused, coherent orientation program for new coaches
- Develop differentiated professional development for experienced coaches
- Ensure that coaches are knowledgeable about the learning needs of special populations
- Enable some coaches to become "coach leaders"

Administrators can provide release time for mentors to work with new teachers. They can offer professional development for mentors to become skilled at coaching. And they can remunerate mentors for their work with new faculty. Administrators who foster and share leadership are able to consider ideas that may be different from theirs, thereby expanding the talent pool for creative innovation and significant problem solving. Another way that administrators may support teacher leadership is to share and utilize a rubric of emerging teacher leadership with interested teachers. Looking with them at their interests and capabilities is a tangible way that administrators may help teacher leaders assess their talents and move beyond their classrooms. (See Figure 10.2, Rubric of Emerging Teacher Leadership and the Continuum of Emerging Teacher Leadership [Lambert, 2003].)

> Everyone has the right, responsibility, and capability to be a leader . . . it is in the adult learning environment that teacher leadership truly develops. Leading and learning are deeply intertwined . . . leading is fundamental to the nature and mission of teaching. (Lambert, 2003, p. 33)

(Text continues on page 193)

Figure 10.2   Rubric of Emerging Teacher Leadership and the Continuum of Emerging Teacher Leadership

From ──▶ To

Dependent	Independent	Interdependent	Leadership
A. Adult Development			
Defines self in relation to others in the community. Considers the opinions of others, particularly those in authority, to be highly important.	Defines self as independent from the group, separating personal needs and goals from those of others. Does not often see the need for group action.	Defines self as interdependent with others in the school community, seeking feedback and counsel from others.	Engages colleagues in acting out of a sense of self and shared values, forming interdependent learning communities.
Does not yet recognize the need for self-reflection. Tends to implement strategies as learned without making adjustments after reflective practice.	Engages in personal reflection leading to refinement of strategies and routines. Does not often share reflections with others. Focuses on argument for own ideas. Does not support systems designed to enhance reflective practice.	Engages in personal reflection to improve practice. Models improvements for others in the school community. Shares views with others and develops an understanding of others' assumptions.	Evokes reflection in others. Develops and supports a culture of self-reflection that may include collaborative planning, peer coaching, action research, and reflective writing.
Does not regularly evaluate practice or systematically connect teacher and student behaviors.	Does not share results of self-evaluation with others, but typically ascribes responsibility for problems or errors to others, such as students or family.	Engages in self-evaluation and is highly introspective. Accepts shared responsibility as a natural part of the school community. Does not blame others when things go wrong.	Enables others to engage in self-evaluation and introspection, leading toward greater individual and shared responsibility.

(Continued)

Figure 10.2 (Continued)

From			To
Dependent	**Independent**	**Interdependent**	**Leadership**

A. Adult Development (Continued)

Dependent	Independent	Interdependent	Leadership
Needs effective strategies to demonstrate respect and concern for others. Though polite, focuses primarily on own needs.	Shows respect toward others in most situations, usually in private. Can be disrespectful in public debates. Provides little feedback to others.	Consistently shows respect and concern for all members of the school community. Validates the qualities and opinions of others.	Encourages others to become respectful, caring, and trusted members of the school community. Recognizes that the ideas and achievements of colleagues are part of an overall goal of collegial empowerment.

B. Dialogue

Dependent	Independent	Interdependent	Leadership
Interacts with others primarily on a social level, and does not discuss common goals or group learning.	Discusses logistical issues and problems with others. Sees goals as individually set for each classroom; does not actively focus on common goals.	Communicates well with individuals and groups in the community as a means to create and sustain relationships and focus on teaching and learning. Actively participates in dialogue.	Facilitates effective dialogue among members of the school community in order to build relationships and focus the dialogue on teaching and learning.
Does not pose questions of or seek to influence the group. Participation is limited to consent or compliance.	Makes personal points of view explicit. When opposed to ideas, asks impeding questions that can derail the dialogue.	Asks questions and provides insights that reflect an understanding of the need to surface assumptions and address the goals of the community.	Facilitates communication among colleagues by asking provocative questions that lead to productive dialogue.

Figure 10.2 (Continued)

From ———————————————————————————————————→ To			
Dependent	**Independent**	**Interdependent**	**Leadership**

B. Dialogue (Continued)

Does not actively seek information or new professional knowledge that challenges current practices. Shares knowledge with others only when requested.	Attends staff development activities that are planned by the school or district. Occasionally shares knowledge during formal and informal gatherings. Does not seek knowledge that challenges status quo.	Studies own practice. Knows the most current information about teaching and learning, and uses it to alter teaching practices.	Works with others to construct knowledge through multiple forms of inquiry, action research, examination of disaggregated school data, and insights from others and from the outside research community.
Responds to situations in rote fashion and expects predictable responses from others. Is sometimes confused by variations from expected norms.	Responds to situations in different but predictable ways. Expects similar consistency from those in authority.	Responds to situations with open-mindedness and flexibility; welcomes the perspectives of others. Alters own assumptions during dialogue when evidence is persuasive.	Promotes open-mindedness and flexibility in others; invites multiple perspectives and interpretations to challenge old assumptions and frame new actions.

C. Collaboration

Bases decision making on personal wants and needs rather than those of the group as a whole.	Promotes individual autonomy in classroom decision making. Relegates school decisions to the principal.	Actively participates in shared decision making. Volunteers to follow through on group decisions.	Promotes collaborative decision making that meets the diverse needs of the school community.

Figure 10.2 (Continued)

From			To
Dependent	**Independent**	**Interdependent**	**Leadership**

C. Collaboration (Continued)

Dependent	Independent	Interdependent	Leadership
Sees little value in team building, but seeks team membership. Participates in teamwork but does not connect activities to larger school goals.	Does not participate in roles or settings that involve team building. Considers most team-building activities to be "touchy-feely" and frivolous.	Participates actively in team building; seeks roles and opportunities to contribute to the team. Sees teamwork as central to community.	Engages colleagues in team-building activities that develop mutual trust and promote collaborative decision making.
Either blames others or takes the blame personally for problems. Is uncertain about the specifics of his or her own involvement.	Plays the role of observer and critic; does not accept responsibility for emerging issues. Blames most problems on poor management.	Acknowledges that problems involve all members of the community. Defines problems and proposes approaches to address the situation. Does not consider assigning blame to be relevant.	Engages colleagues in identifying and acknowledging problems. Acts with others to frame problems and seek resolutions. Anticipates situations that may cause recurrent problems.
Refuses to recognize conflict in the school community. Misdirects frustrations into withdrawal or personal hurt. Avoids talking about issues that might evoke conflict.	Engages conflict as a means to surface competing ideas and approaches. Understands that conflict intimidates many.	Anticipates and seeks to resolve conflicts. Actively tries to channel conflicts into problem-solving endeavors. Is not intimidated by conflict, but does not seek it.	Surfaces, addresses, and mediates conflict within the school and with parents and community. Understands that negotiating conflict is necessary for personal and school change.

Figure 10.2 (Continued)

From			To
Dependent	**Independent**	**Interdependent**	**Leadership**

D. Organizational Change

Dependent	Independent	Interdependent	Leadership
Focuses on present situations and issues; seldom plans for the future. Expects certainty.	Demonstrates forward thinking for own classroom. Does not usually connect personal planning to the future of the school.	Develops forward-thinking skills for working with others and planning for school improvements. Future goals based on common values and vision.	Provides for and creates opportunities to engage others in visionary thinking and planning based on common core values.
Maintains a low profile during school change, and does not get involved with group processes. Tries to comply with changes, and expects compliance from others.	Questions the status quo; suggests that others need to change in order to improve it. Selects changes that reflect a personal philosophy. Opposes or ignores practices that require a schoolwide focus.	Is enthusiastic and actively involved in school change. Leads by example. Explores possibilities and implements changes for both personal and professional development.	Initiates innovative change; motivates and draws others into the action for school and district improvements. Encourages others to implement practices that support schoolwide learning. Provides follow-up planning and coaching support.
Is culturally unaware and naive about the sociopolitical implications of racial, cultural, and gender issues. Treats everybody the same regardless of background.	Is becoming more sensitive to the political implications of diversity. Acknowledges that cultural differences exist and influence individuals and organizations.	Appreciates own cultural identity and the cultural differences of others. Applies this understanding in the classroom and school.	Is committed to the value of cultural differences and builds on those values. Actively seeks to involve others in designing programs and policies that support a multicultural world.

Figure 10.2 (Continued)

From			→ To
Dependent	**Independent**	**Interdependent**	**Leadership**

D. Organizational Change (Continued)

Dependent	Independent	Interdependent	Leadership
Attends to students in own classroom. Is possessive of children and space; has not yet secured a developmental view of children.	Exhibits concern for the level of preparation of students and their readiness to meet established standards.	Is concerned for all children in the school (not just those in own classroom) and their future educational performances.	Works with colleagues to develop programs and policies that take holistic view of child development (e.g., multigrade classrooms, multiyear teacher assignments, parent education, follow-up studies).
Is cordial when working alongside new teachers, but does not offer assistance. Lacks the confidence to provide others with feedback.	Limits information shared with new teachers to that dealing with administrative functions (e.g., attendance accounting, grade reports). Does not offer to serve as a master teacher.	Collaborates with, supports, and gives feedback to new and student teachers. Often serves as master teacher.	Takes responsibility for the support and development of systems for new and student teachers. Develops collaborative programs among schools, districts, and universities.
Displays little interest in the selection of new teachers; assumes they will be appointed by the district or by others in authority.	Assumes that the district will recruit and appoint teachers. Has not proposed a more active role to the teachers' association.	Is actively involved in setting the criteria for and selecting new teachers.	Advocates the development of hiring practices that involve teachers, parents, and students in the schools, district, and teachers' associations; promotes the hiring of diversity candidates.

Figure 10.2 (Continued)

A. Adult Development

Defines self as interdependent with others in the school community, seeking feedback and counsel from others. ⟶ Engages colleagues in acting out of a sense of self and shared values, forming interdependent learning communities.

Engages in personal reflection to improve practice. Models improvements for others in the school community. Shares views with others and develops an understanding of others' assumptions. ⟶ Evokes reflection in others. Develops and supports a culture of self-reflection that may include collaborative planning, peer coaching, action research, and reflective writing.

Engages in self-evaluation and is highly introspective. Accepts shared responsibility as a natural part of the school community. Does not blame others when things go wrong. ⟶ Enables others to engage in self-evaluation and introspection, leading toward greater individual and shared responsibility.

Consistently shows respect and concern for all members of the school community. Validates the qualities and opinions of others. ⟶ Encourages others to become respectful, caring, and trusted members of the school community. Recognizes that the ideas and achievements of colleagues are part of an overall goal of collegial empowerment.

B. Dialogue

Communicates well with individuals and groups in the community as a means to create and sustain relationships and focus on teaching and learning. Actively participates in dialogue. ⟶ Facilitates effective dialogue among members of the school community in order to build relationships and focus the dialogue on teaching and learning.

Asks questions and provides insights that reflect an understanding of the need to surface assumptions and address the goals of the community. ⟶ Facilitates communication among colleagues by asking provocative questions that lead to productive dialogue.

Figure 10.2 (Continued)

B. Dialogue (Continued)

Studies own practice. Knows the most current information about teaching and learning, and uses it to alter teaching practices. ⟶ Works with others to construct knowledge through multiple forms of inquiry, action research, examination of disaggregated school data, and insights from others and from the outside research community.

Responds to situations with open-mindedness and flexibility; welcomes the perspectives of others. Alters own assumptions during dialogue when evidence is persuasive. ⟶ Promotes open-mindedness and flexibility in others; invites multiple perspectives and interpretations to challenge old assumptions and frame new actions.

C. Collaboration

Actively participates in shared decision making. Volunteers to follow through on group decisions. ⟶ Promotes collaborative decision making that meets the diverse needs of the school community.

Participates actively in team building; seeks roles and opportunities to contribute to the team. Sees teamwork as central to community. ⟶ Engages colleagues in team-building activities that develop mutual trust and promote collaborative decision making.

Acknowledges that problems involve all members of the community. Defines problems and proposes approaches to address the situation. Does not consider assigning blame to be relevant. ⟶ Engages colleagues in identifying and acknowledging problems. Acts with others to frame problems and seek resolutions. Anticipates situations that may cause recurrent problems.

Anticipates and seeks to resolve conflicts. Actively tries to channel conflicts into problem-solving endeavors. Is not intimidated by conflict, but does not seek it. ⟶ Surfaces, addresses, and mediates conflict within the school and with parents and community. Understands that negotiating conflict is necessary for personal and school change.

Figure 10.2 (Continued)

D. Organizational Change

Develops forward-thinking skills for working with others and planning for school improvements. Bases future goals on common values and vision.   ⟶   Provides for and creates opportunities to engage others in visionary thinking and planning based on common core values.

Is enthusiastic and actively involved in school change. Leads by example. Explores possibilities and implements changes for both personal and professional development.   ⟶   Initiates innovative change; motivates and draws others into the action for school and district improvements. Encourages others to implement practices that support schoolwide learning. Provides follow-up planning and coaching support.

Appreciates own cultural identity and the cultural differences of others. Applies this understanding in the classroom and school.   ⟶   Is committed to the value of cultural differences and builds on those values. Actively seeks to involve others in designing programs and policies that support a multicultural world.

Is concerned for all childern in the school (not just those in own classroom) and their future educational performances.   ⟶   Works with colleagues to develop programs and policies that take holistic view of child development (e.g., multigrade classrooms, multiyear teacher assignments, parent education, follow-up studies).

Collaborates with, supports, and gives feedback to new and student teachers. Often serves as master teacher.   ⟶   Takes responsibility for the support and development of systems for new and student teachers. Develops collaborative programs between schools, districts, and universities.

Is actively involved in setting the criteria for and selecting new teachers.   ⟶   Advocates the development of hiring practices that involve teachers, parents, and students to the schools, district, and teachers' associations; promotes the hiring of diversity candidates.

Source: Used with permission of the Association of Supervision and Curriculum and Development.

TEACHER LEADERS GAIN AS THEY GIVE

Rejuvenation and Retention of Veteran Teachers

Teacher leadership, in the form of something specific such as mentoring, or through more systemic involvement, has many benefits for veteran teachers. In fact, many mentors and teacher leaders say that they gain more than they give in terms of their own professional development, improvement of their own practice, and deep-felt satisfaction from being a contributing member of the school community. Teacher leadership can promote veteran teacher retention and rejuvenation, as well as new teacher retention and satisfaction.

Roland Barth, founder of the Principals' Center at Harvard University, has identified benefits experienced by teachers who choose the path of teacher leadership (1990).

Reduction of Isolation

Mentors often reach out to reduce new teachers' sense of isolation and are surprised to find how energized they are by the frequent contact and collaboration. In addition, they know their support means a great deal to the new teachers.

Though Colleen, as an instructional specialist, feels two steps removed from the action of teaching students, she acknowledges the impact of her work as the mentors' coach. "I've gotten letters from teachers who are so thankful for their coach. I'm providing something that might not have otherwise been there."

Personal and Professional Satisfaction

The goal of the program Colleen coordinates is to provide compassionate, committed, collaborative support for high-quality teaching and learning at schools with the greatest need. Perhaps that's why she concluded, "Teacher leadership is going beyond one's self to improve the greater picture for children and learning. Teacher leadership is influencing up and out for the greater good."

A Sense of Instrumentality, Investment, and Membership in the School Community

For Colleen, it evolved. "I thought I was going to coach, and then I asked: Who's going to monitor for compliance? Pay the teachers correctly? Organize professional development for them? Set up the rooms?" Not getting any answers, she concluded, "I guess it's me."

Ted mentors three new teachers who are alternative certification candidates. All three have completed their plans for alternative certification, which have been approved, with commendations, by the New Hampshire

Department of Education. In addition, they helped eight other noncertified teachers complete their alternative certification–route plans; they, too, were all approved.

New Learning About the Schools, the Process of Change, and Themselves

Ted noticed that many teachers who were certified were hired and then failed. He decided to do something about it.

> I knew the school board and the administrators. I became president of the teachers' union and negotiated that every new teacher, particularly if they hadn't any experience, have a mentor. Mentors had a job description, and were paid $1,500. That was in 1992, and it was put into the contract.

Judy reported that teacher leadership in mentoring had a tremendous influence on her own professional growth.

> In addition to my self-reflection, the workshops that Martin and I had to produce for the mentoring program were an opportunity for us to focus on the real issues of teaching. Mentoring moved beyond the middle school, gradually increasing communication among other schools in the district. At the same time, Martin and I were asked to present and consult in schools outside our district. That gave me a perspective on our school and program which I never had before.

Colleen provides a great deal of training as a coordinator and coach of mentor coaches. Through her program, coaches participate in a mentor academy through the New Teachers Center of Santa Cruz, a Cognitive Coaching™ book study, and weekly coaching meetings for problem solving and learning. "We're using what some of my mentors did with me: goal setting, scripting lessons, videotaping, giving parent workshops, taking classes, presenting, offering suggestions on practice, engaging in planning and reflecting conferences, and looking at data."

Professional Invigoration and Replenishment

Steve participated in the Governor's Academy and the NNECN, both of which he credits with helping him become more intentional about his practice.

I had a feel for what was the right thing to do. Both trainings forced me to look at the standards—why do I do what I do? Plus, it's changed the way I do things. It forced me to examine what's not been effective.

Judy also found an unexpected benefit of mentoring for herself; she was instrumental in the development of the mentoring program in her district.

The fact that we developed a cognitive coaching part of our program gave us an opportunity to reflect on our practice in ways that we don't typically do. There's been an opportunity for me to reexamine my practice over and over again. I always learned more than the new teachers, in my opinion, because I could reflect with them and that then forced me to think about what I was doing myself, in my own practice.

> "I feel like there's no question that what I do makes a difference to a lot of people: kids, their parents. . . . Change is occurring in a positive way for a large number of people. That affects other people who will affect other people. Those ripples keep traveling."
>
> Steve DeAngelis

RECENTLY RETIRED TEACHERS ARE A SOURCE OF LEADERSHIP

Ted tried to retire from teaching in 2004 after thirty-eight years in the profession. After doing so, he was immediately recruited by the assistant superintendent of his former district to teach a course and mentor some new teachers. Ted noticed ACROSS on the Internet and contacted the central office administrators to discuss the possibility of becoming involved.

In 2005 Ted became the dean of students and he heads the mentoring program. He does this four hours each day, leaving school at 11:00 with plenty of time for gardening and other interests. Ted is an example of a growing trend to involve recently retired teachers in mentoring new teachers. Carefully selected retired teachers may be in an ideal position to mentor because they have so much knowledge and craft wisdom and don't have classroom responsibilities of their own.

Recently retired master teachers (RMTs) can make a significant contribution to their chosen field by mentoring new teachers. There are a number of advantages to recruiting, screening, training, matching, monitoring, supporting, recognizing, and paying them (Yalen, 2004):

- RMTs have accumulated expertise and wisdom and a wide repertoire of strategies to share.
- RMTs have the time and flexibility to meet the new teacher's needs without other school or classroom responsibilities.
- RMTs will benefit personally and professionally as they experience a bridge to retirement and a chance to validate their careers and impact the next generation of teachers and students.
- Using retirees in such a constructive way is consistent with current research on both successful retirement and successful aging.
- Using retirees to support the future of education is supported by both major teacher professional organizations, the American Federation of Teachers (AFT) and the National Education Association (NEA).
- Using RMTs is a cost-effective solution that may provide school systems with significant payback.

ENCOURAGE THE DEVELOPMENT OF ALL TEACHER LEADERS

Just as mentors promote new teachers' reflections by asking questions and looking at data, teacher leaders can grow from reflecting on their leadership.

Figure 10.3, the Coaching Self-Assessment Survey (Dunne & Villani, in press), is a discrepancy analysis tool that helps teachers reflect on the following coaching skills and information:

- Engaging teachers and administrators in your setting
- Adult learning
- Group facilitation
- Professional learning
- Data analysis
- Instructional planning

Figure 10.4, Coaching New Teachers: Essential Coaching Skills (Dunne & Villani, in press), will support reflection by teacher leaders who are mentors or additional support providers. The elements of performance are

- Questioning: the planning conversation
- Data gathering and classroom observation
- Questioning: the reflecting conversation
- Analysis of and response to teacher reflection
- Engaging with content

(Text continues on page 208)

Figure 10.3   Coaching Self-Assessment Survey

The following self-assessment survey is a discrepancy analysis tool that asks you to self-assess your current knowledge and use of specific coaching skills and information. The Likert-type scale ranges from 1 to 5.   1 = no knowledge of or ability to use; 2 = little knowledge of or ability to use; 3 = moderate knowledge of or ability to use; 4 = consistent and solid knowledge of or ability to use; 5 = advanced knowledge of and ability to use.

COACH WORK COMPONENTS	Knowledge of	Ability to apply in your work	Comments
Engaging Teachers and Administrators in Your Setting: *Strategies to*			
Negotiate entry to one third or more of classrooms	1 2 3 4 5	1 2 3 4 5	
Develop plan of relevant work with principal	1 2 3 4 5	1 2 3 4 5	
Present concepts of new initiative in small groups	1 2 3 4 5	1 2 3 4 5	
Communicate to teachers and administrators the resources a coach offers	1 2 3 4 5	1 2 3 4 5	
Communicate progress to the larger community (including using existing communication mechanisms)	1 2 3 4 5	1 2 3 4 5	
Communicate with key leadership groups in the school	1 2 3 4 5	1 2 3 4 5	
Adult Learning: *Strategies to*			
Identify a range of adult learning styles	1 2 3 4 5	1 2 3 4 5	
Identify the learning styles of specific individuals in your school	1 2 3 4 5	1 2 3 4 5	
Effectively respond to people regardless of their learning style	1 2 3 4 5	1 2 3 4 5	
Support adults through the process of change	1 2 3 4 5	1 2 3 4 5	

(Continued)

Figure 10.3 (Continued)

COACH WORK COMPONENTS	Knowledge of	Ability to apply in your work	Comments
Group Facilitation: *Strategies to*			
Facilitate small groups (4-12 persons)	1 2 3 4 5	1 2 3 4 5	
Facilitate medium groups (12-40 persons)	1 2 3 4 5	1 2 3 4 5	
Facilitate larger groups (40-100 persons)	1 2 3 4 5	1 2 3 4 5	
Effectively deal with resistant behavior	1 2 3 4 5	1 2 3 4 5	
Ensure that all members of a group participate and contribute	1 2 3 4 5	1 2 3 4 5	
Facilitate group decision making	1 2 3 4 5	1 2 3 4 5	
Help other groups to facilitate own group meeting	1 2 3 4 5	1 2 3 4 5	
Professional Learning: *Strategies to*			
Conduct a classroom lesson while one or more teachers observe	1 2 3 4 5	1 2 3 4 5	
Give and receive feedback following a classroom lesson	1 2 3 4 5	1 2 3 4 5	
Organize a cycle of peer observation and reflection with a group of 4 to 6 teachers	1 2 3 4 5	1 2 3 4 5	
Offer nonjudgmental feedback	1 2 3 4 5	1 2 3 4 5	
Support teachers in deepening their content knowledge	1 2 3 4 5	1 2 3 4 5	
Teach others to give and receive feedback	1 2 3 4 5	1 2 3 4 5	

COACH WORK COMPONENTS	Knowledge of	Ability to apply in your work	Comments
Data Analysis: *Strategies to*			
Analyze summative assessments	1 2 3 4 5	1 2 3 4 5	
Examine student work and student thinking	1 2 3 4 5	1 2 3 4 5	
Conduct a classroom walk-through	1 2 3 4 5	1 2 3 4 5	
Lead a group in looking at student work	1 2 3 4 5	1 2 3 4 5	
Lead a group in data analysis	1 2 3 4 5	1 2 3 4 5	
Data Use: *Strategies to*			
Use data to change focus or emphasis of instruction	1 2 3 4 5	1 2 3 4 5	
Organize a group to use data analysis to shift or refocus instruction	1 2 3 4 5	1 2 3 4 5	
Instructional Planning: *Strategies to*			
Develop an annual instructional plan focused on specific content	1 2 3 4 5	1 2 3 4 5	
Engage a group of educators to assess needs	1 2 3 4 5	1 2 3 4 5	
Engage a group of educators to develop instructional strategies	1 2 3 4 5	1 2 3 4 5	
Engage a group of educators to identify appropriate measures of goals	1 2 3 4 5	1 2 3 4 5	
Help a group to organize small strategies around a broad vision	1 2 3 4 5	1 2 3 4 5	

Source: Created by Kathy Dunne, Learning Innovations at WestEd, Woburn, MA, and Sonia Caus Gleason, Jamaica Plain, MA. Used with permission of Kathy Dunne.

Figure 10.4 Coaching New Teachers: Essential Coaching Skills

Levels of Performance Elements	1 Emerging	2 Maintaining	3 Sustaining	4 Adaptive
Questioning: *The Planning Conversation*	• Coach asks questions based on the coach's thinking about content, instruction, and assessment	• Coach asks questions that elicit the teacher's inner intent of the lesson in terms of content, instruction, and assessment, and that promote the coach's thinking about content, instruction, and assessment	• Coach asks questions that both elicit the teacher's inner intent of the lesson in terms of content, instruction, and assessment, and that promote the coach's thinking about content, instruction, and assessment	• Coach asks questions that elicit the teacher's inner intent of the lesson in terms of content, instruction and assessment and the coach asks questions of him/herself that elicit the coach's inner intent in the coaching process

Figure 10.4 (Continued)

Levels of Performance Elements	1 Emerging	2 Maintaining	3 Sustaining	4 Adaptive
	• Coach frames and poses questions that elicit teacher responses focused on explanation and clarification	• Coach frames and poses questions that elicit teacher responses focused on explanation, clarification, prediction and assessment	• Coach frames and poses questions that elicit teacher responses focused on explanation, clarification, elaboration, prediction, assessment, teacher's intentionality, and connections to other content/concepts	• Coach and teacher co-create questions that elicit teacher responses focused on explanation, clarification, elaboration, prediction, assessment, teacher's intentionality, and connections to other content/concepts
Data Gathering and Classroom Observation	• Classroom data is subjective and based on judgment and inference by the coach	• Classroom data is mostly objective i.e. measurable and observable with some judgment or inference of the coach	• Classroom data is objective, i.e. measurable and observable	• Classroom data is objective i.e. measurable and observable and includes questions to elicit the teacher's intentions (at particular moments of the lesson) based upon the data gathered

201

Figure 10.4 (Continued)

Levels of Performance Elements	1 Emerging	2 Maintaining	3 Sustaining	4 Adaptive
	• Classroom data gathered is based on what the coach is interested in observing	• Classroom data gathered is mostly based on what was agreed upon between the coach and teacher during the planning conference. Additional data is recorded by the coach based on the coach's opinion of what was important to gather	• Classroom data gathered is based on what was agreed upon between the coach and teacher during the planning conference	• Classroom data gathered is based on what was agreed upon between the coach and teacher during the planning conference and includes additional data the coach is able to gather that pertains to issues that had been discussed between the coach and the teacher during other planning/reflecting conferences
	• Classroom data gathered is not	• Classroom data gathered is not	• A copy of the classroom data	• A copy of the classroom data gathered is provided to the

Figure 10.4 (Continued)

Levels of Performance Elements	1 Emerging	2 Maintaining	3 Sustaining	4 Adaptive
	shared with the teacher	shared with the teacher until the reflective conference	gathered is provided to the teacher immediately following the classroom observation in written format	teacher immediately following the lassroom observation in a variety of formats e.g. written, audio, and/or video
Questioning: *The Reflecting Conversation*	• Coach begins the reflective conversation with her/his interpretation of what occurred during the classroom observation	• Coach begins the reflective conversation-with a question that elicits the teacher's perspective of "how the lesson went" and then adds his/her opinion of how the lesson went	• Coach begins the reflective conversation with a question that elicits the teacher's perspective of "how the lesson went"	• Teacher begins the reflecting conversation by reflecting on how s/he thought the lesson went

Figure 10.4 (Continued)

Levels of Performance Elements	1 Emerging	2 Maintaining	3 Sustaining	4 Adaptive
	• Coach frames and poses questions that are based on the coach's beliefs and values about what happened/should have happened during the lesson	• Coach frames and poses questions that prompt the teacher to examine the data and how it compares with what the teacher intended	• Coach and teacher co-create questions that prompt the teacher to examine the data and how it compares with what the teacher intended and identify what s/he would do the same or differently next time and why	• Teacher identifies and responds to questions that prompt him/her to examine the data and how it compares with what the teacher intended and identify what s/he would do the same or differently next time and why
	• Coach seldom asks questions that focus on student learning	• Coach poses questions that asks the teacher to identify what the students learned	• Coach and teacher co-create questions that ask teacher to identify what students have learned and what evidence the teacher has of student learning	• Teacher shares evidence that demonstrates student learning and any student misconceptions that may exist

Figure 10.4 (Continued)

Levels of Performance Elements	1 Emerging	2 Maintaining	3 Sustaining	4 Adaptive
			• Coach asks questions that prompt the teacher to begin planning for the next lesson	• Teacher identifies what s/he will do next with these students based on the classroom data and her/his own reflections
Analysis of and Response to Teacher Reflection	• Coach assumes what teacher responses mean without checking assumptions or paraphrasing	• Coach inconsistently applies the norms of *pause, paraphrase and probe* when responding to teacher's reflections about a given lesson	• Coach consistently applies the norms of *pause, paraphrase and probe* when responding to teacher reflections	• Coach consistently applies all seven norms of collaboration in conversations with the teacher
	• Coach accepts vague responses without probing for specificity	• Coach occasionally accepts vague responses without probing for specificity	• Coach consistently probes for specificity around vague responses by the new teacher	• Coach consistently probes for specificity around vague responses by the new teacher

Figure 10.4 (Continued)

Levels of Performance Elements	1 Emerging	2 Maintaining	3 Sustaining	4 Adaptive
	• Coach advocates for her/his perspective without inquiring into the teacher's perspective	• Coach inconsistently comes from a place of inquiry first and advocacy second when talking with teacher about how s/he will apply learnings of one lesson to the next	• Coach consistently comes from a place of inquiry first and advocacy second when talking with teacher about how s/he will apply learnings of one lesson to the next	• Coach consistently comes from a place of inquiry first and advocacy second when talking with teacher about how s/he will apply learnings of one lesson to the next
	• Coach uses only her/his preferred style of coaching without consideration of the teacher's need for structure	• Coach modifies coaching style to match the teacher's need for structure some of the time	• Coach consistently modifies coaching style to match the teacher's need for structure	• Coach consistently modifies coaching style to match the teacher's need for structure

Figure 10.4 (Continued)

Levels of Performance Elements	1 Emerging	2 Maintaining	3 Sustaining	4 Adaptive
Engaging with Content	• Coach asks questions that elicit responses about the content goals of the lesson without reference to content/curriculum standards • Coach references content-based mathematics tools and curriculum without using them with the teacher	• Coach asks questions that elicit responses about the content goals of the lesson and about how those goals connect with content/curriculum standards • Coach uses at least one content-based tool and one curriculum unit in her/his work with the teacher	• Coach asks questions and provides examples of how to connect lesson/unit plans to content/curriculum standards • Coach consistently uses most of the content-based tools and curriculum in her/his work with the teacher	• Coach conducts demonstration lessons that provide examples of content-specific instruction and assessment that connect to content/curriculum standards • Coach consistently uses all of the content-based tools and curriculum in her/his work with the teacher

Source: Created by Kathy Dunne, Learning Innovations at WestEd, Woburn, MA.

Teacher leaders need support to stretch their thinking and promote heightened skills in whatever aspect of leadership they choose. It is not enough for administrators to be willing to work with teacher leaders when they initiate a discussion or make a suggestion for school improvement. Administrators need to recruit teacher leaders and nurture their development. Similarly, veteran and new teachers must recognize the contributions that teacher leaders can make and work with them to achieve ways to make schools better places for children and adults to thrive.

Mentoring provides an obvious and needed opportunity for teacher leadership. Teacher leaders, like new teachers, need support structures that enable growth and learning, that foster initiative, and that encourage collaboration; the collective wisdom of any community is greater than its parts.

CONCLUSION

Mentors are often excellent teachers stepping into a new role. They need training and ongoing support, just as new teachers do to fulfill their role. They each may feel as though they are facing the challenge of a ropes course: They are taking great risks to improve their practice while being observed as they do. To be successful, they need training, resources, systemic structures, and acknowledgment. It is the responsibility of all members of the school community to provide what they need.

Mentoring also provides an opportunity for experienced teachers to see their profession from a new perspective. While learning new skills such as cognitive coaching, they are gaining insight into their practice and the practices of those around them—all while they are helping new teachers. For some mentors, this will lead to a sense of renewal and rejuvenation about their own work. For others, it will open up possibilities for reflection and change at an institutional level.

Parallel leadership may be one answer to the growing challenges facing administrators and teachers in today's schools. School communities need to nurture leadership in many different ways if schools are to offer the opportunities for students and adults to learn and achieve at new heights.

REFLECTIONS AND APPLICATIONS

This chapter points out that master teachers are a source of leadership. Exercise 10.1 asks you to reflect on the extent your induction and mentoring program provides opportunities for master teachers to participate. Then, based on the material in the chapter, it asks that you consider how you might provide or extend such opportunities.

Exercise 10.1 Involving Teacher Leaders

Directions: Below, in column 1, are six areas that should be considered when involving master teachers in the induction and mentoring program. In the box to the right of each component, reflect on how that item is currently being addressed by your program. In the next box, speculate how, by applying material from this chapter, you might provide master teachers with opportunities to become even more effectively involved.

Area of Involvement of Teacher Leaders	How Addressed	Potential Opportunity to Apply or Enhance
Formally mentoring new teachers		
Providing professional development sessions to new and veteran teachers		
Arranging coverage so that mentors and new teachers may do classroom observations and coaching conferences		
Training the mentors for the induction and mentoring program		
Being involved in the design, implementation, and evaluation of an induction and mentoring program for new teachers		
Integrating the induction and mentoring program with systemwide professional development		

REFERENCES

Barth, R. (1990). *Improving schools from within: Teachers, parents, and principals can make the difference.* San Francisco: Jossey-Bass.

Bolman, L., & Deal, T. (1994). Looking for leadership: Another search party's report. *Educational Administration Quarterly, 30*(1), 77–96.

Crowther, F., Kaagan, S. S., Ferguson, M., & Hann, L. (2002). *Developing teacher leaders: How teacher leadership enhances school success.* Thousand Oaks, CA: Corwin.

Darling-Hammond, L. (1993). Reframing the school reform agenda: Developing capacity for school transformation. *Phi Delta Kappan, 76*(101), 752–761.

Darling-Hammond, L. (2000). *Solving the dilemmas of teacher supply, quality, and demand.* New York: National Commission on Teaching and America's Future (NCTAF).

Dunne, K., & Villani, S. (in press, 2005). *Mentoring: A resource & training guide for educators* (2nd ed.). Woburn, MA: Learning Innovations at WestEd.

Ferrandino, V. (2000). *Testimony presented to the Commission on Teacher and School Administrator Shortage and Minority Recruitment.* Connecticut State Legislature.

Forster, E. (1997). Teacher leadership: Professional right and responsibility. *Action in Teacher Education, 19*(3), 82–94.

Goleman, D. (1998). What makes a leader? *Harvard Business Review, 76*(6), 93–103.

Holmes Group. (1986). *Tomorrow's teacher: A report of the Holmes Group.* East Lansing, MI: Author.

Katzenmeyer, M., & Moller, G. (1996). *Awakening the sleeping giant: Leadership development for teachers.* Thousand Oaks, CA: Corwin.

Lambert, L. (2003). *Leadership capacity for lasting school improvement.* Alexandria, VA: Association for Supervision and Curriculum Development.

Lieberman, A., & Miller, L. (1999). *Teachers: Transforming their world and their work.* New York: Teachers College Press and Alexandria, VA: Association for Supervision and Curriculum Development.

Lieberman, A., Saxl, E., & Miles, M. (1988). Teachers' leadership: Ideology and practice. In A. Lieberman (Ed.), *Building a professional culture in schools* (pp. 148–166). New York: Teachers College Press.

Lord, B., & Miller, B. (2000). *Teacher leadership: An appealing and inescapable force in school reform?* Newton, MA: Education Development Center.

Meckel, A., & Rolland, L. (2000). BTSA models for support provision. *Thrust for Educational Leadership, 29*(3), 18–20.

NEA. (1995). *Retired projected K–12 professional retirees by decade and sex: 1990–2020.* Alexandria, VA: Decision Demographics.

Neufeld, B., & Roper, D. (2003). *Results.* National Staff Development Council Staff Development Library. Retrieved 8/16/04 from http://www.nsdc.org/library/publications/results/res10–03neufeld.cfm

Rice, E. M., & Schneider, G. T. (1994). A decade of teacher empowerment: An empirical analysis of teacher involvement in decision making, 1980–1991. *Journal of Educational Administration, 32*(1), 43–58.

Schein, E. (1992). *Organization culture and leadership.* San Francisco: Jossey-Bass.

Schon, D. (1983). *The reflective practitioner: How professionals think in action.* New York: Basic Books.

Senge, P. (1992). *The fifth discipline: The art and practice of the learning organization.* New York: Doubleday.

Sparks, D. (2004, Spring). Broader purpose calls for higher understanding: An interview with Andy Hargreaves. *Journal of Staff Development, 25*(2), 46–50.

Spillane, J., Halverson, R., & Diamond, J. (2001, April). Investigating school leadership practice: A distributed perspective. *Research News and Comment,* pp. 23–27.

Texas Center for Educational Research. (2000). *The cost of teacher turnover.* Austin, TX: Texas State Board of Educator Certification.

Villani, S. (1999). *Mentoring teachers: A good, strong anchor.* In M. F. Hayes & I. K. Zimmerman (Eds.), *Teaching: A career, a profession* (pp. 19–26). Wellesley, MA: Massachusetts Association of Supervision and Curriculum Development.

Villani, S. (2001). Mentoring: An opportunity for teacher leadership. *Perspectives.* Wellesley, MA: Massachusetts Association of Supervision and Curriculum Development.

Villani, S. (2002). *Mentoring programs for new teachers: Models of induction and support.* Thousand Oaks, CA: Corwin.

Yalen, T. (2004). *The retired master teacher as mentor: Meeting a national need.* Retrieved April 11, 2004, from http://teachersnetwork.org/TNPI/research/prep/Yalen/

11

Promoting Quality Programs Through State-School Relationships

Janice L. Hall

I f you are convinced as I am that new teacher induction and mentoring programs are critical to the retention and development of new teachers, then I want to impress upon you that I believe at the heart of the success of induction and mentoring programs is the relationship between the state agencies and the school districts. Show me a state where they have a collaborative working relationship between the state and the school districts, and I'll show you a state with strong teacher induction and mentoring programs.

MANDATED MENTORING PROGRAMS

There are about as many working models of new teacher mentoring programs as there are states that have them. A study by the American Federation of Teachers (AFT Policy Brief, 1998) examined each state as to whether it required a mentor program, whether that program was funded, and whether mentor training was mandated. I wondered what might have changed over the six years since that study, so I set out to discover what was happening around the country through examining the various states' Web sites, e-mailing questions posed to state personnel, and finally calling the state agencies for information and verification. The results of this search and its comparison to the earlier data may be found in Table 11.1, the accuracy of which is left to those who disclosed the information.

An examination of the data reveals some interesting facts. In 1998, 44 percent (twenty-one) of the reporting states had mandated new teacher mentoring programs as opposed to 66 percent (thirty-three) of the states in 2004. The earlier study reported that 67 percent (fourteen) of the states mandating programs had full or partial funding for these programs. The later study also showed 67 percent (twenty-two) funded. The significance of these figures is that there has been an increase in mandated new teacher mentoring programs and the state level funding has increased proportionately. There was close to a 25 percent increase in mandated mentoring programs. These facts as they stand are encouraging; however, there were ten states that told me that they were looking to cut back on their funding and were afraid of the negative impact that would follow. All were trying to find ways that they could work with legislators and with school districts to come up with creative ideas to continue their programs.

Five of the states with no mandated programs reported that they were piloting programs through grants that they hoped would be picked up by the state when completed. On a sad note, five states lost funding entirely within the past six years with one dropping its program altogether. Only one state dropped the mandate for training mentors, the cause being the loss of funding.

It's not a surprise that funding was reported to be one of the major stumbling blocks to states not mandating new teacher mentoring programs. As reflected in the statement from one state, "We encourage it, but cannot fund it, therefore we do not mandate it." While some strong programs existed within states that have no mandates, the participation in mentoring programs in these states was inconsistent. The larger school districts and those closer to universities who could help often had wonderful programs, while smaller or rural districts would have little or nothing.

One state without a mandated program (Tennessee) was committed to the idea of mentoring new teachers and therefore had helped their school districts by coming up with guidelines and offering a mentor training manual. They felt that they had to help their school districts establish strong programs even though they did not have the funding to support the programs themselves. I found no other states without mandated mentor programs which had established mentoring standards or guidelines. I was even told by one state official that it was not their responsibility but that of the university's. The general gist of the conversation was that they felt that if the colleges of education wanted their graduates to succeed, they would follow them into the schools and help them. They had basically washed their hands of assisting new teachers. I wondered what would happen

Table 11.1   State Mentoring Comparison Chart

	1998 AFT Report			2004 Hall Study Data			
	Mandated Mentor Program	Funded Mentor Program	Mandated Mentor Training	Mandated Mentor Program	Funded Mentor Program	Mandated Mentor Training	Funded Mentor Training
Alabama	No			No			
Alaska	NR			Yes	Yes	No	
Arizona	No			No			
Arkansas	No			Yes	Yes	Yes	Yes
California	No	Yes	No	Yes	Yes	Yes	Yes
Colorado	Yes	No	No	Yes	No	No	
Connecticut	Yes	No	Yes	Yes	Yes	Yes	Yes
Delaware	No	Yes	No	Yes	Yes	Yes	Yes
Florida	No			No			
Georgia	No	Yes	No	No			
Hawaii	No			No			
Idaho	No	Yes	No	Yes	No	No	
Illinois	No			Yes	Yes	Yes	Yes
Indiana	Yes	Yes	Yes	Yes	Yes	Yes	Yes
Iowa	No			Yes	Yes	Yes	Yes
Kansas	No			Yes	No	Yes	No
Kentucky	Yes	Yes	Yes	Yes	No	Yes	No
Louisiana	Yes	Yes	Yes	Yes	Yes	Yes	Yes
Maine	Yes	No	No	No			
Maryland	No			No			
Massachusetts	Yes	No	No	Yes	No	Yes	No
Michigan	Yes	No	No	Yes	Yes	No	
Minnesota	No			No			
Mississippi	Yes	No	No	Yes	Yes	Yes	Yes
Missouri	Yes	No	No	Yes	Yes	Yes	Yes
Montana	No			No			
Nebraska	No	Yes	No	No			
Nevada	NR			No			
New Hampshire	No			No			
New Jersey	Yes	Yes	No	Yes	No	Yes	No
New Mexico	Yes	No	No	Yes	Yes	Yes	Yes

(Continued)

Table 11.1 (Continued)

| | 1998 AFT Report | | | 2004 Hall Study Data | | | |
	Mandated Mentor Program	Funded Mentor Program	Mandated Mentor Training	Mandated Mentor Program	Funded Mentor Program	Mandated Mentor Training	Funded Mentor Training
New York	No			Yes	No	Yes	No
North Carolina	Yes	Yes	Yes	Yes	Yes	No	
North Dakota	No			No			
Ohio	Yes	Yes	No	Yes	Yes	No	
Oklahoma	Yes	Yes	No	Yes	Yes	No	
Oregon	No			No			
Pennsylvania	Yes	No	No	Yes	Yes	No	
Rhode Island	Yes	No	No	Yes	No	Yes	Yes
South Carolina	Yes	No	No	Yes	Yes	Yes	Yes
South Dakota	No			No			
Tennessee	No			No			
Texas	Yes	No	No	Yes	Yes	No	
Utah	Yes	No	No	Yes	No	Yes	No
Vermont	No			Yes	No	No	
Virginia	No			Yes	Yes	Yes	No
Washington	No	Yes	Yes	Yes	Yes	Yes	No
West Virginia	Yes	Yes	Yes	Yes	Yes	Yes	No
Wisconsin	No			Yes	No	Yes	No
Wyoming	No			No			

to teachers in school districts not close to a university or to graduates of universities outside of that state who had been hired to teach in that state.

MANDATED MENTOR TRAINING

With respect to mandating training for mentors who work with new teachers, the 1998 study reported that seven states, 33 percent of those mandating programs, required mentor training, while the 2004 study showed twenty-three states (70 percent) with this requirement. The increase in mandated mentor training clearly shows that this training has become an important focus in the past six years.

Early mentoring programs concentrated on the successful pairing of mentor and mentee and on the qualification of a caring and insightful mentor. But as mentoring programs have matured, it has become apparent that caring and insightful classroom teachers do not necessarily know how to mentor new teachers. As Daresh (2003) explains, "Training people for the role of mentors serving teachers is a critical aspect of any effective program. It is simply not effective to identify people as mentors and then throw them into service in that capacity" (p. 28). According to Nash and Treffinger (1993), although mentor training can increase mentor effectiveness, many who are setting up teacher induction programs are afraid to suggest that any training might be necessary for mentors. These fears often stem from the prospect of "turning off" mentors. However, without training and support for the mentors, an induction program may be "little more then a haphazard effort at pairing new teachers with veteran teachers and hoping some good will come from the match" (Black, 2001, p. 47). Sweeny (2001) cautioned,

> The most critical weak links in ineffective mentoring programs are mentor training and support. These two elements are often missing because people assume that an excellent employee will naturally make an excellent mentor. In fact, that is often not the case. Mentoring is a professional practice with its own knowledge and research base, strategies, and best practices. Without access to these "tools" of effective mentoring, the quality of mentoring is frequently inadequate to produce the kind of impact that the program was designed to produce. (p. 21-c)

A search of the literature revealed that in most programs, mentor training consists of an introduction to mentoring at the beginning of the school year, perhaps followed by some kind of ongoing training (Ganser, 2001; Hutto, 1991; Sweeny, 2001). Ganser (1995) warned that "one of the shortcomings of many staff development programs is that they are 'front-end loaded' . . . with little opportunity for systematic application, practice, and follow-up" (p. 9). One mentor related, "In my first year of mentoring, I felt like a new teacher. The information was given to us quickly, and I felt lost. You are fumbling around trying to look like a mentor, but what you really need is someone to mentor the mentor" (NEA Foundation for the Improvement of Education, 1999). Initial and continuing support for the mentor is crucial.

In the presence of concern for mentoring the mentor, as the beginning mentor expressed above, mentor training has become the center of legislation in twenty-one states such as my own state of Utah, where there had been legislation for nine years mandating a new teacher mentoring program. In January 2002, Utah legislators changed one word in the law (R277-522-3) from stating that "each beginning teacher would have a mentor teacher . . ." to "each beginning teacher would have a *trained* mentor teacher . . ." (emphasis added). This started a flurry of activity within the state to establish mentor training at the school district level since there was no state funding allocated for that purpose. In response to the legislation, the state formed a Quality Teaching Committee. One of the committee's charges was to come up with state guidelines to assist school districts to set up mentor training programs. These guidelines may be found at their Web site (http://www.usoe.k12.ut.us). The committee was composed of representatives from the state, the state education association, school districts, and universities.

To follow this down to the school district level, one school district in northeastern Utah, Cache County School District, has taken the guidelines and will introduce a new mentor training program in the 2004–2005 school year. The training program will incorporate the efforts of the Utah Education Association, who will provide the training for a group of experienced mentors who will become mentor trainers for the district. These trainers will, in return, train the mentors in their district and become a resource for them. In my data collecting, the only other state that reported a similar model was Tennessee.

The above example shows that the relationship between the state agency and school district was very important in assisting the district to set up a mentor training program by first mandating mentor training and then providing state guidelines for implementation, although the funds were acquired through a grant with Utah State University. The example also shows the collaboration between the state, the school district (which also extended to the university), and the state's education association. Similar collaborations between states and school districts were reported by other states, but in all states reporting a collaborative effort, the main stakeholders were the state agents and the school districts.

NCLB IMPACT

The effectiveness and quality of teachers is at the center of the No Child Left Behind (NCLB) legislation. According to the National Governors Association (NGA Center for Best Practices, 2002), "Early studies suggest that not only do good induction programs improve teacher retention, but they also influence teaching practices, increase teacher satisfaction, and promote strong professional development and collegial relationships" (p. 6). Research done by the American Educational Research Association showed that "beginning teachers who are paired with a mentor are more likely to move beyond concerns about classroom management and concentrate on student learning" (p. 6). As I spoke with the various representatives at the state agencies, it soon became apparent that the NCLB legislation was fueling some of the interest in mentoring new teachers and in training the mentors. There were state agents who felt that mentoring their new teachers could help keep their highly qualified teachers in the profession. At the same time, there were school districts in some states that, in the face of NCLB, were asking their states to help by providing funding for developing new mentoring programs or setting up mentoring and mentor training guidelines. It is noteworthy that the NCLB legislation was causing more states and school districts to talk about collaborating to set up new programs and maintain existing ones.

THE IMPACT OF COLLABORATION

As I finished my study, I became more convinced than ever that a collaborative relationship between state agencies and school districts is significant in creating and maintaining new teacher mentoring programs and mentor training. Even though it is usually perceived that mandates create a top-down relationship, in this instance, such was not the case. The mandates from state agencies created an atmosphere in which the state began working closely with the school districts to establish guidelines, standards, and training manuals. As pressures to maintain high quality teachers in the schools came from federal legislation, the school districts turned to the states for help with their new teacher mentoring programs.

Even in the absence of funding, states could still assist with creating guidelines, encouraging and supporting school districts in their efforts to establish new teacher mentor programs, offer mentor training, and assist in coming up with innovative ideas. As an example of innovative ideas, two states reported that they were beginning an online mentoring program in the fall of 2004: Michigan was working to set up their "Virtual Learning Community," and North Dakota, their "Electronic Mentoring." Dorothy Gotlieb, the director of the Office of Professional Services and Educator Licensing in the Colorado Department of Education, shared with me her idea of an incentive which might help school districts that could not afford to pay their mentors for their service to new teachers. Referring to her comments at a conference she had just attended in which her state's fiscal crisis was being discussed, she told me,

> My own initial suggestion was to, at the very least, allow [license] renewal credit to mentor teachers who had taken on new licensees. Having an induction/mentoring program, with strong support, will obviously lead to more effective teaching and much better retention in the field, so it would be a good thing on which to focus, even though the incentives may have to be creative.

WHAT STATES CAN DO TO DEVELOP RELATIONSHIPS AND IMPROVE PROGRAMS

Not all states understand the tremendous impact they can have by taking an active role in establishing funding and guidelines to promote consistent statewide mentoring programs, program guidelines, and standards or creating mentor training standards or guidelines. Those who lack this vision need to look to the excellent working relationships that exist between some states and their school districts. For example, there are states that have created mandates which forced participation, and in many instances had helped to create consistency, in the school districts across the state, whether they were small rural districts or large urban districts. The states with the most consistency have mandates with some kind of accountability in place. A little less consistency occurred in states where they had no mandates but still had worked collaboratively with school districts to set up guidelines for programs and mentor training.

States can also create consistency through funding. States where there are funded mandated programs are where the most consistency and accountability are found. The states with the least consistency have left everything up to the school districts or to universities. States that take an active role in securing funding for mentor training programs will find that doing so is much more cost-efficient than recruitment and hiring initiatives. For example, an NGA Center for Best Practices report (2002) states that in California "after only one year, participating school districts saved 31 cents for every state dollar spent; after two years, the savings amounted to 68 cents for every state dollar spent" (p. 7).

I may be going out on a limb here, but I truly believe that the more one considers the data, the more one will come to the conclusion that states cannot have a hands-off approach to mentoring new teachers. If funding is not possible, the state can still actively support school districts in their attempts to mentor new teachers. For one thing, the state could be active in gathering and disseminating information to school districts about what other school districts within the state are doing that are successful. They could also research ideas from other states in similar circumstances and pass the information along to their school districts. I lost track of the number of times I would be talking to a state agent and say, "We have that same situation in Utah." Or as I spoke with them, I would say, "That sounds similar to what they're doing in [another state]." Inevitably the state agent to whom I was speaking would ask for more information about that state or how to contact that person. Sometimes looking at long-established mentoring programs can be discouraging, especially to states struggling with funding. But when state agents would hear of others who were struggling in the same way they were, they were interested in obtaining information from those states. In other words, states do not have to reinvent the wheel. There are other states with which they could share information and ideas.

CONCLUSION

Public schools cannot afford to lose our well-trained, highly qualified teachers. Legislation and results from extensive research demand that we give the best education possible to our children. States need to take a more active role in establishing a collaborative relationship between themselves and school districts. It is reassuring to know that there was an increase between 1998 and 2004 in states that have awakened to the realization of the necessity of this collaboration. We need to keep this trend going.

REFLECTIONS AND APPLICATIONS

This chapter emphasizes the importance of state involvement in district induction and mentoring programs. Exercise 11.1 asks you to reflect on the impact your state has (or does not have) on your district's mentoring program and then to consider what your state can do to enhance that support.

Exercise 11.1   State-District Collaboration

Directions: Below, in column 1, are ways states may be involved in mentoring programs that impact districts. In the box to the right of each area, reflect on the extent to which that area impacts your mentoring program. In the next box, speculate how, by applying material from this chapter and other sources, your state might be able to enhance its support in that area.

State Involvement	Impact on District	Potential Enhancement
Program is mandated		
Program is funded		
Mentor training is mandated		
Mentor training is funded and/or provided at no charge		
Other support such as guidelines, consultation, materials, and conferences provided		

REFERENCES

AFT Policy Brief. (1998). *Mentor teacher programs in the states.* Retrieved May 11, 2004, from http://www.aft.org/edissues/

Black, S. (2001). A lifeboat for new teachers. *American School Board Journal, 188*(9), 46–48.

Daresh, J. C. (2003). *Teachers mentoring teachers: A practical approach to helping new and experienced staff.* Thousand Oaks, CA: Corwin.

Ganser, T. (1995). *A road map for designing quality mentoring programs for beginning teachers.* ERIC Document Reproduction Service No. ED 394 932, Springfield, VA.

Ganser, T. (2001). *Building the capacity of school districts to design, implement, and evaluate new teacher mentor programs.* ERIC Document Reproduction Service No. ED 452 168, Springfield, VA.

Hutto, N. (Ed.). (1991). *Mentor training manual for Texas teachers.* ERIC Document Reproduction Service No. ED 359 182, Springfield, VA.

Nash, D., & Treffinger, D. (1993). *The mentor kit.* Waco, TX: Prufrock Press.

The NEA Foundation for the Improvement of Education. (1999). *Creating a teacher mentoring program.* Retrieved November 8, 2003, from http://www.nfie.org/publications/mentoring.htm

NGA Center for Best Practices. (2002). *Issue brief: Mentoring and supporting new teachers.* Retrieved May 10, 2004, from http://www.nga.org/center/divisions/1,1188, T_CEN_EDS^C_ISSUE_BRIEF^D_3011,00.html

Sweeny, B. (2001). *Developing, evaluating and improving peer mentoring and induction programs and practices to deliver a higher impact.* Wheaton, IL: Best Practice Resources.

12

Applying Ideas From Other Countries

Ted Britton

Lynn Paine

I magine if the entire United States required and paid for induction programs for two or more years. In these programs, beginning teachers have multiple support providers, who are coordinated and serve complementary roles. New teachers don't merely survive. From the get-go, they thrive by also learning more about teaching. Such programs exist in a few other countries.

WestEd's National Center for Improving Science Education in collaboration with Michigan State University examined how five countries provide new middle and high school science and mathematics teachers with substantial, ongoing support (Britton, Paine, Pimm, & Raizen, 2003). The three-year, million-dollar-plus investigation was funded by the National Science Foundation (NSF). In this chapter, the principal investigators of this study elaborate results, implications, and issues that arise from the research. The programs in these five countries are exemplars by their nature, longevity, and level of effort. We chose them by first surveying about 20 countries to find robust programs that would help U.S. audiences think outside the box. Over three years, we spent two months visiting schools to observe and interview beginning teachers and the people who support them.

Some people feel that while hearing about other countries' educational systems is nice, it doesn't have much utility for changing anything here in the United States. So, first, here are some reasons one might want to examine induction programs in other countries.

WHY LOOK AT OTHER COUNTRIES' INDUCTION SYSTEMS?

Many people find it hard to take an interest in research about education in other countries. Educational systems in other countries can seem so foreign that one is tempted to give up on trying to figure out how to apply the results to our U.S. situation. Perhaps it would be easier not to even try thinking about adaptations in the first place.

Indeed, translating practices from abroad often is a complex and demanding endeavor. Successfully implementing programs or policies can be even more daunting. Some U.S. implementations of practices from abroad have been glaring failures. For example, U.S. school systems in the 1960s were quick to restructure school buildings into open classrooms found then in the United Kingdom. U.S. teachers promptly used boxes, crates, or anything else they could find to recreate walls for their classrooms. Incidents like this make it understandable when people are biased toward not considering what is happening around the world in education.

This chapter attempts to describe policies, programs, practices, and principles of other countries' induction systems in a way that discourages simple-minded implementation. It illustrates the promise of some fresh ideas, while still giving a flavor of the complexity of their local contexts. As encouragement to pay attention to international research, we note that there are examples of more fruitful attempts to make use of ideas from other countries. It seems, for example, that the current spread of Japanese- or Chinese-style "lesson study" approaches may have positive value and staying power. Here are some arguments for taking a look at other countries' induction systems.

Exhortation for the Spread of Teacher Induction

The number of countries that are implementing teacher induction systems is growing. This chapter elaborates on a few that have been making a substantial effort for at least ten years, but recently some other countries have been launching induction efforts. For those in the United States who still are not offering induction at all, one can use knowledge of induction abroad when making the case for the start-up of teacher induction. The section below on "Status and Trends of Teacher Induction Abroad" will address this point.

Affirmation of the U.S. State of the Art

Many readers of this book are most likely aware of progressive induction programs under way in the United States. Therefore, this chapter emphasizes the following: Some leading edge issues and practices in U.S. teacher induction already are in place in other countries. This knowledge could encourage some in the United States who are considering trying state-of-the-art approaches to become early adopters of them.

Existence Proof for Testing Emerging U.S. Innovations

Selling the most state-of-the-art practices to other people is hard. People often are skeptics (often with good reasons), thinking along these lines: "That innovation only happens in one place that I know about. The project must have special or peculiar circumstances. The idea probably isn't even possible most places. Even if it is possible, how do people even know this new thing works and is worth the cost?"

Well, some leading-edge ideas for U.S. teacher induction already are in place abroad. Therefore, the foreign examples can serve as proof that such things can be done, becoming what scientists call an "existence proof." Further, one can look out for foreign programs that can serve as sort of a test bed or laboratory experiment for what we would like to try in the United States.

Ideas for New Policies, Programs, and Practices

In addition to bearing out the validity of U.S. state-of-the-art approaches, our research has found some policies, programs, and practices that are rare or nonexistent in the United States. In other words, some foreign practices could be innovations in the United States. This perspective is where the foreignness of practices abroad can actually be helpful to U.S. readers, helping us think outside the box. A natural, human perception is to become desensitized to structural aspects of our educational system, regarding them as fixed and not amenable to change. Some of these givens of our system work strongly against new teachers. For example, we take as given that our newest teachers will be assigned the worst initial teaching loads. We may not even contemplate trying to do something about it. Finding out that other countries structure their systems quite differently might help U.S. programs take the blinders off.

STATUS AND TRENDS OF TEACHER INDUCTION ABROAD

What are the global status and trends for teacher induction? A growing number of countries are starting or strengthening such programs. But let us quickly add that the United States is nowhere near the lone country that can be characterized as having a "sink-or-swim" model of teacher induction. At the outset of our research in 1997, many of our international colleagues from the Third International Mathematics and Science Study (TIMSS) reported weak or no teacher induction programs in their countries. However, many of them also emphasized that they had a rapidly growing conviction of the need to strengthen the learning of their beginning teachers. They were contemplating creating teacher induction programs in the future.

Teacher Learning First, Retention Second

The most prevalent purpose of teacher induction programs abroad is to help beginning teachers reach their potential. These countries perceive teacher induction as an investment that will enhance the learning of hundreds and thousands of students during a teacher's career. Teacher recruitment also was a motivating factor in establishing the current induction approach in France, and teacher retention is an issue in some of these sites today. Yet, induction is not simply or primarily to decrease teacher turnover. Instead, it stands as a key juncture of learning, growth, and support. It is not primarily about fixing a problem. It is about building something desirable—a teacher, a teaching force, a profession, a kind of learning for pupils in schools. Rethinking induction, in ways that can encompass not only support and assessment but also learning, we feel that a more comprehensively envisioned induction can also have more far-reaching benefits than we often hope for it.

It is critical that U.S. advocates of teacher induction broaden their current appeal among policymakers from enhancing teacher retention to launching early career learning. If not, when the fluctuating cycle of teacher oversupply and undersupply tilts toward oversupply, policymakers' newfound support of teacher induction could evaporate. If there are plenty of teachers around, policymakers won't be worried about retention anymore. The situation in New Zealand illustrates how a different perspective can give staying power to teacher induction. The program there has been ongoing for over twenty-five years, through several ups and downs in the teacher supply cycle. In fact, the government maintained teacher induction funding even in moments when severe budget cuts became necessary for the educational system overall. New Zealand officials steadfastly approve funds for teacher induction because they want beginning teachers to develop the best possible knowledge, skills, and practices.

Long-Standing, Growing Programs

A few countries have had comprehensive teacher induction systems for a long time. This chapter emphasizes a recent investigation by us and colleagues in countries that each have had induction programs for at least ten years. These five countries are China (limited to the city of Shanghai), France, Japan, New Zealand, and Switzerland. Ten years ago, a study by Moskowitz and Kennedy (1997) initially described the induction programs in some of these same countries. It also illustrated programs in additional countries, such as Australia and Taiwan.

Although these programs have been going on for a decade or more, they are being strengthened rather than being allowed to wane. France was considering adding a third year to its program, while some in Japan would like to add a second year. New Zealand has steadily offered more support to its beginning teaches over the long history of its program.

Rapidly Growing Interest

A number of additional countries have in the past five years launched teacher induction programs: The United Kingdom is a prominent example. In 2003, Swedish researchers hosted a Scandinavian conference for educators in that region who are interested in teacher induction (Lindgren, 2003).

The global interest in teacher induction has become so heightened that a TIMMS-like, cross-national comparison of teacher induction will take place during 2005–2008. The Teacher Education *and Development* Study (or TEDS, emphasis added) will be conducted under the auspices of the International Association for the Evaluation of Educational Achievement (IEA, forthcoming). The TEDS organizers originally planned to focus only on understanding how different countries prepare their teachers. At a 2003 meeting, however, representatives from dozens of countries voted that TEDS should also include some research on teacher induction.

Comprehensive Versus Limited Induction

Deeply addressing all the needs of beginning teachers requires

- A lot of effort
- By a lot of people having different roles and expertise
- Using a variety of activities
- Tailored to the novices' needs

This tall order is rarely filled around the world, even though research has long documented that novices come with a very wide range of needs. Most induction programs tackle only some kinds of needs; common ones are improving classroom management or orienting teachers to their school's facilities and procedures.

However, induction systems in the studied countries go beyond limited support. They launch novice secondary teachers into early career learning; for example, they offer detailed understanding of how to plan and teach lessons in their subjects, how to assess student understanding, and how to work with parents. They also promote reflection on teaching, which encourages continuous learning throughout a career.

Table 12.1 illustrates these and other distinctions between what we term "more limited" teacher induction programs and the "more comprehensive" ones we found abroad. The table begins with goals, because tackling more comprehensive goals necessitates the other features of comprehensive systems. Addressing more and more diverse needs of beginning teachers requires more effort, more resources, participation by all sectors of the education system, more kinds of people, more kinds of activities, more time in the year, a longer period of time, and so on.

Together, these educational systems reflect great variation in their level of centralization, the organization of the teaching force, and the educational philosophies and reforms in play. For example, France has a very centralized school system, while New Zealand's system is more decentralized, like ours. Yet as we look across the sites, we note a surprising pattern of similarity. They employ comprehensive teacher induction—both in terms of what induction is intended to support and ways such learning is fostered.

Multiple Sources of Support

In all five countries studied, induction programs coordinated support from multiple sources. Such induction systems are organizationally complex, requiring coordination and articulation of induction activities across multiple levels of the education system. Figure 12.1 makes use of New Zealand teacher induction to illustrate this principle of induction program design. Most support in New Zealand was within schools because there are no school districts in the country; each school interacts directly with the national ministry of education. In other countries, school districts, district or regional professional development centers, and teacher preparation institutions also played a strong role in teacher induction.

Novice science teachers are assigned one primary mentor, usually the science department head. Department heads formally and informally observe beginners' classes, hold one-on-one meetings with them, permit beginners to observe their teaching, arrange for novices to observe other teachers, and alert them to professional development opportunities outside the school.

Every school has an advice and guidance (AG) coordinator, usually a deputy principal, who is the novices' second main source of support. The administrators' flexible schedules give them the availability to meet beginning teachers for one-on-one meetings whenever the novices have free periods. Coordinators also bring together new teachers on a regular basis, typically every two weeks, to grapple with whatever practical, emotional, or other needs the teachers are facing. Thus, beginning teachers help each other through these facilitated, peer-support meetings.

Table 12.1 Key Features of Limited Versus Comprehensive Induction Programs

Program Feature	Limited Induction	Comprehensive Induction
Goals	Focuses on teacher orientation, support, enculturation, retention	Also promotes career learning, enhances teaching quality
Policies	Provides optional participation and modest time, usually unpaid	Requires participation and provides substantial, paid time
Overall program design	Employs a limited number of ad hoc induction providers and activities	Plans an induction system involving a complementary set of providers and activities
Induction as a transitional phase	Treats induction as an isolated phase, without explicit attention to teachers' prior knowledge or future development	Considers the influence of teacher preparation and professional development on induction program design
Initial teaching conditions	Limited attention to initial teaching conditions	Attention to assigned courses, pupils, nonteaching duties
Level of effort	Invests limited total effort, or all effort in few providers, activities	Requires substantial overall effort
Resources	Does not provide resources sufficient to meet program goals	Provides adequate resources to meet program goals
Levels of the education system involved	Involves some levels of the system, perhaps in isolation	Involves all relevant levels of the system in articulated roles
Length of program	One year or less	More than one year
Sources of support	Primarily or solely uses one mentor	Uses multiple, complementary induction providers
Conditions for novices and providers	Usually attends to learning conditions for novices	Also provides good conditions and training for providers
Activities	Uses a few types of induction activities	Uses a set of articulated, varied activities

Source: Britton, E., and Paine, L., Pimm, D., & Raizen, S. (2003). *Comprehensive Teacher Induction: Systems for Early Career Learning.* Kluwer Academic Publishers and WestEd.

Figure 12.1   Support providers for beginning secondary science teachers in New Zealand

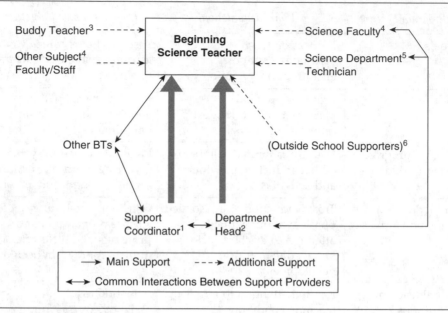

[1] Usually a deputy principal.	REQUIRED
[2] Sometimes an experienced teacher.	REQUIRED
[3] Often an accomplished, early career teacher.	OPTIONAL
[4] Usually through faculty coffee breaks, department meetings, or impromptu interactions.	UNOFFICIAL
[5] Depends on disposition of science department lab technician.	UNOFFICIAL
[6] Science teachers in other schools, regional advisers, workshops, courses.	OPTIONAL

Source: Britton E. & Paine L. (2003). *Comprehensive Teacher Induction: Systems for Early Career Learning.* Kluwer Academic Publishers and WestEd

Buddy teachers usually are a secondary source of support, and their roles vary. Some buddy teachers help substantively—for example, by observing novices' classes and offering advice. The following comment by an induction support coordinator illustrates that others have a quite different view of the buddy teacher's role: "I assign a buddy teacher who lives nearby and can give them a ride if need be, bring some work home to them if they're sick, etc."

Beyond the school, regional science advisers and leaders of workshops or short courses at colleges and universities also aid novices. Although not a formal part of the induction program, other people in the New Zealand schools support beginning teachers; these include other science teachers, science department laboratory technicians, and teachers in other subjects.

AN AMBITIOUS "CURRICULUM OF INDUCTION"

These countries see induction as a distinct phase in a teacher's learning career, one where particular knowledge, skills, and understandings can only and should best be learned. There is unusual, broad cross-national similarity in what teachers need to learn in their first several years of teaching and the help they need to do so. Even in settings like Switzerland, where extensive teacher preparation occurs that provides a solid grounding in both subject specialization and pedagogy, there is the assumption that a beginning teacher, even one with prior classroom experience (as a substitute teacher, for example), needs opportunities to learn. The induction goals among the countries included in our study speak loudly to the importance of developing knowledge and skill in

- Effective subject-matter teaching
- Understanding and meeting pupils' needs
- Assessing pupil work and learning
- Reflective and inquiry-oriented practice
- Dealing with parents
- Understanding school organization and participating in the school community
- Understanding self and current status in one's career.

The first goal seems to be an accentuated difference between foreign and U.S. teacher induction. In contrast to most U.S. teacher induction programs, attention to the subject area specializations is a prominent feature of the programs abroad, particularly those in France, Japan, and Shanghai. In every country, a beginning teacher has a mentor who teachers the same subject (but they may also have additional mentors). Serious effort is exerted to achieve this. In Japan, for example, we witnessed *prefectures* (districts) where a science teacher was relocated from her school to be a mentor to a new science teacher in another school. In New Zealand, a new and only science teacher in a rural school was given time and travel support to visit a science mentor in a school hours away. For middle or high school mathematics teachers in France, the induction system overwhelmingly focuses on their mathematics knowledge and pedagogical content knowledge for mathematics teaching. Their yearlong action research program—the *memoire*—must focus on a mathematics-specific aspect of their mathematics teaching. We are now embarked on a three-million-dollar-plus, NSF-funded examination of subject-specific issues in secondary teacher induction in the United States, by focusing on the experience of new mathematics and science teachers in several programs around the country.

VARIATION WITHIN PROGRAMS

In New Zealand, induction involved both school-based advice and guidance discussions and out-of-school seminars. In France, the first-year teacher not only teaches part-time in a school but also each week takes courses at the IUFM, a higher education institution designed to support teacher learning, and assists an experienced teacher in a second school. The range of options for novice teachers in Switzerland include beginning teacher practice groups, individual counseling made available to any new teacher, observation of other teachers, seminars, and courses. In Shanghai, there is a menu of possibilities both in and out of school that includes demonstration lessons, school-level and district-level mentoring, teaching competitions, school orientations, district seminars, subject-specific hotlines, and more. Beginning teachers, these programs assert, need a range of different approaches—different formats and different teachers—to support the broad range of learning and development required of novices.

Facilitated Peer Support

While many U.S. programs mandate that novice teachers work with experienced teachers, induction providers in these studied countries also create regular opportunities for novices to share, discuss, plan, investigate, and vent with other beginners. Peer observation, peer reflection, and joint inquiry projects all reinforce the idea that novices can learn from each other. The Swiss practice groups offer perhaps the clearest example of the attention and value given to such connections. The authority for the direction of the group discussion is given to the novices themselves, based on a view that, as adult learners, they are problem solvers.

Self-Reflection

Induction can also push beginners to look closely at their own practice by creating activities that focus on reflection and inquiry. Beginning teachers develop a reflective stance, personally and professionally. The *Standortbestimmung* in Switzerland exemplifies the importance Swiss educators give to the individual's personal life. For example, with the aid of a counselor or facilitator, the beginning teacher reflects on the demands that teaching makes on his or her private life.

In France, the yearlong professional *memoire* typifies the French interest in teachers developing analytical and reflective skills which they can bring to bear on aspects of their own emerging practice.

Opportunities Beyond Their Classrooms

Learning can be amplified by participating out of one's primary teaching context. Thus, each system also provides opportunities for beginners to participate in activities out of school: regularly visiting another teacher's classroom through the "accompanied practice" as well as the IUFM-based work in France, the occasional seminar in New Zealand, the practice group in Switzerland, even as far-ranging as Japan's teacher cruise ship which each year takes about 20 percent of the nation's new teachers for a summer cruise that emphasizes cultural activities.

Adequate Time

The total number of hours for teacher induction is significant: Shanghai beginners are committed to a minimum of 100 hours of induction activity, although we consistently observed novices engaged in more intensive induction. French first-year mathematics teachers, one could argue, have their entire week arranged to support induction—with a day and a half at the IUFM, solo teaching of a single class in one school throughout the entire year, developing and presenting a professional memoir, and supporting and observing weekly at another school (for some twelve weeks in a block during the year). New Zealand's national ministry of education requires that all public schools give first-year teachers 20 percent paid release time, and the ministry provides the funds for it. Typically, that means new teachers are assigned four classes rather than five, which gives them three to five more free periods a week than their more experienced colleagues. In 2002, the government strengthened the induction program by extending 10 percent release time to second-year teachers. In Japan, the out-of-school induction component alone involves ninety days.

Also important is that any single activity is, for the most part, a sustained one. Working with a mentor, constructing a professional memoir, and participating in a practice group all involve repeated interactions over a substantial period of time, affording opportunity to develop relationships, dig into a topic, consider alternative views, and gather and explore data.

Broadening Induction Even Further

In addition to having comprehensive induction program activities, the definition or purview of induction is broader than typical U.S.-defined induction. First, some systems address initial teaching conditions of beginning teachers. Second, there are features of some educational systems that, although not regarded as teacher induction, especially impact beginning teachers. The New Zealand system best illustrates these points.

No Rites of Passage

As a former faculty representative to a teachers' union, the lead author notes that a prevalent mentality among veteran U.S. teachers is to obtain the best classes and students in the school, leaving the worst for beginners to teach. Their conscience is assuaged by a "rite of passage" mentality: "I had to do it; it's part of the process of beginning as a teacher; it tests whether they should be a teacher or not."

New teachers in New Zealand are usually not assigned to the most difficult classes or given the most demanding loads. For example, we noticed that a new science teacher had his own classroom even though the school did have other science teachers who had to circulate in this overcrowded school: "They knew I was coming, and voted that I should have my own class. They didn't think it was fair for me to have to run around the school all day on top of coping with everything else in my first year." To achieve this, an experienced teacher gave up her classroom for the year.

At another New Zealand school, we noticed that the beginning science teacher seemed to have better students than those in some other classes. The science department head explained: "Goodness, I'd never assign the difficult students to a new teacher; I take them because, after all, they are the ones who need my expertise the most. It's about the children."

A CULTURE OF SUPPORT

One aspect of the New Zealand educational system that makes beginning teacher support programs effective is a commitment throughout the educational system to beginning teacher support. Players at all levels of the system assume that new teachers have particular needs and, therefore, that the system must pay explicit attention to addressing them. Many new teachers state that they feel free to approach most anyone in their department for advice. For example, new teachers feel they can ask other teachers to drop in to see how they teach some specific topic or activity. This strong culture of support makes it easier to implement beginning teacher support programs and activities.

As shown in Figure 12.1, New Zealand teachers also receive assistance from teachers other than their main support providers in the official induction program. The most common way that other science teachers help is through informal means such as conversations at "interval" and lunchtime. All secondary schools have a 15- to 20-minute interval in the morning when the entire school faculty comes to the faculty lounge for coffee and refreshments while the pupils have a recess. In our school visits, it appeared that over 90 percent of the teachers regularly show up for these collective breaks. As a result, new teachers have a chance to briefly discuss anything on their minds with virtually any other teacher.

In some schools, even the science department laboratory technicians offer advice to beginning science teachers. In New Zealand (and Australia, the United Kingdom, and some other countries of the former British Commonwealth), most secondary schools employ science technicians who order, maintain, and prepare all the apparatus and reagents for teachers to conduct hands-on science lessons. In some schools, these technicians went out of their way to help new science teachers learn how to operate equipment or even conduct the science activities.

INDUCTION INTO INTERNATIONAL INDUCTION

The five countries that we studied have some of the most comprehensive teacher induction programs in the world. They illustrate what can be done.

We do not mean to suggest that a lot of other countries have such robust teacher programs, as yet. Undoubtedly, there are some U.S. induction programs that have some features of these programs from abroad.

There are caveats about these programs. For example, while every school in New Zealand receives financial support for its new teachers' induction, not every school is providing a rich program for its novices. Therefore, we are not advocating wholesale adoption of another induction system. One should learn more about these systems to seriously consider trying out ideas from them. Consider this chapter an induction into international induction, rather than a primer on how to adopt these foreign models. However, we do hope that learning about these five programs can catalyze the global trend of empowering more beginning teachers to reach their potential and spark specific, new ideas for doing so.

REFLECTIONS AND APPLICATIONS

Exercise 12.1 asks you to reflect on the extent to which your induction and mentoring program emulates the ways some foreign programs provide multiple support to new teachers. It then asks that, by reflecting on material from this chapter and other sources, you speculate on how your program might be able to incorporate or enhance its support in those areas.

Exercise 12.1   Multiple Sources of Support

Directions: Below, in column 1, are five ways some other countries provide multiple support to their new teachers. In the box to the right of each item, reflect on the extent to which your mentoring program provides that support. In the third box, speculate how, by reflecting on material from this chapter and other sources, your program might be able to incorporate or enhance its support in that area.

Source of Support	How Currently Provided	Potential Provision and Enhancement
Department heads hold one-on-one meetings with beginners, permit novices to observe them and other teachers, and alert them to professional development opportunities outside the school.		
Coordinators bring together new teachers in facilitated, peer-support meetings on a regular basis to grapple with whatever practical, emotional, or other needs the teachers are facing.		
School and district subject area teachers, advisers, and leaders of workshops or short courses at colleges and universities also aid novices.		
New teachers are usually not assigned to the most difficult classes or given the most demanding loads.		
Attention to the subject area specializations is a prominent feature of the program. Beginning teachers have mentors who teach the same subject (but they may also have additional mentors).		

REFERENCES

Britton, E., Paine, L., Pimm, D., & Raizen, S. (2003). *Comprehensive teacher induction: Systems for early career learning.* Dordrecht, The Netherlands: Kluwer Academic Publishers and San Francisco: WestEd.

International Association for the Evaluation of Educational Achievement (IEA). *Framework for the teacher education and development study.* Amsterdam: Author.

Lindgren, U. (2003). *Proceedings of an international conference on mentoring.* Umea, Sweden: University of Sweden at Umea.

Moskowitz, J., & Kennedy, S. (1997). Teacher induction in an era of educational reform: The case of New Zealand. In J. Moskowitz & M. Stephens (Eds.), *From students of teaching to teachers of induction around the Pacific Rim* (pp. 131–168). Washington, DC: Department of Education.

Note: The research serving as the foundation of this chapter was supported by a grant from the National Science Foundation.

Afterword

The Gift That One Generation
of Educators Gives the Next

Dennis Sparks

Well-designed and skillfully implemented induction programs—which include mentoring as an essential core element—are critically important in creating schools in which students experience quality teaching in every classroom. These programs apply research and leading-edge practice to provide individually customized (mentoring and coaching) and group-based (workshops, study groups, etc.) professional learning. Such programs communicate clearly to both teachers and the broader community that a school system values high levels of learning for all students regardless of the preparation and previous experience of its teachers.

Well-designed induction programs recognize that even the very best teacher preparation programs cannot provide entry-level teachers with all the knowledge, skills, and attitudes required in their first years of teaching. It is only on the job that the full extent of the complex intellectual and emotional demands of teaching make themselves known to new teachers, and it is only in this context that particular understandings and practices can be developed and honed.

The primary means by which those understandings and practices are acquired and sustained is through professional learning that is built into the structures and culture of schools. Such professional learning is part of what teachers do every day rather than an "add-on" or "pullout" from their jobs. Induction programs provide beginning teachers with their introduction to career-long, team-based professional development through which they continuously improve their teaching and student learning.

These improvements occur as teachers acquire deeper understanding of the content they teach, expand their repertoire of instructional strategies, learn how to strengthen relationships with students and colleagues, and use various sources of information about student achievement to plan more powerful lessons.

MY EXPERIENCE

When I began teaching in 1968, "induction" in the school system in which I was employed meant orientation sessions provided by administrators and the assignment by the district of a mentor-like "tenure coach" with whom I had few if any discussions about teaching and learning. During my first three years of teaching, though, I had the good fortune to be part of several teams in which teachers planned together and helped one another solve the common problems of teaching. On the other hand, the benefits of team teaching were offset by the inexperience of my teammates, who were neophytes like myself. More than once during my first few years in the classroom, I recall feeling incompetent and seriously doubting if I had chosen the right profession for myself.

Today such an approach to the induction of new teachers might appropriately be labeled malpractice, given the challenges faced by new teachers as they enter classrooms filled with students of tremendous diversity in background and ability. In addition, teachers who serve this nation's most vulnerable students too frequently come to their positions with inadequate preparation. All too often, they face intense pressures for performance from the testing requirements of No Child Left Behind and from other powerful forces shaping public education.

MY ASSUMPTIONS

My views regarding teacher induction are based on the following assumptions:

* *The success of induction efforts depends on the organizational context in which they exist.* The benefits of mentoring and various formal learning experiences that convey the knowledge, skills, and attitudes expected of teachers are limited if a school's leadership and culture send contrary messages regarding performance standards. It is essential that school and school system leaders create high-performance cultures that promote quality teaching in every classroom and the continuous improvement of teaching and learning through sustained, team-based professional learning.

* *Responsibility for induction can't be "outsourced"; its planning, implementation, and evaluation are core responsibilities of district and school leaders.*

While district and school leaders may choose to contract with consultants or with organizations such as universities to perform particular functions, it is essential that they are closely involved in formulating program goals, determining the most effective approaches for achieving those goals, selecting providers, monitoring progress, and evaluating the overall effectiveness of the induction program. Such leaders understand that few things are more important to a school system's future success than the thoughtful and thorough induction of new teachers.

• *Effective induction programs apply what is known about high-quality professional development.* As the authors of this book emphasize, effective induction programs are not simply a parade of district administrators lecturing new teachers on district and school procedures during an orientation program. Well-designed programs address essential subjects such as classroom management, effective instruction, and teachers' content knowledge using group-based learning methods and in-classroom coaching that are sustained over teachers' initial years of service.

• *School and district leaders select mentors as embodiments of the desired future of teaching and learning in the school or school system.* While the customized support provided by mentors is essential in high-quality induction efforts, unless mentors are carefully selected and well supported, this relationship may simply serve to further entrench current practice and heighten resistance to the serious reform of teaching and learning. Consequently, mentors serve as both symbols and exemplars of the teaching the school desires in every classroom. To that end, mentors benefit immensely from thorough training and the supportive supervision of their work.

• *Mentoring relationships provide continuous cycles of learning through which both mentors and new teachers learn from one another throughout their relationship.* In the best mentoring relationships both parties enter the relationship with a teachable state of mind. Mentors understand and convey to new teachers that they are learners as well as teachers, a point of view that eloquently expresses the critical importance of career-long professional learning.

• *Every challenge facing schools in this first decade of the twenty-first century is compounded in schools serving high proportions of poor and minority students.* Not only are the instructional challenges greater and the pressures for performance heightened, but these schools are far more likely to be staffed by inexperienced and ill-prepared teachers with minimal attachment to the school and its students.

Strong induction programs are the starting point of a continuum of professional learning that can extend across a teacher's career. When embedded in school cultures that value collaboration, view professional learning as part of teachers' daily work rather than as something separate from it, and promote continuous improvement in teaching and student achievement, induction programs are the starting point for a career-long commitment to professional growth and innovation.

Well-designed induction programs reveal a school system's deep commitment to quality teaching and the professional learning that feeds it, from even before a teacher's first days in the classroom through retirement. There are few greater gifts that one generation of educators can give to the next and that schools can give to their communities—teachers who continuously improve their teaching for the benefit of all their students.

Index

**CORWIN
PRESS**

The Corwin Press logo—a raven striding across an open book—represents the union of courage and learning. Corwin Press is committed to improving education for all learners by publishing books and other professional development resources for those serving the field of K–12 education. By providing practical, hands-on materials, Corwin Press continues to carry out the promise of its motto: **"Helping Educators Do Their Work Better."**